W9-BIG-294

Your Resonant Self

YOUR RESONANT SELF

Guided Meditations and Exercises

to Engage Your Brain's Capacity for Healing

SARAH PEYTON

FOREWORD BY BONNIE BADENOCH

W.W. NORTON & COMPANY

Independent Publishers Since 1923

New York • London

Copyright © 2017 by Sarah Peyton
Illustrations by emily chaffee

For information about permission to reproduce selections from this book, write to Permissions, W. W. Norton & Company, Inc., 500 Fifth Avenue, New York, NY 10110

For information about special discounts for bulk purchases, please contact W. W. Norton Special Sales at specialsales@wwnorton.com or 800-233-4830

Manufacturing by Maple Press
Production manager: Christine Critelli

Library of Congress Cataloging-in-Publication Data

Names: Peyton, Sarah, 1962- author.
Title: Your resonant self : guided meditations and exercises to engage your brain's capacity for healing / Sarah Peyton ; foreword by Bonnie Badenoch.
Description: First edition. | New York : W.W Norton & Company, [2017] | Includes bibliographical references and index.
Identifiers: LCCN 2016058508 | ISBN 9780393712247 (hardcover)
Subjects: LCSH: Meditation—Therapeutic use. | Mental healing. | Mind and body. | Neurobiology.
Classification: LCC RC489.M43 P49 2017 | DDC 616.89/1652—dc23 LC record available at https://lccn.loc.gov/2016058508

W. W. Norton & Company, Inc., 500 Fifth Avenue, New York, N.Y. 10110
www.wwnorton.com

W. W. Norton & Company Ltd., 15 Carlisle Street, London W1D 3BS

1 2 3 4 5 6 7 8 9 0

To Nick and Ben with gratitude, love, and tenderness.

Contents

List of Meditations

Acknowledgments and the Birth of This Book

In August of 2012, after I had spent seven years weaving together the healing that resonant words bring to emotional pain, and the deepening understanding about brains in relationship from the field of interpersonal neurobiology, three women came to me and said, "Sarah, we want a book, and we want you to write it, and we're going to support you to do that."

There was a flutter in my chest, a mixed-up feeling of delight, dread, and pain. I felt surprise at being offered solid support, as I felt so lonely when I was writing. Until I began this seven years' journey, the inside of my head had not been a good place to live. So the thought of spending time alone with my brain in a writing process was a little scary. Had I healed enough to be able to live what I was teaching? Or would I be so relentlessly critical with myself that I would tear each sentence to shreds and never get beyond the first paragraph? I agreed with my friends—the book needed to be written. But could I do it?

The team said they would get on the phone with me, in groups or one-on-one, so that I would be talking to them instead of writing alone, and they would take notes. They called our efforts the Dandelion Project, in honor of the way that the seeds of self-compassion are spread from person to person, where they take root, flower, and spread further.

These three women were Tamyra Freeman, the initiator of the whole idea, whose project management skills let us break down the unimaginable overwhelm of "a book" into doable chunks and chapters; Deb Solheim, the second team member, who has traveled with me on this journey, coteaching this material with me at the women's prison for the last six years; and Mika Maniwa, with her capacity to build and sustain warm community, who has been the central pillar of support and encouragement in breathing life into this material for the general public.

As we started the process, this team held my hand every step of the way, as if I were a toddler learning to walk. They had weekly phone sessions with me, where they would give me emotional support for my fears and my shame and then let me speak the material aloud and transcribe our conversations. As the chapters took form, they read and reread every word, supporting the book in becoming its full self.

I would not be here in any condition to write this book at all if it were not for Penny Walden, who knew everything here before I ever saw it in the research, and who remains my most beloved friend and inspiration. My husband, Matt Wood, and my younger son, Nick Wood, are my sources of delight, play, and rest, making writing possible. Susan Fusillo and Carol Ferris, there aren't enough words to say what I would like to express.

During the writing of this book, my adopted son, Benjamin Brick, died at the age of thirty-two from the aftereffects of childhood trauma. I learned everything I have written about here in the hopes of stopping his trajectory. I hope that even though we lost him, this synthesis will support others in finding an easier path.

Bonnie Badenoch is my model for living this work, teaching it and writing about it. She recommended this book to Norton. Thank you, Bonnie, for being the midwife.

Neuroscience consultant Alan Fogel and Norton vice-president Deborah Malmud, I'm not sure you've ever been appreciated for being doulas before, but I remain so humbly thankful for your help on this journey of birth.

And emily chaffee worked step by step with me to create the gorgeous illustrations, visiting neuroscientists and consultants to bring the most accurate and beautiful renderings of the brain possible.

Over a decade ago, I had the good luck to hear Susan Skye speak about the neuroscience of healing trauma with resonant empathy. I attended all her presentations and quickly became her apprentice for five years. She was the creator of the neuroscience and NVC New Depths program that we taught together for many years.

Dan Miller and Gloria Lybecker, thank you for your support, mentorship, and constant friendship. The same to Patrice Schanck, who didn't want to die before she saw this book, but who was taken from us by cancer on Sept. 18, 2016.

I am deeply appreciative to neuroscience researchers Michael Andresen and Laura Paret, who spent precious time to support the accuracy and clarity of several chapters of this book. Any points of inaccuracy or lack of clarity are entirely my responsibility.

To the women of Coffee Creek Correctional Facility in Oregon and the men of the Twin Rivers Unit in Washington, I am eternally indebted to you for the development of meaning and clarity in teaching this work.

To the people doing this work internationally, Olga Nguyen in Russia and Malaysia; Pernille Plantener and Joanna Berendt in Denmark and Poland; Yuko Goto, Tsyuoshi Goto, Ken Anno, and Shigeko Suzuki in Japan; Nat Fialho Bravo in Portugal; and Vera Heim and Sylvie Hoerning in Switzerland, I hope that this book provides support and nourishment.

And in North America: Amanda Blaine, Carolyn Blum, emily chaffee, Gail Donohue, Leigh Galbraith, Sandra Harrison, Satori Harrington, Clemie Hoshino, Celeste Kersey, Susan Jennings, Mika Maniwa, Jim Manske, Jori Manske, Vika Miller, Marilyn Mullen, Wendy Noel, Klarissa Oh, Mali Parke, Darilyn Platt, John Porter, Sam Qanat, Rosemary Renstad, Katherine Revoir, Peggy Smith, Sharran Szeleke, Kangs Trevens, Jessica Van Hoogevest, and Angela Watrous—thank you for your empathy, your support, and your commitment to this work and to passing it on to others.

I would also like to acknowledge the crew of secondary readers: Melissa Banks, Bruce Campbell, Sofia Campbell, Susan D. Dixon, Alfred Joyell, Daniel Kingsley, Becky Lewis, Carol Lindsay, Alison McDonald, Jean McElhaney, Jonna Morgan, Dianna Myers, Nina Otazo, Bev Parsons, Carl Plesner, Shana Ritter, Rita Schmidt, Sharon Seymour, Peggy Smith, Philip D. Stewart, my beloved Carmen Votaw, and Carla Adwell Webb. Thank you for your care and your thoughtful comments.

The other voices I would like to thank for these years of love and support are my brother James Peyton, Elena Peyton-Jones, Jennifer Jones, Kathryn Krogstad, and Mikaela Wyman. Also Mari Alexander, Chuck Blevins, Eric Bowers, Jocelyn Brown, Phyllis Brzozowska, Janice Eng, M'Lyss Fruhling, Turiya Gearhart, Annie Harkey-Power, J.J. Jackson, Finn Ludlow, Daliah Lundquist, Frith Maier, Kristin Masters, Jane Peterson, Pam Raphael, Art Resnick, Evie Rolston, Kerridwyn Schank, Michael Smyth, Noah Smyth, Liam Smyth, Tryg Steen, Kelly Stevens, Anastasia Stevens, Carolyn Stuart, Lia Stuart, Colleen Tootell, Elena Veselago, Kelly Wilson, Elizabeth Wood, Pat Wood and Charles Wohl.

As a final note to my gender-neutral friends, this book was originally written in gender-neutral language in honor of you. It didn't all make it through the editing process, but I hope you will hear it even so.

Foreword

Bonnie Badenoch

People who write from a combination of passion, wisdom, and personal experience have something unique to offer their readers. Their words have a whole-mindedness and whole-heartedness that can reach into our minds and hearts in a way that changes something. Sarah is such a person.

When I first met her eight years ago, I noticed that she was curious about everything, and immediately dug into the research to answer her questions. She delighted in the nuances of brain science (and many other things), and had a particular knack for synthesizing the pieces she was accumulating. Then she began to diligently practice what she was uncovering about how brains work independently and in relationship. With humility and humor, she shared her obstacles as much as her successes, her ongoing wounds as much as her healing. This made her an extraordinary friend and teacher whose own vulnerability made it safe for others to open as well. When I heard she was thinking of writing, I was so glad to be able to connect her with Norton so her voice could be more widely known.

Now, with this book, we have the fruit of these years of study and practice, offered to help each of us develop a more compassionate and gentle relationship with our inner voices as an entryway to the path of healing. Developing this capacity inevitably leads to greater understanding and care for others as well. It couldn't come at a better time. Our world is facing severe challenges to our inborn potential for connection, empathy, and appreciation of differences. I believe we all feel it, no matter what our views on how our society's struggles can be ameliorated. The practices of self-warmth that Sarah offers can be a foundation on which we can rest to access our inherent surge toward healing, perhaps an essential ingredient in long-lasting cultural change. Because of the challenges we are experiencing, it is indeed a rare and most helpful resource.

Each chapter couples clearly stated core concepts with guided meditations, along with introductions to relevant parts of the brain. This lovely design will first engage our understanding and then offer the opportunity to deepen into experience as we visit and revisit the meditations. It is an invitation to move slowly and with kindness into the territory of our inner world. The neuroscience that is offered, sometimes with beautiful illustrations, can help us picture what is unfolding within our embodied and relational brains when we have these experiences. It turns out that our brains are so supportive of our well-being, and so available for healing, that we might find these sections fostering even more hope and gratitude than science knowledge. I can imagine reading, practicing, and absorbing each chapter more than once before moving on. In fact, it would likely be helpful to check in to see when our inner world is ready for the next chapter. While this isn't our usual way of reading, it would certainly be respectful practice for the very skill Sarah is offering—deep listening, deep inside.

Several beautiful overarching ideas are explored in this book. We are built for connection at every stage of life, and if we don't have others who can provide that, it is possible to become our own compassionate self-witness. Our minds hold the capacity both to be engaged in an experience and to be held with kindness when we are in that state. This is an ability that can be cultivated so no one is barred from healing for lack of companions. (Although I will say that Sarah is a most wonderful and resonant fellow traveler on this journey through her compassion-infused words.)

The second principle that has potential to ease our way is that every voice, no matter how distressing, has the intention to help. That single realization begins to calm the war that often wages inside between the parts of us we love, or at least tolerate, and the parts we hate and want to get rid of. When we open to the possibility that every part has value, something enormous starts to shift. Sarah's fierce and compassionate dedication to these often-unwanted parts is a valuable encouragement for us to soften and open to them as well.

The third message is that healing is a gradual and doable process, with its own logic and timing. Sarah moves from what are likely more accessible and tolerable inner journeys to those that may be more challenging for many of us. Her kind understanding, born of her personal experience and so many years of working with wounded others, makes room for each of us to find our pace, to be with our difficulties with compassion rather than judgment, and to even be with our inevitable judgments more gently. Such a broad space of acceptance sets a beautiful milieu for our gradual unfolding.

I trust this book will hold each of us well on our journey toward greater resonance and compassion. Whether we are healers of various stripes, teachers, parents, clients of IPNB-informed therapists, or simply people who want to find more inner harmony, Sarah's offering will be a cherished resource for growth and healing.

Bonnie Badenoch
Vancouver, Washington
December 2016

"And the day came when the risk to remain tight in a bud
was more painful than the risk it took to blossom."
—Anais Nin

Introduction

What does your inner voice sound like? The one that's inside your head, that only you can hear? If you stop for a moment to notice what it feels like to be you, you will find that you have a particular attitude about yourself. You might be delighted in who you are and happy to be engaged in your passions and the contributions you are making. (If this is so, you are probably reading this book so that you can make your contributions to others even more meaningful.)

People can also feel disappointed in themselves. They can ache for success, or competence, or grace. They can long to know and express their gifts more fully. They can feel angry at themselves, or they can feel depressed, or they can feel more grief than they can bear. For these people, the emotional tone of stopping for a moment might be so overwhelming and painful that they avoid being alone with their thoughts at all costs, even to the point of hurting themselves with an electrical shock that they previously said they would pay to avoid, rather than just sitting and thinking.[1] When people struggle with **depression** and shame or with the threat of rage overtaking them, they learn sidestepping techniques that stop them from being alone with their brains: always staying busy, endless games of solitaire, staying plugged into social media on their phones, being a workaholic, or addictions to change what it feels like to be themselves. (As I introduce new terms in this book, I will both define them and put them in boldface so that you, the reader, will know that you can look them up in the glossary in the back of this book. For example, a good working definition of depression is a persistent feeling or state of sadness, loss of a sense of pleasure, and loss of interest in life; can be accompanied by fatigue and constant overwhelm.)

Every person has an inner voice.[2] In some people, it is expressed in words; in others, it is more of a tone. The inner voice can be a constant flow of **emotional warmth**; it can be expressed as a river of difficult emotions; for still others, it might seem emotionless, consisting of reviewing the layers of conceptual planning of our social lives and relationships, and checking to see if our lives are on track and if all the moving pieces are running in the right direction.

Emotional Warmth

Emotional warmth is the experience of being met or meeting others with affection and welcome. On the body level, when we are close enough to feel one another's body heat, there is warmth, so this concept also encompasses closeness and the possibility of comfort with physical contact.

What does it feel like? Like gentle heat in our heart, spreading inside our chest and abdomen. It comes with relaxation and comfort. It brings us a sense of belonging.

Where does it come from? From a feeling of being cared for, nourished, and nurtured. We experience warmth when we know we matter.

What forces, thoughts, or actions diminish warmth? Self-hate, self-criticism, and self-judgment greatly diminish warmth. Spending time with people who roll their eyes at us, lift only one side of their mouth when they talk to us, define or label us, or tell us how we feel—all these diminish warmth. Asking ourselves to be perfect diminishes warmth.

How can emotional warmth be nurtured? By finding out what feels really good and is really good for us. Touch that feels good and relaxing can nurture warmth. Resonance plants seeds of warmth and lets it grow, strong and resilient. Gatherings where nourishing and delicious food is shared and people laugh together can nurture warmth. Being unconditionally accepted can bring us warmth. The surprise of being loved nurtures warmth.

Often the inner voice can seem devoid of emotion altogether, but whatever its tone, it tends to flow in an endless stream of chatter about the good, the bad, and the ugly: who we are, what we've done, what we've forgotten, and what the other people in our lives have done, haven't done, or are going to do.

Don't believe it? Stop reading for several moments and see what happens. Wait long enough so that the thoughts that these words have stirred up have settled. The pattern that runs automatically in our heads, when our brain is not engaged in doing something intentional, is our inner voice. Even if we can't hear this voice, we might guess what its tone is from the way we treat ourselves or from the way we are thinking about others. If we have had experiences of being known and delighted in by people who have been important to us (such as parents, grandparents, teachers, or even a kind neighbor), our thoughts may have an easy, gentle tone.

If people have had other life experiences—such as having parents or spouses who want to improve them and only speak to them to make them "better," who are exhausted and want their children or partners to be seen and not heard, or who are surrounded by too much busyness or are too overwhelmed to see them at all—then a person's inner voice may sound very different. For many people, this inner voice can be unrelentingly negative and sometimes even vicious.

Even with all of that, there is good news. You can hear, understand, and transform your inner voice if you don't enjoy the way it treats you. As people take in the self-compassion and self-understanding encouraged in these pages, they will often let go of distracting themselves by being continually busy; keeping the television, computer, or smartphone turned on 24–7; eating comfort foods; or having a couple of drinks.

Instead, there will be tendrils of a different possibility. There is a gradual hope of being able to respond in a new way. As the inner voice becomes calmer and more supportive, people start to like themselves.

This happens inexorably once something called **resonance** comes into the picture. Resonance is the experience of sensing that another being fully understands us and sees us with emotional warmth and generosity. It is the sense that *we know* that they could try on our skin and that our feelings and longings would make sense to them.

What's the difference between empathy and resonance? There are many definitions of empathy, including walking in other people's shoes, understanding their experience, interpreting the emotional states of others, and experiencing related emotions. None of these captures the necessity of being a "we," that is, part of a resonance. In resonance, the person who is receiving says, "Yes, you are with me. You understand me." This can happen verbally, or it can happen with a sigh and with physical relaxation. I can have empathy for homeless people when I drive by them, and they will never know. We cannot be resonant with a person unless we are being relational—resonance is a two-person experience. Someone else can't simply declare a resonance with us. The receivers are the ones who get to say whether or not someone else's presence or language feels resonant.

You might be thinking, "If feeling better is dependent on something that is supposed to happen between two people, then my goose is cooked. I don't have anyone else. I am alone in this world." That is the reason I wrote this book, to offer a way for people to learn to be with themselves. This is why the title is *Your Resonant Self*. In order to be resonant with yourself, you have to notice two different parts of yourself: your emotional self and your resonant self. Your emotional self is the one who gets to say whether the part of you who is trying to be resonant is hitting the mark. It is still a two-person experience, but both of the people are inside you.

- If you sometimes feel sad and need hope that healing is at hand, this book is for you.
- If you ever look at old patterns and long for positive change, this book is for you.

- If you sometimes feel like you are on shaky ground and would like a solid foundation under your feet, this book is for you.
- If you ever feel anxious and want calmness, this book is for you.
- If you sometimes feel bewildered and want to be able to like the human race, this book is for you.
- If you ever feel depressed and would like a reason to keep moving, this book is for you.
- If you sometimes need a little hope that you are essentially just right, this book is for you.
- And, if you love to learn about the brain, this book is for you.

You are reading the best words I could put together to invite your brain to come on a journey of learning with me to transform your inner voice. This journey follows a healing path of connection with the body, learning about the brain, and **resonant language**. Resonant language is language that gives people a sense of being understood. It has a feeling tone and references relationship, shared memories, and acknowledgment. This type of language includes wondering about and naming emotion; dreams, longings, and needs; body sensations; and fresh metaphor, visual imagery, and poetry.

RESONANCE SKILL 0.1: WHAT IS A RESONANCE SKILL?

People can use language to create connection, and they can use language to separate themselves and to push people away. There is a joining with others or the self when words are resonant, while words that are critical, judgmental, or objectifying split the brain and stop warmth in its tracks. The way a person speaks matters, as it reveals whether their thoughts are coherent, whether they speak with integrity, how they use their brains, and what are their deeply held attitudes toward self and other.[3] The way people speak to themselves can lead to long-term self-support and well-being or to stress and lack of resilience. When people change the way they speak to themselves, they change the way their brain works. Language is a starting point for the movement toward warmth for the self, and throughout this book we will be building an understanding of how to use language in ways that are supportive of brain integration. These are called **resonance skills**. When people let go of comparing and criticizing themselves and move toward warm self-understanding to care for themselves, they are moving toward brain health.

Each chapter provides a chance to experience how resonant language can change the brain through guided meditations and empathy. Then you'll learn something about how the full-body brain works, in order to support self-knowledge and self-compassion.

When we find out that we make sense and that our ancient habits of self-disparagement are just our brain's best attempt to take care of us, a new gentleness enters the picture. As we learn about our brains, we are creating new connections that allow a more generous and relaxed way to see the self. The big picture of who we are becomes bigger and more complex as we begin to take into account the way we are wired, the effect of other peoples' brains and behaviors on us, and the effect of past generations of brains on our own patterns of thinking and feeling. A lively and warm curiosity about humans and their behavior is born, making life richer and more interesting at every turn.

So while you are reading, I will ask your brain to link things together in a new way. An example of this is happening right now, as I invite you to bring your sense of self to mind and simultaneously to feel affection, curiosity, and welcome for yourself. You may never have been asked to look at yourself with emotional warmth before.

Our brains are always growing and changing in response to the experiences we have. When we bring our attention to (1) how we feel about ourselves and (2) our capacity for gentle understanding, then all of a sudden we are cultivating a new way to be with ourselves, and that is the essence of this book. As I introduce these new ideas by writing about them and you immerse yourself in them by reading about them, we are asking your brain to change so that it is a better place for you to live.

During this journey through the brain and through the basics of resonant communication, I will invite you to notice your body sensations and your emotional responses as much as possible. The more you allow yourself to feel, both physically and emotionally, and begin to see the connections between your deepest longings and your emotions, the more change is possible.

This book invites you to make this learning your own and to look at your life story with new eyes. Despite what you may believe, you are not defined by the story you have lived up to now. You are not set in stone or frozen in ice. As you find and melt the history of self-blame and frozen **emotional trauma** (the moments when what is happening around you is too difficult, terrifying, or painful for your brain-body to bear and it is impossible for you to integrate the experience), you will learn what your true and generous life story really is. Once all the pieces influencing you are on the table, you will start to braid together an understanding that your decisions have always made sense. No matter how often you have called yourself an idiot or regretted what you have done, once you understand the brain effects of freezing and self-protection, you will know that you have always been making the best moves available to you. In this movement toward healing, we are physically changing our brains.

BRAIN CONCEPT 0.1: NEUROPLASTICITY

The scientific word for the brain's capacity to change is **neuroplasticity**. For a long time that word didn't make sense to me, because I was thinking about plastic as being something firm and hard, but in this case the word plastic means moldable. The word *neuroplastic* means that the **neurons**, the basic cells of our brains, grow and shift in response to life experience, and the way that they link with one another changes, too.

Most people, when they hear the word *brain*, immediately think of the bumpy walnut-shaped organ inside the skull. However, the cells that make up this organ are indivisibly linked to the body's **distributed nervous system** (all the body's nerves, including the neurons of the skull-brain). The more that people study the brain, the fewer distinctions they make between the skull-brain and the entire body-brain. In this book, when I'm writing only about the brain in the skull, I will write **skull-brain**. When I write the word **brain**, I am referring to the entire nervous system running throughout the body, including the brain in the skull. Every so often I'll use the words *brain in the entire body*, or *distributed nervous system*, or *brain-body* to remind you that I'm really talking about a full-body-and-skull experience.

The inside of the skull-brain is closely packed with billions of neurons (the most-studied type of brain cell) and other supportive brain cells.[4] It is an inner world entirely different from the outer world, so it is tricky to try to describe it using images from our familiar landscape. It runs more like quantum space, instead of abiding by the regular rules of physics. At the same time, images from the familiar world can help people orient themselves to new learning, so I will try to use comparisons where possible, all the while naming the ways in which my similes fall short of the complexity and essential difference of the brain. For example, neurons look a little like trees (and some scientists even call them trees), each with multiple branches (called **dendrites**) and a single root (called an **axon**). They are different from trees, though, in many ways. While trees communicate with one another with gases through their leaves and with chemicals through their roots, neurons align themselves branches to roots in every direction in the densely packed matter of the brain and use different brain chemicals to communicate different messages to one another, almost always running energy and information from the axon of one neuron to a dendrite of another. Neurons are also much more responsive and changeable than trees are. On a tree, once a branch has grown, it stays there until is it knocked off or falls off. In contrast, the branches of neurons (its dendrites) are in a constant state of change, depending entirely on how we are using our brain.

All humans, even adults, grow thousands of new neurons in their skull-brains every day.[5] This is called **neurogenesis**. These new neurons help us hold new information and learning. But the major way that the brain learns is by forming and strengthening **associations** between already existing neurons—in the mysterious world of the brain, neurons and brain areas that are not even touching one another can be linked and read by the brain as a whole.

Memories are collections of multiple inputs from many sources. What we call "learning" is an interneuronal connection and association process that takes place across millions of cells. The structural organization and reorganization of the neurons that are at the root of learning are the essence of neuroplasticity. Here are some of the ways that the brain changes in response to learning:

- Neurons grow new bumps on their dendrites, called **spines**, that can receive information from the axons of other neurons to form new connections. Sometimes this learning is remembered for a long time, and the spines stay in place, even turning into dendrites themselves. Sometimes things are forgotten and the spines and connections disappear. This process is called **neuronal remodeling**.[6]
- Connection sites between neurons, called **synapses**, form and disappear.
- Synapses can change the way they create and receive brain chemicals. For example, the brains of methamphetamine users decrease the number of **receptors** (the areas on the ends of dendrites that receive chemical messages) that can detect a brain chemical called **dopamine**, to try to create balance in response to the sudden "high" from methamphetamines (caused by the synapse receiving a much greater rush of dopamine than the brain usually produces). In other cases, the number of receptors might be increased, looking for particular brain chemicals that may be lacking. As we introduce emotional warmth and integration to our brains through our heal-

ing, it is possible that we are physically changing the balance of some of the brain chemicals that maintain our mood and influence how we see the world.

- With repetition, the number and strength of the connections and associations increase. Individual neurons tend to make connections and associations similar to those experienced in the past. This means that experiencing threat or trauma would make neurons more prone to form connections that respond to threat. In this way, trauma survivors tend to "see" or "feel" threats even when none are present.[7]

As you read this book, your brain will build new associations between your own past knowledge and experience and what you learn here. This will create new learning and ways of thinking about yourself. The aha moments, the times when things come together in novel ways, strengthen our new associations and help us make new sense of the world.

This book focuses on the field of **interpersonal neurobiology**, which pulls together research from every field that studies the relational brain (not just the brain by itself but how brains affect one another), such as cognitive and social neuroscience, attachment research, and psychology. (The ideas behind this concept are laid out primarily in a series of books published as the Norton Series on Interpersonal Neurobiology, Daniel J. Siegel, founding editor.) When we add to that research an understanding of the importance of the body's voice and how resonant empathy supports us, we start to see what needs to be in place for brains to change.

While we so often want to resolve our problems all by ourselves, we cannot do it alone. We need other people and their kindness in order to heal and thrive. We are social animals created to live in groups, like honey bees, ant colonies, or parades of elephants. Our brains are made to be soothed by other human brains. Our nervous systems are formed so that we focus on human faces and voices whenever we feel safe (unless we have learned that other people are never safe, as shown below).[8] Words and language allow our love and care for one another (as well as our hatred and contempt) to be carried from person to person, from parent to child, between partners, between friends, even across distances and time, over continents and generations.

If, on the other hand, a person has learned that other people are not safe, then it may only be possible to relax when there are no people around, in nature, alone, or with animals. In such a case, this person might choose to work with a therapist who focuses on rebuilding relational attachments and restoring the possibility that safety can happen with other people. Some of the learning that is touched on here can help in such an effort.

RESONANCE SKILL 0.2: PEOPLE MAKE SENSE

As we will see in our journey through the brain and body, we make sense. Our panic comes from somewhere, our worries are more coherent than we realize, and the pain we have always carried serves a purpose. There is a way to transform the painful parts of our relationship with self, a way that is simple and doable, although not always easy. As we learn about our basic thought patterns and the way that every brain uses itself to function, we start to understand that our stuck places and inefficiencies, our struggles, and even the acts that we regret can be seen with compassion. At the same time, we have new opportunities to take responsibility for these acts and to make repairs and make up for them. In addition, we may start to hold ourselves with warmth and understanding while we show up as best we can for ourselves, our families, and the world. The more we understand about our human brain and the things it tends to do, the more we can bring a cheerful skepticism to our own voices of contempt, dismissal, and judgment.

As we travel more deeply into this world of intermingling brains, we will discover the stamp that is left on us by every important relationship. Not only are we deeply affected by the world of our mother's womb and by our early childhood with our parents and caregivers,[9] but we can also be transformed by caring adult relationships that make up for past trauma.[10]

For ten years in the early part of this century I offered classes at various prisons once a week on the brain and how we use language. In this book, I bring stories and experiences from those classes to illustrate the learning that can happen. As you read these stories, I invite you to think about the ways that each of us is imprisoned by our own habits and patterns. The main human patterns of distress, such as anxiety, depression, and addiction, are uncomfortable and painful, and people often judge themselves for being caught in them. We will learn that each pattern has contributed to survival in some way, even if it is no longer helpful. In the coming pages we will look at these patterns and ways to work with them.

This introduction opens the door to the healing journey and the changes that can happen when we understand our own brains. It has shown you that brain change is real by bringing in the concept of neuroplasticity. Here is an overview of the rest of our journey, moving through each chapter of this book. Our physical brain-body will be introduced, part by part, chapter by chapter, sharing the relatively new scientific discoveries from the worlds of social neuroscience and attachment research, both because they are fun and because knowing how our brains work creates self-compassionate ground to stand on.

As you read through the outline of the chapters, think about the ways that your life could be better by understanding these brain systems and changing these patterns. I want us to get to know ourselves, love ourselves, and be kinder to ourselves.

Chapter 1. How We Talk to Ourselves: The Default Mode Network
This chapter helps with the belief people can have that there is something wrong with them. It introduces the role that self-warmth plays in resonance. The guided meditation supports learning the basic skill of having warmth for our attention, a seed that can grow into more general care for the whole self. We establish a basic understanding of the geography of the brain. Additionally, we start to hear the way we talk to ourselves (meeting our default mode network, or DMN) to begin to imagine how warmth might change the tone of that voice.

Chapter 2. Staying in Emotional Balance: Healthy Self-Regulation

This chapter addresses the benefits of warm accompaniment and how being warm with ourselves supports us in staying in balance and becoming resilient. It invites the move from warmth for our attention to warmth for a part of the self. We begin to support the skills of attunement and see how resonance unfolds. The guided meditation supports this by starting small, with just one cell. In this chapter we learn how our emotions are regulated. We meet the amygdala and the prefrontal cortex, or PFC, and learn how to foster a healthy relationship between the two.

Chapter 3. Developing Self-Kindness: Introducing the Resonating Self-Witness

This chapter introduces the concept of continually having access to our own self-warmth and self-understanding. The guided meditation invites readers to discover their own self-witness. The importance of a nuanced vocabulary of emotions is revealed. This chapter discusses oxytocin, Jaak Panksepp's care circuit, and their relationship with the neural fibers of self-regulation.

Chapter 4. Taming the Inner Critic: Hearing the Attempt to Contribute

In this chapter we start to understand the function and desires of the self-critical voice, opening a path to self-compassion. We also find out why people dismiss themselves and why they don't believe that their pain matters. This chapter introduces the importance of "big ideas," or longings, and explores the link between feelings and big ideas. The guided meditation offers one approach to dialoguing with the inner critic. Neuroscience research is introduced that helps us to understand and differentiate the ways that the left and right hemispheres attempt to support us.

Chapter 5. Calming Anxiety: Moving Toward Trust

This chapter explores the foundations of anxiety to find out how to transform worry into dynamic peace. The guided meditation for this chapter takes readers into relationship with their very earliest existence to offer acknowledgment for the experience of living this life. The reader learns the skill of self-empathy. This chapter's neuroscience concepts include learning from Panksepp's circuits of emotion that anxiety can be either loneliness or fear, and looking at the anterior cingulate cortex, or ACC, as the skull-brain's hamster wheel of worry.

Chapter 6. Time Traveling With Resonance: Healing Old Hurts

In this chapter, we start to understand why painful memories are so vivid and how we can time travel to our previous self at difficult moments to begin to heal trauma. Surprisingly, the aliveness of old memories helps us heal more quickly. The guided meditation offers a personal experience of this movement. The neuroscience concepts in this chapter include the timelessness of the amygdala's hold on memory and an exploration of implicit and explicit memory and their implications for posttraumatic stress disorder (PTSD).

Chapter 7. Claiming Anger's Creative and Protective Gifts

We begin to understand the gifts of anger, why people might believe it is bad, and how to shift old patterns of pain toward healthy expression. We bring together what we have learned so far to help us see that there are at least two parties to every conflict. The guided meditation in this chapter lets us start to decode what is happening for us in moments of anger. We learn about anger's impacts on others when it is directed against them and about how to make repairs to improve relationships. In this chapter we get our first look at sympathetic activation and the way the body responds to our fight-or-flight directives.

Chapter 8. Vanquishing Ancient Fears

By this chapter we have built enough understanding and resilience that we can begin to encompass the enormity of our emotions. We take a look at how fear can overrun the nervous system, and we hold terror with tenderness. With the help of a guided meditation we explore creating a safe place that will let us find relief from any persistent fear. This exploration helps integrate the implications of disorganized attachment. The new neuroscience concept in this chapter is the enteric nervous system, or the gut brain.

Chapter 9. Returning From Dissociation

In this chapter we uncover patterns of shame and dissociation and learn to use exquisite gentleness to return to ourselves. We learn that shame can be an attempt to bring about human belonging. We discover the roots of our sense of self and how our interactions with other people help us know who we are. The skill of bringing gentleness to shame is introduced, and the guided meditation invites the dissociated self to come home. This chapter further explores the vagus nerve, specifically the dorsal nerve complex and its "immobilization" effect.

Chapter 10. Attachment: How Brains Respond to Accompaniment

We start to understand the importance of our earliest relationships. We see how the brain patterns of our parents and grandparents live on in us, bringing self-regulation and dysregulation patterns down through the generations. Learning about healing old attachment wounds and disentangling nervous systems supports both differentiation and linkage. The guided meditation contributes a sense of how warm community brings us another kind of secure attachment. Mirror neurons make an appearance, as well as a general outline of all four attachment styles, integrating our understanding of the vagus nerve.

Chapter 11. Healing Self-Hate and Disorganized Attachment

In this chapter we learn how people can use self-hate to try to manage themselves when they don't have access to resonance. As we understand the purpose we are trying to serve with self-hate, we move toward self-compassion, and we become skeptical about the voice of the savage DMN, taking steps to heal self-hate. The two guided meditations in this chapter take the reader through a possible way to transform a savage story about the self, and a way to find emotions a little easier to live with. All the previous skills contribute to integration in service of working with our own disorganized attachment with ourselves. This chapter addresses the neuroscience concept of the window of welcome regarding self-hate. Our capacity to welcome ourselves is stabilized and expanded by understanding and by trauma repair.

Chapter 12. Gently Healing Depression

A major component of depression is negative self-talk. As we bring gentle acknowledgment and resonance, as well as the sense of being supported with warmth, to the depressed brain, we are supporting healing and resilience. We explore dialogues between two parts of the self and with others. This chapter has two guided meditations, acknowledging and providing support for the two major forms of depression: negative self-image and lifelong loneliness. As we develop learning, we find leverage points for empathy and resonance. The neuroscience concept in this chapter is a look at brain patterns of depression.

Chapter 13. Leaving Behind Addictions and Compulsions:
The Contributions of Self-Understanding and Resonance

Just as with depression, negative self-talk tends to exacerbate addictive behavior. We use the tools and concepts from earlier chapters to make headway toward living with emotional ease and not depending on external substances or activities for self-management. We see the effects of past generations' traumas on our present-day body. The guided meditation invites exploration of cravings to see if there are trauma bubbles that lie at their root. We use neuroscience research to reveal the roots of addiction and how dopamine, self-regulation, dysregulation, and the circuits of attachment play a role, and we meet the nucleus accumbens.

Chapter 14. Joy, Community, and Our Outside Voice:
Bringing Our Resonating Self-Witness to Others

In this chapter we learn the importance of empathizing with experiences of excitement, delight, and joy. We review our path through this book and the world of interpersonal neurobiology. The final neuroscience concept is understanding and enjoying the gifts of social engagement and the ventral channels of the vagus nerve. The reader is bid goodbye and good journey.

Appendices

The self-assessment review gives you a chance to see where you are and where you would like to focus your efforts. This appendix may also be useful as questions to review right before reading a chapter, and then after finishing each chapter, as a learning and self-awareness tool.

It is followed by the Online Resources page, which gives you the URL for my website, where you can download the recordings of the guided meditations. It also lists websites for further exploration of the researchers and healing modalities referenced throughout the book. And then there is a Recommended Readings page, in case you would like to follow up with more books on interpersonal neurobiology. Finally, the Glossary is provided as a resource for learning and reference.

This book will accompany you on this journey as a caring, compassionate, and imaginative friend. You can do the exercises and meditations on your own, with a listening partner or a friend, with a therapist, or in small groups. People are not designed to suffer in silence, thinking they are idiots and beating themselves up in isolation. As a human being, you are made to be loved. When you feel safe, you are at your best and you can start to know who you really are and what you really want. As an added bonus, you will also be able to understand your fellow humans with more ease and nuance.

The meditations form a bubble of safety and care that you can step into, whether your hand is touching the page, you are listening to a recording, or your eye is looking at the words on a screen. This guided imagery extends an experience of a world where you matter, where you are deeply accepted, and where you make sense. As people grow a good place to live in their brain, they learn to be on their own side. They stop shaming themselves with irritation, impatience, or frustration.

You are invited to walk your own healing journey as your own best friend, accompanied by everyone else who has also walked this path. Welcome to this book. Welcome to your own sweet life.

Your Resonant Self

CHAPTER ONE

How We Talk to Ourselves: The Default Mode Network

———————

"Suck it up." "What kind of idiot am I?" "Will I ever learn?"
(Or maybe I could ask, "Can I be kind to myself, even now?")

Many people believe something is wrong with them. They believe something is wrong with them because they believe their own brains. And a brain that is unused to warm respect believes that either there is something wrong with it or there is something wrong with everyone else.

Do you believe that you are too much? Too noisy, too big? Do you believe that you are not enough? Too sensitive, not tough enough, not smart enough, not strong enough?

If you have any of these beliefs, how do you manage them? Do you try not to think about them? Do you stay busy to keep your automatic thoughts quiet? Do you use substances or distract yourself to put the belief in the background?

Whether you have this belief or some other idea about yourself that is less than pleasant, there are ways to make your brain an easier place to inhabit. Your brain is actually capable of warmth and affection for you—it's just a matter of starting small. This next section takes what we learned in the introduction and continues unfurling the concepts that make resonance possible: the feeling of being deeply known, either by someone else or by ourselves.

RESONANCE SKILL 1.1:
START SMALL TO DISCOVER SELF-WARMTH

For people who have never experienced much warmth, having affection for the self can be close to impossible to imagine, so it is important to make the discovery process as simple as possible. We make it easier if we don't begin by trying to like our whole grown-up self all at once with all our layers of guilt and shame. Instead, we will begin small (sometimes small as in a young part of the self, and sometimes physically small, like a single cell) and come at this question from as many different starting points as possible. Sometimes your brain will be surprised into self-warmth, sometimes there will be some modeling of how to direct your attention to make self-affection a little easier, and sometimes the stories and language used will encourage you to develop tenderness for yourself, so that you don't have to do it all alone.

Our Primary Tool for Growth and Healing:
Practicing Guided Brain Meditations

The primary tool that this book offers is a series of guided brain meditations, at least one in each chapter. As the meditations invite our attention to awaken different parts of the brain at the same time, it is like we are introducing areas that have never known one another before.

As you encounter each meditation, you are welcome to read through it first and then close your eyes, remembering the general flow, and allow yourself to experience it. If you would like to hear my voice speaking the meditations and you have access to the Internet, please go to www .yourresonantself.com to download the meditations for free. I personally practice all of the meditations regularly. I recommend a daily commitment to connect with yourself in ways that feel good, and some of these meditations might be resources for you in pursuing that intention. See what works for you. Notice how each meditation affects you. See what it is like to think of them as medicine for your mind, using them for the effect they bring to you. If the meditations don't feel good to you, simply ignore them, or try them again after you have read the book and have had time to more deeply understand the concepts. The meditations seem simple, but they can help your learning and create profound change. This guided meditation is your first invitation to a warmer relationship with self, flavored with ease, self-acceptance, and self-welcome. It is the first promise of hope that all of our cells are actually in the right place—they just need to know what to do with one another.

GUIDED MEDITATION 1.1: Breathing (1–5 min)

This very short guided meditation lies at the heart of our explorations. It is a breath practice that can give birth to the first glimpses of hope of having warmth for oneself and is the basis for all the meditations that follow.

Before you begin this meditation, do this breath experiment so that you become more familiar with your own relationship with your breathing: start counting your breaths. See how many breaths you can count before you forget that you are counting and catch yourself thinking about something else. What took you away from your counting? Can you identify the emotional tone of your distraction? Is it worry or anxiety? Is it shame? Is it a flood of emotions and sensations that might drown you if you stop running, if you stop the distracting flow of your daily life? (If you find that there is a lot of emotional pain, or that it is unbearable or boring when you try to count your breaths, reassure yourself that this makes sense, because without loving acceptance for yourself, your brain might not be a pleasant place to rest.)

If you experienced pleasant focus and relaxation with your attention on your breath, then you are already well along the path of healing and well-being.

Now we'll actually start the guided meditation. Try following along and breathing again, this time with a clear intention of warmth for self.

> If you are listening to someone read this, and you like closing your eyes, go ahead and close them. If you are reading this to yourself, simply imagine as you read. Notice that you have a body. You have

elbows, and toe knuckles, and ear lobes, and you have a torso. And your torso is where your lungs are, and where you are bringing breath and life-giving oxygen into your being. Now, notice that you are a breathing being, and that you might be able to feel the sensation in your body where the movement of your breath is most alive. Stop for a moment and close your eyes, to see if you can feel the breath coming into you and going out of you. Where can you feel that sensation the most? In your nose, your upper sinuses, your mouth, or your throat? Is it in your lungs? In your ribs? Wherever the sensation has the most intensity, invite your attention to rest there. (If you would like a way to track your focus, you can count breaths to see how long you can stay with the invitation to keep your attention on the sensation of your breath.)

Whenever your attention wanders, as attention does, gently and with warmth invite it to come back to your breath. Your attention always wants to make sure that you are focusing on whatever is most important, and in the beginning of learning meditation, it usually believes that almost anything else is more important than your breath. Thank your attention for its commitment to keeping you going with its alertness to what it thinks is important, and see if it is willing to come back to the sensation of breathing.

You may find yourself noticing other body sensations, like discomfort, aches, or pains. Acknowledge that your attention is trying to help you, and find out if it is willing to come back to your breath.

Sounds or changes in your environment may pull you away. Using warm acknowledgment, bring your attention back to your breath.

You may find that you are trying to plan your day. Gently and with kindness, invite your attention to come back to the sensation of breathing. You might express the warmth by saying, "Hello, attention, how are you doing? Did you get distracted by something you thought was really worrisome? Did you want to contribute to my well-being and take care of me? We can worry about that later. I wonder if, right now, you'd be willing to come back to my breath?" You might notice your voice tone in your thoughts, bringing quiet, respectful, and affectionate notes to the sound you make inside your own head. You might not speak with words at all, instead visualizing a gentle hand affectionately nudging your attention back to your breath.

Repeat this reunion of attention and breath several times, and see if this feels any different from how you have done a guided meditation in the past.

Whenever it feels right to you, thank your attention for its efforts, and let the lens of your focus expand out to include your body as a whole, and a sense of yourself being part of your world. What sounds do you hear? How does your body feel? Can you feel your feet on the floor? What are your hands doing? Let yourself gently wiggle or move a body part as you bring yourself fully back to whatever your attention would like to move toward in your regular life.

WHY PRACTICE THIS MEDITATION?

How was this meditation for you? What was it like to attend to your sensation of breathing with warmth? Was it possible to have kindness for yourself? Can you feel a little more affection for yourself and for your attention after experiencing this mediation?

Or, did you have a sense that you might have done this mediation "wrong"? So often people are more critical with themselves than with anyone else. When we look at the brain from the outside, we are inviting the inner judges to rest for a bit by giving them information about themselves and about what it means to be human. We will explore taming the inner critic in more detail in Chapter 4.

Often when people are first invited to count their breaths, they don't even make it to two. Even counting to one, there can be horror at having to stop and experience the inside of the brain. It can be a rocky and inhospitable place where the self is not welcome. Before people learn about the possibility of self-warmth, they can spend years white-knuckling through guided meditations, battering away at themselves for doing it wrong, while continually restarting their count and judging themselves for not being able to focus.

For such people, breath meditations can leave them in the middle of their own rockslide of shame, self-contempt, horror, depression, and bewilderment. It is not until these people are specifically invited to bring their attention back to their breath with warmth and gentleness, with something like the meditation that we've just done, that they can begin to make it to a count of two or even three without falling into their own personal hell.

As people begin to have a deeper sense of the possibility of loving themselves with warmth, their relationship with the inside of their own head can begin to change, and they can start to be at peace with and even welcome invitations to be quiet and pay attention to themselves.

I live in daily gratitude to Bonnie Badenoch (author of *Being a Brain-wise Therapist*, a beautiful book on bringing all these concepts into healing relationships) for first introducing me to a similar breath meditation in a university class on the science of the interpersonal brain. The warmth in this exercise caught me by surprise and transformed my relationship with myself. It is something that I still practice multiple times every day.

To foster the understanding of the brain that leads to self-compassion, it is helpful to know our way around the inside of our skull. Again, the skull-brain is only a part of the entirety of the nerves that run throughout the body, so this next section is only a partial exploration of the whole.

BRAIN CONCEPT 1.1:
BASIC SKULL-BRAIN GEOGRAPHY

Before neuroscientists had much of an idea what the different parts of the skull-brain did, they could tell the sections apart because they looked dif-

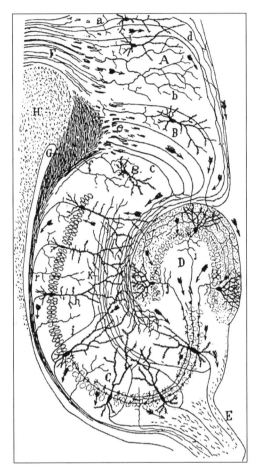

Figure 1.1. Ramón y Cajal's hippocampus

ferent. The earliest anatomists were naming different parts of the brain in the 1500s. When the microscope came along, Santiago Ramón y Cajal was inspired by the beauty of what he was seeing in the brain. Because there were no microscopic cameras, he drew what he saw by hand. Cajal drew hundreds of delicate, precise pictures of the arrangement of brain cells, called neurons, that he was seeing in his microscope. He drew the picture shown in Figure 1.1 in the late 1800s, but it was almost another hundred years before scientists started to discover that this structure helps us form memories. It is the hippocampus (the Greek word for "seahorse," which was the shape the early anatomists saw when they cut into the hippocampus). We will learn about the hippocampus when we learn about memory in Chapter 6.

As the brain scientists started to be able to tell which parts of the brain were used for which functions (such as speech, vision, or memory), they discovered that all brains were arranged very similarly: the part of one person's brain that held speech would be very close to the same area that held speech in another's. They also discovered that the coils of tissue in one person's brain were very similar to the arrangement of coils in another person's brain.

This meant that if they gave the parts names, they could talk with one another about the different parts of the brain, share research, and build knowledge together about the mysteries of neuroscience. So they sectioned the brain into **lobes** (skull-brain parts), and they named the lobes and the parts of the lobes based on where they were located (Figure 1.2).

The **cortex**, Latin word for "bark," is the part of our brain that thinks. It is like a skin covering the whole brain—if the skull-brain were a walnut, the cortex would be the brown skin that covers the white meat of the nut. The cortex (also called gray matter) and the deeper neuronal connections below it (also called white matter) are divided into lobes. The **frontal lobe** is so named because it is at the front of the head. Scientists get even more specific with divisions of the frontal lobe, such as the prefrontal cortex (PFC), which means the front of the frontal lobe, right behind the forehead. (We will learn a lot more about the PFC in Chapter 2.) The **temporal lobes** are located inside a person's temples. The word *parietal* in **parietal lobe** comes from the Latin word *paries*, which means the walls of a house. The **occipital lobe** also comes from Latin: *occiput* is Latin for the back of the head. The **cerebellum**, Latin for "little brain," is in the back bottom of the brain.

These early brain scientists were anatomists, so they used all their anatomy terms to describe to each other what they were finding and to locate their discoveries, pointing one another more toward or away from the midline, or more toward or away from the front of the head.

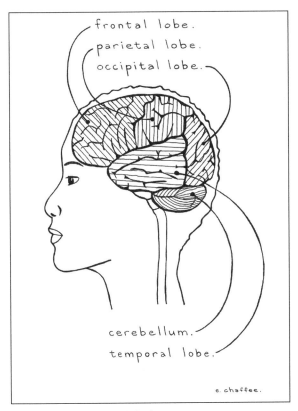

Figure 1.2. The lobes of the brain

Up is **superior**, down is **inferior**, toward the midline of the brain is **medial**, away from the midline is **lateral**, toward the front is **frontal** or **anterior**, and toward the back is **dorsal** or **posterior** (Figure 1.3a). And finally in the frontal lobe there is a dividing line, shown in Figure 1.3b, which scientists use to segment the PFC into forward and down, called **ventral**, and slightly back and up, also called **dorsal**. This dividing line makes sense because the scientists were used to working with animal brains. If a human were down on all fours, with the chin pulled forward to be able to see, instead of standing, the dorsal part of the brain would be more oriented in the direction of the spine, like the dorsal fin on a dolphin.

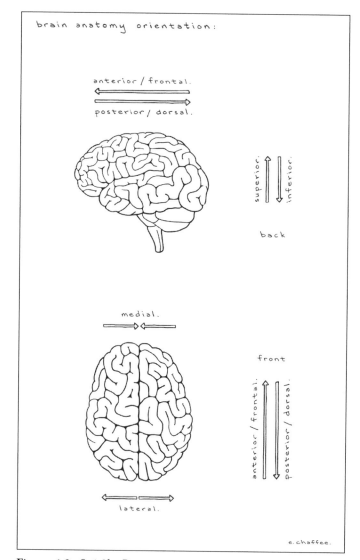

Figures 1.3a & 1.3b. Brain anatomy orientation. (a) Top-bottom, front-back, inside-outside. (b) Dorsal-ventral (on next page)

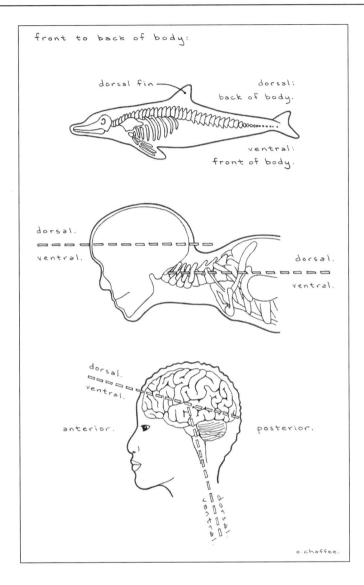

What We Actually "Know" About the Brain and the Mind

There are things that we know absolutely about the brain and how it works. And every day researchers are gathering more data that reveal how complex the brain is and how little we know. Just during the four years that I have been working on this book, the world of neuroscience has been revolutionized by new discoveries and concepts. With each discovery, we learn again how little we know—structures that we thought we understood turn out to be involved in many other functions that we thought were the responsibility of entirely different structures.

There is a lot of mystery here. Some people differentiate between the "mind" and the "brain," saying that the mind is what the brain manifests. Others sense that the word *mind* hints that we are something greater than brain tissue. I see the brain as infinite and indefinable, something that gives me bubbles of excitement in my chest and about which I love to muse and wonder and research. I am boggled by the brain. For me, the word *mind* takes me into the dichotomy of my childhood, mind versus body, so it is a word I tend to use when I am talking about human thinking, intending, and decision making. I invite each of you to discover which words work best for you. If you prefer to use the word *mind* rather than *brain*, and it takes you farther into mystery and wonder, I encourage you to use it.

The neuroscience in this book is based as closely as possible on the latest research with the full admission that things will change and change again, just in the months after I finish writing and before the book is published. For this reason, I will be fairly general with the concepts, since what is most important is the understanding that we all have similar brains, that our brains all behave in similar ways depending on our life experience, and that the way we use our brains, even when it doesn't feel very good, makes perfect sense. Our brains, even when they are misguided, are just trying to take care of us.

Exploring the Workings of the Brain

Now that we know how scientists organize the geography of the skull-brain, and we have acknowledged the limitations of research into how brains work, let's return to our explorations. First, I invite you to use your brain to think about something external: how many blocks, counties, states, or countries lie between the place you were born and where you are right now?

This question has nothing to do with this book. I'm just giving your brain something intentional to do. Now stop thinking about this question of distance and let your mind range freely wherever it wants to go. What is your brain's next thought? Is it a creative thought, a social consideration, or a worry? Are you suddenly remembering something you forgot to do?

As we saw in the introduction, if a person is under stress, the brain might start doing one or more of the following: worrying about things that can't be controlled, remembering tasks and social niceties that have been forgotten, rehashing events, rehearsing and planning future conversations, reviewing obligations, evaluating past performances, running dialogues, going over grudges, criticizing self and others, ruminating, blaming, or revisiting shame.

When there is less stress or there has been less trauma in our lives, our brain might spend its energies more neutrally or even pleasantly: mind wandering, daydreaming, reflecting on memories, considering the future, running mental simulations, speculating on why people do things, or thinking creatively.

Which of these patterns are most familiar to you? What does your brain do when you stop directing its attention to the outer world? Which of these are your brain's favorite ways to try to make your life go better? As we will see in our next section, neuroscientists have recently discovered that as soon as we stop asking our brain to do something that has an external focus, it will automatically start to try to integrate our life and manage the world of social interconnection.[1]

BRAIN CONCEPT 1.2:
THE DEFAULT MODE NETWORK

The default mode network (**DMN**) is the way the human brain uses itself automatically to:

- Remember everything it needs for social interaction
- Review what we and others have said and done, or not said and not done

- Integrate new experiences
- Be creative

The DMN is active when we are not paying attention to the external world. Our brain automatically brings together memory and thought and integrates both of these with our sense of self. Research shows that the DMN is universal in all humans and that it starts up immediately, as soon as we stop focusing on externals, in as little time as one second between algebra problems and in the tiny brains of two-day-old infants.[2] We get to use the DMN intentionally, too, when we are reaching for autobiographical memory, envisioning the future, using our imagination, or putting ourselves in someone else's shoes.[3] We can become aware of this spontaneous brain patterning as soon as we wake up. It is the background of our days and is with us continually, even under anesthesia,[4] as well as when we fall asleep at night. It appears to be the garden in which our night dreams grow.[5] It changes during the day, as we integrate the day's events, and this may be why the way we feel when we wake up can be so different from how we feel when we fall asleep.[6]

Scientists are still discovering the secrets of the DMN and which parts of the brain it draws upon most routinely. The most important thing is that the parts of our brain that we use for this automatic integration of self and social connections are almost entirely different from the parts we use when we are concentrating on getting things done in the external world. So, for example, when we learn a new task, the DMN goes offline as focused attention comes online, and then, as the task becomes more automatic, the DMN starts to become active again.[7]

We can focus our skull-brains in a number of different ways, each of which shows up differently in our patterns of thought. Take a look at Figure 1.4, which shows seven different major networks, seven different ways the brain uses itself, depending on what we are doing. The largest image, at the bottom of the figure, is the DMN. Note how it is different from all of the other patterns of brain use.

Take a look at the **dorsal attention network** in Figure 1.4. This is

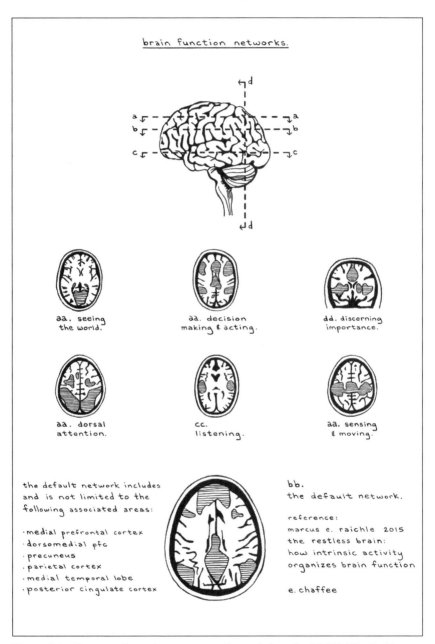

Figure 1.4. The major brain function networks, including the DMN[8]. The double letters in front of the different types of networks show which plane of the brain the visual slice has been taken from.

the network that most completely turns off the DMN—it comes online when we are doing new or absorbing things, like video games. It may be that video games are so popular because they are able to turn off the DMN entirely.[9]

Here are the names of the brain parts that the DMN pulls in (if brain parts make your eyes cross, just skip the rest of this section)—you will recognize these directional words and areas from our earlier section on brain anatomy:

- the **medial PFC** for retrospective and prospective memory and for putting ourselves in others' shoes[10]
- the **dorsomedial PFC** (near the midline, moving up and back from the forehead) for considering our own autobiography and helping us put ourselves into the past, present, and future social context of our world[11–13]
- the **ventromedial PFC** (near the midline, moving down and forward from the dorsal-ventral line—see Figure 1.3b to make sense of this direction) for connecting the body and emotional awareness and helping manage emotions[14] (more on this brain part in Chapter 6)
- the **precuneus** (a word that in Latin means the front part of a wedge; located in the rear part of the parietal lobe) for holding memories of and reflections about the self and tracking what others do[15]
- the **parietal cortex** for overall self-recognition and self-tracking[16]
- the **medial temporal lobe** for memory[17]
- the **posterior cingulate cortex** (the rear part of a girdle-shaped bit of cortex tucked inside the brain) so that we can integrate everything[18]
- the anterior cingulate cortex (**ACC**), in front of the posterior cingulate cortex, for integrating emotions and thoughts (included by some but not all researchers as part of the DMN)[19]

Remember, the word *medial* means close to the center line of the brain where the two hemispheres meet. This midline area of the brain holds most of the places dedicated to us knowing who we are, so the DMN network seems to pull on these areas for social memory. (I haven't tied the names directly to the DMN areas activated in Figure 1.4 because the names cover very specific areas, and the diagram is too small to provide that level of specificity. This list is not exhaustive, and different researchers name different areas as parts of the DMN.)

Our social world as humans is extraordinarily complex. It is exciting to begin to catch a glimpse of the way that our DMN is always trying to help us stay afloat socially. Memories don't just help us to remember things; our DMN seems to use them to make predictions about what is going to happen next and what people are likely to be intending or thinking[20] that help us move and grow with our communities.[21]

A number of things change the way our DMN interacts with our externally focused brain, including anxiety (which we talk about in Chapter 4), trauma (Chapter 6), and depression (Chapter 12). Additionally, as we get older, the boundaries between our external consideration of the world and our DMN become more and more porous, perhaps pointing toward older adults' ability to bring past experience to bear on present-day life.[22]

When the Default Mode Is Painful: The Savage DMN

The normal DMN, which helps the brain integrate the experiences of life, requires that all the regions of the DMN be interconnected and functional. When the interconnections between the DMN regions are disrupted (which can happen because of trauma, anxiety, depression, or other illnesses that disrupt brain connectivity and neurotransmitter function), we can expect the brain to start spinning "negative" and self-debilitating thoughts whenever it is trying to rest. In other words, depending on people's early experiences with others and how much trauma they've lived through,[23] the DMN can automatically default to self-blame and self-abuse rather than neutrality. This means people can be in the habit of walking around beating themselves up without even having to take a breath (or of blaming others without so much as a conscious thought). If people feel badly about themselves, then this emotional tone can run through their automatic thoughts, and it can come out like a knife in the darkness whenever consciously directed activity stops.[24]

The main problem in the working of the savage DMN is connectivity. One of the brain areas that needs to be properly joined with the DMN is a part of the front of the brain called the **inferior frontal gyrus** (Figure 1.5). Problems with connectivity between this area and the DMN appear

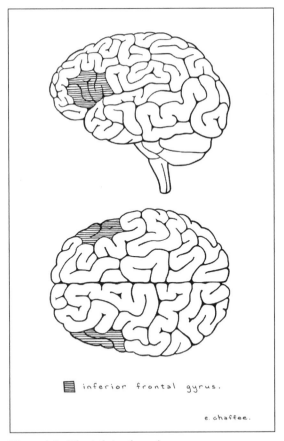

inferior frontal gyrus.

e. chaffee.

Figure 1.5. The inferior frontal gyrus

to lead to a linkage between negative thoughts and interpretations of life and the sense of self.[25] This area appears to evaluate the meaning of what is going on and, when it is working well, helps keep the brain calm.[26]

The more emotional pain a person has survived, the more likely it is for the DMN to be toxic. As we will learn in this book, the kind of emotional support that provides the best health and well-being for humans (and other mammals, too) is warm, responsive nurturing. The less care and attention humans receive, especially when something diffi-cult or painful has happened, the less well-being they experience in the long run. And when people actually receive harm from others (all kinds of abuse and neglect), their brains show the physical effects of that harm.

Some of these physical effects show up in the connectivity of the dif-ferent parts of the DMN, and some in the way the DMN connects with other parts of the brain. These faulty connections are part of what fuels depression, anxiety, and any or all of the other standard mental health diagnoses. When the DMN is savage, it makes general unhappiness or diagnosed disorders worse. It leads people to devalue themselves and to be cruel to others and brings helplessness and hopelessness in its wake. When people are in the grip of their own savage self-dislike, they can't believe that they are cared for by others, so they can't reach back to build relation-ships, and isolation is more likely. Changing the tone of the automatic way people speak to themselves is essential to making the world a better place.

As mentioned in the introduction, either boredom with the self, undeniable curiosity, or the need to stay away from one's own thinking and manage the DMN is such a drive that many people left alone in a room for fifteen minutes will give themselves small electrical shocks rather than just sitting and doing nothing.[27] It is possible that part of the ongoing stream of distraction and social media in our world helps people to manage the traumatized and unkind self-talk that starts as soon as they are quiet. All of this can happen below the level of conscious aware-ness. That's why it is important to know about the DMN, recognize it, and name it when it is savage. People may learn to keep themselves busy, text while they drive, stay numb, play video games,[28] smoke cigarettes (which also turns off the DMN completely),[29] or turn to other addictions or compulsions without even realizing that they have a cruel self-witness and that these activities let them silence it.

On the other hand, if people have grown up with responsive, warm parents and without much trauma, their DMN may (almost unthinkably for so many) have a positive or encouraging tone. The DMN is starting to seem so important for people's mental health that some researchers even want to measure well-being by using the way the DMN shows up in **functional magnetic resonance imaging** (fMRI; a way to take pictures of the inner workings of the brain by detecting changes associated with blood flow).[30]

The life that we live when we have integrated self-compassion (when we can be gentle and welcoming with ourselves and others) feels very different from one lived inside a savage DMN. For those of us who were not so lucky in our families of origin and have to heal our savage DMN, what are some helpful approaches to feeling comfortable and welcome inside our own heads? Here are some tangible steps that can be taken. You can start anywhere. Choose a starting point that feels good to you:

- Start a meditation practice that has self-warmth and is doable.
- Learn about the brain to be able to see the self with compassion and recognize the savage DMN.
- Learn resonant language and make self-resonance the new default, putting words to emotional experience and meeting the self with understanding.
- Develop body awareness, which can improve full body-brain connectivity and even increase the well-being of the heart.[31]
- Detoxify the DMN by healing trauma, which helps transform the tone of social musings from self-annihilation to self-compassion.
- Read fiction and literature, which develops theory of mind and integrates the DMN.[32]
- Act in the theater and read plays aloud with others—this also improves a person's theory of mind.[33]

[As a side benefit, both body awareness and trauma healing reduce post-traumatic stress disorder (**PTSD**), a condition where the brain has difficulty recovering from a traumatic event, which can include intrusive memories of the event or persistent dissociation.]

The first five steps are supported by the offerings that we are working with here. All of these activities are things that can be done by anyone reading this book. The last two surprised me and brought me delight when I discovered the research, so I have included them here because they may bring you some pleasure, too.

Surprisingly, meditation, despite its internal focus, is a different animal from the DMN. At the same time, there is something about meditation that calms, soothes, and integrates the DMN. There are physical changes in the way the brains of long-term meditators respond to both self-criticism and self-praise (they become much less reactive), and changes in the DMN that make it more efficient and integrated, that are visible with fMRI.[34] The guided meditations offered here are not traditional mindfulness meditations, except for the first one, in this chapter, with its focus on breath and acceptance of the present moment. The rest of the meditations invite you to begin to name emotional experiences for yourself and to have a sense of being warmly accompanied within your own brain.

Sometimes, even though mindfulness meditation is supposed to integrate the brain, the network used for meditation and the DMN can remain distinct. This is important to know, because it explains how a person can have a decades-long mindfulness practice and still have a savage DMN that comes into play once that person gets up off the cushioin,[35] and why it is important to focus on both of these aspects of brain support to heal a toxic DMN. The guided meditations offered here provide focused tools for changing the tone of the DMN and support development of a personalized and warm mindfulness practice.

To convince you to keep reading, even if there's a part of you that believes it is selfish to start caring for yourself, consider this: the ongoing self-attack of living with a savage DMN is a sign that we might be living with PTSD.[36] Using fMRI, researchers are just starting to see that the different names we give to anxiety, including general anxiety, social anxiety, posttraumatic stress, obsessive-compulsive disorder, and panic, each have their own way of taking over our DMN and giving us a hard time.[37]

No matter which of these flavors of savagery a person's DMN has, they bring trouble with **cortisol** levels (a chemical that the brain and body work together to produce to mobilize resources when there is stress and to turn off the stress response when safety has returned), as well as anxiety, depressive tendencies, exhaustion, and compromised immune systems.

These troubles may be hard to read about, but remember, every movement that is made toward gentleness with ourselves moves us closer to well-being. To make the sign posts of self-compassion clearer, we know that the tone of the DMN is changing for the better when we:

- Understand why we do things
- Let go of our self-resentment
- Recognize our savage DMN
- Pause and listen to its voice with compassion
- Heal our broken hearts
- Become more and more present, releasing the survival strategy of dissociation
- Grow from irritation, anger issues, temper, and road rage to stable calm and resilience
- Shift out of fatigue, exhaustion, and insomnia into rest, relaxation, and rejuvenation
- Move from lack of self-esteem to self-confidence and self-trust
- Stop being afraid of loneliness and start to enjoy being alone
- Move from shame to belonging just as we are
- Leave self-hatred behind and start enjoying who we were born to be
- Feel our panic attacks and fear lessen and start to have a sense that we are fairly safe in this world
- Shift from envy and jealousy to satisfaction and delight

e). The thumb represents the **limbic system**, a brain area deep
e skull-brain that helps us with emotions, memory, bonding, and
g for danger (it includes the amygdala and hippocampus, which
mportant to us later). The limbic system is tucked into the center
rain. The fingers show the bumps that we usually think of when
k about the skull-brain, the surface of which is called the **cortex**
prets our world; stores all the sensations and perceptions that
b memory; does all our planning, creating, and sense making; and
ur body).

e limbic system lies deep in the heart of the brain and is also,
confusingly, the gateway for everything that's coming in. All
ons (from the inner world) and all perceptions (from the outer
enter the brain through the limbic system. This is where the star
emotional brain, an organ called the **amygdala**, holds emotional
nconscious memory and filters everything that comes in. It auto-
lly sorts present-day experience to identify similarities to difficult
gerous situations from our past and sounds the body's emotional
when it finds a match. When a person is awake, the amygdala is
pating in full brain waves of energy that occur twelve to one hun-
imes a second,[2,3] essentially asking the questions, "Am I safe, do I
? Am I safe, do I matter?"

e amygdala makes rough matches between experience and emo-
importance.[4,5] For example, if someone smells the familiar aftershave
by an unstable uncle during his childhood, that person might go on
even if the uncle died decades ago. Or if a person sees a friendly hand
g toward her for a fist bump but has experienced physical abuse, she
flinch instead of enjoying friendly touch. The amygdala sets off the
onal alarm whenever there is a sense of historical or present-time
r, but it also makes positive connections: if a person sees someone in
e and is reminded of a beloved teacher, his body might relax.

he more a person was originally parented with warmth and affec-
the stronger the connections are that run from the prefrontal cortex
) to the amygdala and the less reactive that person is.[6] The more
na a person has survived, and the less emotional support that per-

- Make choices that support our well-being, including choosing
nourishing food, thirst-quenching liquids, safe environments,
warm friends, meaningful contributions, work that sustains
us, and time for play

Believe it or not, sometime not too far in the future, when you hear
your inner critic saying, "How could you be so stupid?" instead of feeling
ashamed, you might respond by asking that voice, "Are you really wanting to contribute to me succeeding in the world?"

Once the solid how-tos of self-warmth have started to enter our systems, we can relax, and any negative automatic emotional tone can be
transformed. When this happens, we can start to create warm community for ourselves, our bodies will relax, and our lives will start following
their true, organic design. As we detoxify our inner voice, we can start to
cultivate openness to experience, which means that we have a tendency
to engage in imaginative, creative, and abstract thinking—this makes
our DMN function particularly well.[38]

The most important thing to remember is that we invite our brains
and bodies toward health when we feel care and tenderness for ourselves.
Our brains don't develop easily when we are not able to see ourselves with
affection. But if no one we know has really held themselves with warmth,
then we have no model for how to do this. That is the purpose of this
book. No matter how old we are, we can turn our compassion for others
back toward ourselves and follow this invitation back home to self-care.

Now that we have this experiential base to work with, Chapter 2
takes us into how and why resonance—having someone else deeply, truly
understand what things are like for us—changes us. Chapter 2 also introduces us to some of the implications of having structures in our brain that
carry the capacities both for alarm and for self-response.

CHAPTER TWO

Staying in Emotional Balance:
Healthy Self-Regulation

"I'm too reactive," or "I'm too sensitive."
(actually, "Self-resonance creates ongoing
support, calm, and balance.")

Just for a moment, imagine yourself resting on the pages of this book, physically being held with deep acceptance and welcome. Are you surprised by this image? Is it possible for you to conjure, even for a heartbeat? Sometimes we can be surprised into warmth, even if it never felt possible before.

Why is it important to bring in warmth when we are talking about emotional balance? Because what lets children be steady and resilient is the understanding, responsive accompaniment of their parents and their community. When we have a sense of belonging and mattering in the world, everything becomes easier, we relax, and we move toward unflappability and a kind of sweet curiosity for ourselves and others.

Life is easier with warmth. When we have integrated resonance for ourselves as our fallback, we don't need to use props or substances to take care of ourselves. We don't have to medicate ourselves with chocolate or wine or bourbon. When we can come back to balance after we've had a hard time—without medicating ourselves with substances or behaviors, and without harming ourselves or others—we feel better, and we can

make solid, well-founded decisions more oft
brain geography of coming back into emoti

BRAIN CONCEPT 2.1: THE BF
OF THE HAND—A TOUR

It is possible to get a sense of the brain by
a model, with the fingers closing down over
ure 2.1).[1] Here, the forearm represents the
hand represents the brainstem (the part of the
that is automatic, such as breathing and adjus

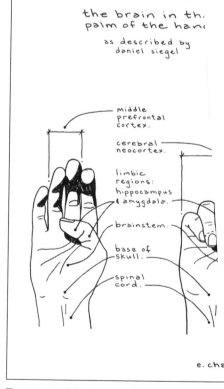

Figure 2.1. The brain in the palm of your har

heart ra
inside t
watchin
will be
of the
we thin
(it inte
make u
moves

Th
a little
sensati
world)
of the
and nc
matica
or dan
alarm
partic
dred t
matte

T
tiona
worn
alert,
comi
migh
emot
dang
profi

tion,
(PFC
trau

son received, the more the amygdala will be the dominant force, with more robust streams of energy and information going the other way, from the amygdala to the PFC. And this means that a traumatized person will be more reactive. For these people, every time the amygdala sounds the alarm, they have to figure out how to deal with their own amygdala-fueled, knee-jerk reactions to the world. Their reactions can be intense and persuasive. Sometimes people believe their own alarm no matter what outer evidence tells them. (For example, one spouse might never really believe that the other is faithful, even though that other is rock solid in her commitment to the marriage.) Sometimes people don't believe their own emotional alarm at all, no matter what's happening in the outer world. (For example, these people can blindly persist in a course of action, even though they're getting lots of signals that it isn't safe, like continuing to go out with a partner who is sexually coercive.) Of course, neither of these situations is ideal—the very best option is when a person can use the thinking part of the brain, the cortex, to listen to the voices of the amygdala and to intuition and make the best decision, taking all the evidence, factual and emotional, into account.

Anthea's Story

One afternoon at a women's prison, Anthea, a woman who hadn't spoken at all during the first ten weeks of the twelve-week class, raised her hand. "I wanted to share with you what happened to me yesterday," she said. "I have been in prison for twelve years. I have six different mental health diagnoses, and I have been through ten anger management classes, with no change in my self-control. But yesterday, I was with my probation officer, and she made me so mad I wanted to hit her. Always in the past I would have just punched her. But yesterday I remembered you standing there talking about the brain, and opening and closing your hand to show what happens when we get mad. I couldn't remember which one was better, whether my hand was supposed to be open or closed, but for the first time in my life, I didn't punch someone that I thought about hitting."

Daniel Siegel, the synthesist who created the field of interpersonal neurobiology, has shared this very supportive way of using the hand to represent the brain with most of his audiences. People all over the world are now using this model, including the thousands of students that I have taught about the brain and language in prison. Many of them have told me that they now walk the halls (and those of them that have left prison now move through their lives) opening and closing their fingers around their thumbs to help themselves remember self-regulation.

BRAIN CONCEPT 2.2: SELF-REGULATION

Go back to Figure 2.1 for a moment and look at how the fingers can close over the thumb representing the amygdala, part of the limbic system. When the fingers are closed, the pads of the second and third fingers easily touch the thumb. This part of the brain (represented in the hand by the first two knuckles of the fingers) is the PFC. When the PFC supports and regulates the amygdala, people are able to respond to their own fears, irritations, and worries with flexibility, care, resonance, and responsiveness.[7, 8] This is a brain-based definition of our new favorite concept, **self-regulation** (Figure 2.2). A common language definition would be *having the ability to control bodily functions, manage powerful emotions, and maintain focus and attention.*

In contrast, we could call all of the other strategies that we use to respond to stress **self-management**, including controlling the self, others, and the environment; self-criticism; and even self-hate (we'll learn about this in Chapter 11). Addictions and compulsions in particular can be used as a way to escape the "savage" resting-state thought patterns created by the default mode network (DMN). And we can call the lack of success of those strategies **dysregulation**, which occurs when people have temper tantrums, act out violently and abusively, or have to live with the aftereffects of posttraumatic stress disorder (PTSD). As mentioned in the last chapter, PTSD and its intrusive memories are part of what make the

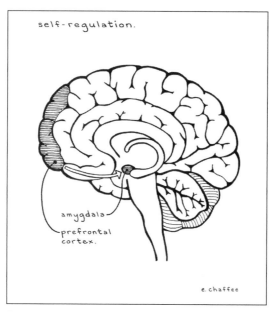

Figure 2.2. Self-regulation: prefrontal cortex and amygdala

brain into a savage and painful place to live when the DMN turns on its own person, altering the sense of self.[9]

Even though it starts with the word *self*, self-regulation doesn't mean that a person has to do it all alone. Self-regulation and self-management are the different strategies for self-care that we have inside ourselves, based on the way that our caretakers treated themselves. In science speak, self-regulation is always internalized coregulation; it comes from healthy relationships. The same thing is true for dysregulation—people develop unhealthy regulation habits based on unhealthy relationships. As our lives continue past the point of trauma, the amygdala is no longer reacting to real threats; rather, it is reacting to internal voices and perceiving them as threats, which is part of the looping stress of the savage DMN.

In the case of self-regulation, someone else, somehow, somewhere, has given us the feeling that we are known, that we make sense, and that we can depend on them. But as we have been learning, not everyone has had the opportunity to be held with warmth so that they can internalize it and carry it with them. For those of us who didn't get to bring that warmth inside from our original relationships, this is the work that lies before us now. As we learn to soften the savage thoughts of the resting-state DMN, the whole brain quiets. Let's learn more about how to bring ourselves warmth.

The Self-Responsive PFC

Researcher Moshe Szyf says that our mother is in every cell of our PFC.[10] This means that people who have grown up with a traumatized mother have the responsibility of transforming their internalized original mother into one who is warm, understanding, and resonant, in order to support long-term health and well-being. Again, the tricky part of this idea is that it necessitates learning how to turn warmth and resonance inward. This may seem hard, but it is doable, and it is key to long-term well-being and brain health. Happily, since brains always seem to be reaching for whatever will help them work better, it is helpful to find models in action or writing that make it possible to understand and that make the voice of a warm, understanding, and resonant mother come alive.

> A note about gender of "mother": Research shows that whatever gender our parents have, the primary parent functions as the "mother"—this person could be a man—and fosters our relationship with ourselves. The secondary parent functions as the "father"—this person could be a woman—and fosters our expectations of relationship with the world.

In any effective experience of receiving resonance, in other words, of having another person attune to us with warm curiosity and giving us the sense we are understood, we get to know ourselves a little better. And every time this happens, we are creating memories we can draw upon of what it would feel like to nurture the part of us that feels the emotion.

(You can wrap your fingers snugly around your thumb to represent this.) This improves our capacity for self-regulation and for self-empathy and begins to change the inner thought patterns of the DMN in more positive directions.

The PFC is a very large area of the brain, and it contributes to our humanity in many ways besides self-regulation, including decision making and planning, abstract thought, and problem solving. It will help us learn what is helpful from this book and steer us toward exploring new possibilities.

Let's take a look at the tools and skills of self-regulation, which lead to self-warmth and self-responsiveness, so that we can begin to learn them if we weren't given them in childhood. Researcher Matthew Lieberman has found that brains find their way back to emotional balance in three main ways:[11]

1. Identifying what we are feeling (**naming emotions**)
2. Thinking about the situation in a different way (**reframing**)
3. Thinking about something else instead of what is bothering us (**distraction**)

Another researcher, James Coan, has added one more piece to the puzzle of how brains return to calm:

1. The real or imagined presence of a person whom we feel cares about us (**accompaniment**).[12]

Here is a short description of each approach to self-regulation.

Naming our emotions

If you have doubts that talking about feelings will help you, you are in good company. Research shows that most people don't believe that putting words to emotions helps at all. People don't think that it makes things better to name what's happening, even though the effectiveness of this approach can be seen with fMRI.[13] Perhaps this is because many people cope by paying no attention to their emotions or their bodies and the naming of feelings is unfamiliar and thus uncomfortable. But the experience of naming what is happening not only works to calm us down; when it is done with a caring other it can also create relationships of warmth and trust, no matter how old we are. Bringing these relationships inside (importing them into our own brain and carrying them there as memory) helps people feel more secure in the world.[14] This can have unexpected long-term benefits, including improving immune system function; the sense of meaning and purpose in life; resiliency in the face of trauma, depression, or posttraumatic stress; and relationships with others and with ourselves.[15]

So why don't people talk about their emotions, if it is so helpful? There can be very good reasons that people have turned off the part of their brain that tells them about their body's emotional response to the world.[16] If a person's skull-brain has no way to respond to messages from the body-brain (for example, if the burning, bubbling, cramping, twisting sensations that come with intense emotions have never been acknowledged, or if every one of these unchanging sensations feels like a driving hunger or a craving for an addictive substance), then a person may need to learn to ignore the body-brain. In other words, if emotions are an unbearable trip to unrecoverable emotional hell, then turning off body sensations can help people manage their world. It can be a solid survival strategy to have no idea what is happening in the body. Connection with the body can be unendurable. So it is important to take this journey slowly and acknowledge that reading about this information may seem simple and unemotional but can awaken old trauma and restimulate old pain.

If you find this to be true for you, slow down. If we move slowly enough, we can simultaneously build a capacity for resonant, calming response at the same time that we awaken the voice of the body.

It seems to be important to capture the completeness of an emotional experience. In the naming work that I do, if we get only part of what's happening emotionally, and not the whole thing, the client doesn't relax. This is partially demonstrated by research showing that we can tell the difference between the words we use to name emotion and that we are affected by whether those words match our experience. The activity in the amygdala decreases when the right word is matched with the right emotion,[17] and when there is less activity in the amygdala, there is relaxation in the rest of the body, and stress levels also decrease. Herbert Benson's discovery of the relaxation response[18] shows us that there is an additional layer of relaxation that happens when we connect with words about "big ideas," words like *love, care, tenderness, exploration, integrity, play,* and *support.* (We will work with this in more detail in Chapter 3.)

Even though it is so life-serving to pay attention to the body's messages, it can be hard to find support and breathing room to do this in this fast-paced world. Take the opportunity to use your reading as a reminder to slow down for self-connection.

Putting words to inner experience is helpful in another way, too. When people can't read the messages being sent by the body, they are in what scientists call **alexithymia**, or body blindness. Did you ever meet anyone who was stressed out and angry but didn't seem to realize it? They might not even have known that they had an increased heart rate or tension in their belly or that their eyebrows were pulling together. These people have a hard time knowing what their emotions are, let alone being able to talk about them. When people don't know what they are feeling, there's nothing they can do to remedy the situation. People who are body-blind show increased stress on their immune system[19] and have a harder time with their relationships. There is also a link between being body-blind and being depressed.[20] These people also suffer more from posttraumatic stress,[21] and some research even shows that they have shorter lives.

To sum up, developing a conscious practice of naming emotions is one of the sweetest and most counterintuitive forms of self-regulation (in which the brain takes care of itself without accessing external behaviors or substances, as opposed to self-management, which uses work-arounds, such as addictions). When naming emotions is done with warmth, it can foster the mothering relationship between the PFC and the amygdala that securely attached children receive effortlessly from their childhoods. Happily, as people start to name what is happening, they can learn to accompany themselves through emotional experience and support themselves and their immune systems while doing so.

Reframing

People use reframing every time they change their perspective on an issue or event. For example, if a person is cut off on the freeway by someone going faster than the speed limit, she might let go of her angry response by imagining what sort of emergency the person is in: driving someone to the hospital or picking up a sick child from school.

Another way that reframing is used is the shift to seeing the big picture of the self. We do this when we remember that we were hurt in the past and that it may not be necessary to be angry or afraid in the present time. (Reframing by reminding the self of what is true often arises from bringing together naming and accompaniment; see below). When it happens spontaneously, we know that old brain patterns are starting to change. The shift in perspective often lets people release resentment or shock and supports the return to calm.

We are also reframing when we start to look at our brains as "just brains." As we see the similarities between our brains and the brains of other animals, we begin to notice the previously invisible structures that have innate relationships with one another, and we start to appreciate the "beautiful constraints" that we live within. Human beings are a marvel of infinite essence, suspended on the webbing of our neural connections. With this information, we can both mourn and embrace our humanness and find our own neuroplasticity—our capacity for change and growth.

Reframing is self-regulation, rather than self-management, because it too is the brain taking care of itself by accessing its own resources. People reference their spirituality, their integrity, and their understanding of the world in order to find their way through this ethically and emotionally challenging life we all live. Placing value on warmth for the self can be one way of reframing that supports the growth of the neural fibers of affection and resonance that are potentially life-changing.

Distraction

Another way that people can bring themselves back to calm is by distracting themselves from what has happened or from what they were thinking about. This is done by deliberately thinking about something else. People will bring their thoughts to such subjects as remembering someone who loves them, prayer, meditation, thinking about a happy time in their life, rerunning sports events or movie scenes, picturing a beautiful place in nature, or even planning for the holidays.

Distraction is another way to self-regulate (rather than self-manage) as it is an internal brain choice that does not depend on taking external action. When we shift our thoughts in ways that include warmth, perhaps choosing subjects for thought that calm and soothe us as if we were giving ourselves gifts, we seem to be growing the fibers that support long-term well-being.

Accompaniment

Neglected children who have been left alone without relationship, even with all the food and shelter they need, are so starved that by the age of five years their brains weigh significantly less than the brains of children who have been nourished by relationship, or accompanied.[22]

James Coan's research, which shows that hills are less steep and pain is less intense when someone is with us,[23] invites us to begin to understand how profoundly social we are as humans. When someone is with us, the brain's alarm center, the amygdala, calms down. When we feel like we are supported, cortisol and stress levels drop. We feel pain less. Tasks become easier. Our entire brain-body is made to carry the memory of supportive people with us *all the time*. We are not meant to be alone.

Being accompanied is more important than everything else: stress, trauma, overwhelm, and tragedy. When we have a sense that we can count on people to be solid and loving, we can import them into our brains, and their care for us is integrated into the web of connections between the PFC and amygdala, as part of the larger picture of self-regulation.

This can be tricky, though, if humans have been a source of pain and distrust. This also shows up in the full brain-body structure. The senses of "safety" and "threat" are different states of the complex neural network that includes both the brain and parts of the nervous system that extend into the body. The amygdala supports this by altering the flow of brain chemicals that communicate when the entire brain-body should prepare for danger. The whole alarm process can be regulated or dysregulated depending on the kinds of connections there are between the PFC and amygdala, which in turn depend on life experiences, memories, and skills. Relationships can be coded as essentially dangerous, even not survivable, depending on a person's life experiences, memories, and skills that may or may not have been acquired. When experiences have been negative, people may automatically reject others' warmth for them as untrustworthy. Contrary to such a lifetime of expectations, it may actually be true that people like us, are inspired by us, want to be around us, and appreciate our gifts. But when we have encoded all relationships as dangerous, we might not even be able to conceive that we could be liked.

It's true, people are flawed: they get irritated with us, they suddenly disappear when we wish they were there, they say they'll do something and then forget or get overwhelmed and can't show up the way we (and they) wish they could. Then, if we aren't careful, it is possible to write off them and their warmth and love and not bring them inside us to become part of our team. There is a part of allowing ourselves to be accompanied that is intentional. We have to deliberately open the door to real-life relationships. We have to let ourselves be loved by humans. We can't hold out for perfection in the experience of being accompanied.

Ask yourself if you are willing to be loved by humans, and if you are willing to accept warmth, love, and reassurance from people who are essentially flawed, occasionally unreliable, and sometimes in the grip of their own trauma. This is not an invitation to stay in an abusive or neglectful relationship, but it is a gentle offering of the possibility that those people have felt and even continue to feel warmth or care for us, and we get to carry their love with us even when it's hard, or even after a difficult relationship has ended.

Combining Naming and Accompaniment

Once we start to name experience, especially when the naming is combined with warmth, we may find that our bodies become more fluid and responsive. It becomes more compelling to know what we are feeling because when we know, we can resolve things in a new way and feel better, instead of being stuck forever in the unbearable sensations connected to difficult (but unnamed) feelings.

When emotional experience has not yet been named, it is still present in the body. It might show up as a fleeting facial expression or gesture. It can also influence the way we think about people or events. As Alan Fogel writes in his book *BodySense*, "Just as emotions of which we are not aware can show up in our actions and expressions, thoughts may reveal embodied experiences of which we may not be aware." Sometimes we can discover what the emotional basis of our thoughts is by listening to our words. Is there judgment? Might there be contempt or irritation that has not been named? Is there an old resentment? Is it possible that we are feeling some hopelessness or discouragement?

Many people have never had the combined experience of naming and warmth, so their bodies remain unchanged. If people get irritated with a coworker, and no one understands them, they can stay irritated for years. An ancient heartbreak can continue to ache like a sore tooth, flaring up whenever it is touched by a stray thought. And it is possible to still feel anxious and ashamed when thinking of childhood pain, even after seventy years have passed. When the emotion is finally known and named, it is possible for the body-brain to begin to relax into the message being received by the brain in the skull.

Objections to Being Compassionate With the Self

It's all well and good to talk about self-kindness, self-compassion, or self-resonance when the concepts might be foreign and impossible. Trying to imagine these ways of being with self can go against the culture of the family or community. The belief that others are more important, or that the self is not worth warmth or compassion, can get in the way. People can also imagine that, if they are kind to themselves, they'll be stuck the way they are and they'll never improve.

It might also be possible to hear the word *compassion* but have no idea what it might mean. People may even be able to recite the dictionary definition but still be so bewildered by the word that they don't know what direction to point themselves in to find it.

Even hearing all the benefits of turning toward the self with understanding, it can seem dangerous to move in the direction of self-warmth. If we speak vulnerably and with generosity to and especially about ourselves, does it lay us open to accusations of self-centeredness or selfishness? Self-connection can seem more like something that should be hidden than something that should be shared. People might hear the word *self-compassion* and think that it means excusing themselves for doing things they regret, rather than seeing it as being forgiving, seeking internal understanding, finding self-acceptance, and coming to a sense of self-worth.

Sometimes just bringing such possible objections and accusations out into the light of day can pop them like soap bubbles. But sometimes these self-accusations do not shift. One possible root cause for this unchangeability is the human need for belonging. People can live in family and country cultures that highly value modesty and humility and even self-recrimination, cultures that might make it difficult to turn toward the self. In such cultures, self-compassion can seem like a violation of integrity. If this is true for you, bow to this important voice within you and keep reading if possible, since the kind of self-warmth that is described here is very different from pride, self-aggrandizement, or justification.

In the best of all possible worlds, our parents were able to talk with us with understanding when we were upset, combining our two golden regulation strategies, naming and accompaniment, creating the integrated other regulation that we call self-regulation. If we were lucky, we got to know ourselves more deeply and more generously through our relationship with our mother and father.[24] If this is true for us, we have a natural ability to do this for other people and for ourselves. It is like how our fingers, representing our PFC, naturally curl over, nestle, and support our thumb, representing our emotional center—our amygdala. Few of us, however, have grown up in this best of all possible worlds.

So what can we do if we grew up without naming or accompaniment? Is there any hope for us? Yes! We just have to grow robust new connections to support the pathway of self-regulation. All of the information, activities, and meditations offered here are designed to strengthen our neural connections for self-care. Learning about the brain is part of what lets us know why it's important to name emotional experience (*naming*) and helps us see the big picture of ourselves in the context of the important relationships in our lives (*reframing*). It also lets us identify healthy ways to distract ourselves (*distraction*) and reminds us why being accompanied is so helpful (*accompaniment*). And happily, these pathways of self-regulating neurons are in the brain areas that can become more effective as we age,[25] making our hopes for healing even more attainable.

Something profound happens when we stand back and look at ourselves, rather than just being reactive without self-reflection. We can rest in a place of nonjudgment when we see ourselves as naturally automatic brains, trained through our lives to respond in certain ways, and simultaneously capable of change. When self-gentleness is offered as an option, it brings the hope that we could be held with affection no matter what our past looks like. Once we learn that is possible, we can't unlearn it. This may be even more important than all the factual information that could be taught. At the same time, learning about the brain supports the big idea that we actually make sense and that we are worthy of warmth and understanding.

Self-gentleness can be a radical and unfamiliar notion. The following guided meditation will give you a chance to experiment with having warmth and tenderness for yourself. If you have an inner voice that tells you it's selfish to care for yourself, remind the voice that this practice makes your love for others more powerful and lets you give your children, your friends, and even your animals the best possible and most health-contributing brain to model themselves on.

GUIDED MEDITATION 2.1: One Cell

What is it like to be asked to hold yourself with warmth? If this is a tall order, here is a meditation that might make it easier. Instead of having to feel kindness for your whole self, the one-cell meditation asks you to just be gentle with one small part of yourself.

> If you are listening to someone read this, and it supports your imag-ination, close your eyes. If you are reading this to yourself, simply imagine as you read. Gently begin by wondering, what is your sense of your whole body? Notice that you have toes, ankles, knees, hips, fingers, wrists, elbows, shoulders, ribs, a stomach, and a back, and that as you breathe, you can feel your breath go in and out. Yes, you are a breathing being, and you might be able to feel the sensation in your body as your breath moves. Where is your sensation of breath-ing most alive? Invite your attention to rest there.
>
> As you ask your attention to stay with that place of alive sensa-tion, be warm and accepting, no matter where your focus goes. You can see your attention as a curious or wary puppy, or as a gung-ho toddler, and see if that brings you any more ease.
>
> As you speak to your attention, allow your voice to be gentle and warmly curious: "Hello, attention, would you be willing to come to my breath?" As you ask your attention to change its focus, let your touch or intention be soft and respectful. When your attention is drawn to other parts of your body, or to other thoughts, thank it for its persistent efforts to support your well-being by going to what it thinks is most important, and gently and with kindness ask it to return to your breath.
>
> Now, with your eyes closed, put one hand out in front of you, palm up. In your imagination, bring one tiny live cell from your body out into the palm of your hand. See how you feel about this one, small, pulsing entity. Can you see that it is in relationship with the larger world? That it has a tender skin that keeps it separate from all

your other cells, but still lets communication happen? That it notices the tone of the emotions that it lives in, and responds to them? Sometimes as we connect with different parts of our body, we find that these parts really want to contribute to the whole of us. Do you find that this cell cares for you and wants the best for you? Can you feel warmth and care for it? How about gratitude?

Notice whether this one cell, as a representative of your whole, spends much of its time in any particular emotion. If it had an emotional tone, would it be lonely or sad? Is it needing reassurance and comfort? Is it fearful or anxious, and longing for safety and predictability? Is it irritated or angry, and wanting respect and consideration? Is it a happy cell? Glad to be acknowledged and appreciated? Would it enjoy company in its satisfaction? Notice whether it is possible for you to feel appreciation for its contribution to your life. How is this cell feeling with your attention on it? Is it relaxing a bit?

Now, in your imagination, return this cell to your body, and let it communicate its experience to the cells around it. What is that like? If this experience was pleasant, it may be that this cell will let all the other cells in your body know that it is possible to be held with warmth and care, and a warm glow may begin somewhere, and ripple gently through you.

Bring your attention back to your body as a whole. Is it any easier to feel warmth for your whole self, after having done it for a tiny part of you? Whether it is or it isn't, invite your attention to notice what it is like to be you as a physical being in gravity. Where do you feel your body touching surfaces? Can you feel your own weight and presence? Are your feet on the floor? Is your bottom on a chair? Where are your arms and hands? What is holding them up? How is the balance of your head on your spine? Notice that you are being supported by the earth. Just for one small moment, allow gravity to be the earth's love for you and your weight. And gently let yourself return to present time, to whatever you are bringing your attention to next. . . .

WHY PRACTICE THIS GUIDED MEDITATION?

We are all capable of feeling warmth and care for others, but we often have no idea how to bring our natural capacity for compassion inward, to the very core of our being. By taking one of our cells and putting it outside our body, we are able to fuel this meditation with our natural capacity to have warmth for others. Then as we bring the cell back into ourselves, we invite the neural fibers to carry messages of acceptance and resonance in a direction we aren't used to, backward and downward to the sense of self and to the amygdala. This builds the nest of neural fibers that will cradle our emotional being.

With this meditation, we are exploring whether connecting with the self becomes more possible if we reduce the difficulty level by focusing on just one cell and bringing gentleness and warmth together with the idea of who we are. Since this strengthens the fibers of self-regulation, it is one of the cornerstones of the healing power of this work.

Strengthened by hope and the beginnings of self-compassion, we will use the next chapter to meet our resonating self-witness and learn more about naming experience, specifically our emotions and our longings.

CHAPTER THREE

Developing Self-Kindness:
Introducing the Resonating Self-Witness

"No one understands me; I am alone."
(actually, "I can always be accompanied.")

Self-kindness is a tricky concept. **Attunement** is the experience of someone focusing on us with warmth, respect, and curiosity. This person wonders what it is like to be us,[1] using all available human sensitivities to tune in to us.

Attunement is essential for **resonance**, and both together are the glue of solid relationships. As you may remember, resonance is what happens when we have a sense that the other person really gets us. That person focuses on us, which we can tell from words, facial expressions, gestures, sounds, or a warm, caring nonverbal presence. And when we have a sense of being gotten, there is a temporary merging into one whole pair.[2] When we experience resonance, no matter how old we are, it's like being a plant that receives the nutrients and the water that it needs to grow. Resonant attention and language change the way we hold memory. They change the way we see ourselves. And with our new eyes, we start to transform our experiences of shame, rage, terror, and self-doubt into the sense that we are enough, just as we are. We start being able to believe the world is safe, to trust ourselves, and to advocate for ourselves.

Resonance, the very experience that calms us the most, is in short supply. It is a tragedy that what supports us to become more whole, creative, and self-empowered is not explicitly taught anywhere. It is a natural human capacity, and available to us all—we just need to be reminded of its power and to be guided to live it. The intention here is to model one way to use words to create resonance, break the process down so that we can see its moving parts, and remind ourselves how to do it, in particular with ourselves. I say "remind" because it seems to be a forgotten birthright of being human.

When I am attuning to other people, I begin to wonder what might be happening for them. I start to pay attention to them. I notice what their face and body look like; I notice the sound of their voice; I notice the content of their words. As I take them in, I am attuning to them. If we each start to have a sense that what is being perceived is true for the other, we begin to resonate together.

Just as we are able to attune and resonate with another human being, we are also capable of bringing that level of focus and care to the self. It means learning to turn inward with the warmth and generosity that we usually reserve for others. It can be unfamiliar and awkward in the beginning, because this turning toward oneself is something we have rarely seen modeled. We may not quite know how to do it.

It is a little easier to imagine what it really feels like to have warmth for ourselves if we personify the parts of the brain that are capable of self-warmth and self-regulation, by calling this complex and healthy integration of brain and body the resonating self-witness (**RSW**). If we want to move toward transforming a traumatized or previously unaccompanied brain into a comfortable and supportive place to live, we need to awaken that brain to the hope of holding the self with care and resonance and remind ourselves that we are capable of warm curiosity, caring self-regulation, and continual self-accompaniment.

All of this means that the RSW is what emerges when people step more fully into self-warmth. The RSW is the experience of feeling supported and held. In the brain, it shows up as an easy self-supportive dialogue between the prefrontal cortex (PFC) and the amygdala/limbic system, which has the effect of shifting the savage and traumatized default mode network (DMN), the automatic voice of self-hate and self-recrimination, into the self-accompaniment of a kind, resonant DMN. And where does this happen in the brain? The key area for self-regulation, as you may remember from Chapter 2, is the PFC (see Figure 2.2), where emotion is noticed and named and where we can hold the intention to bring attunement to self and other.

BRAIN CONCEPT 3.1: THE ROOT OF WARMTH—CARE

Many people, when they start to learn about the importance of warmth, realize that they grew up in families that were so stressed by trauma and addiction, or so focused on achievement, that there were no or very few experiences of affection. They can even feel confused or disoriented by use of the word *warmth*. They rarely say, "I love you." Physical touch can seem intrusive and demanding. For these people it is important to know that every human being is born with the brain parts that are used for bonding and connection. Even if you have never had the chance to feel warmth for yourself, your brain is ready and waiting to learn how to do it.

Another very important part of the RSW picture is the deeper brain structures that run through the brain stem and link into the body, making self-care a rich, fully embodied, and complex experience that unifies the skull-brain and the body-brain.

Humans are used to thinking of themselves as different from other animals, but when it comes to brain structure, we are obviously part of the animal continuum. Emotions researcher Jaak Panksepp has shown that all mammals, including humans, have seven basic emotional networks, or **circuits of emotion**, that carry our different life energies.[3] There is one circuit that handles **RAGE** (Panksepp writes their names in all capital letters so that we can tell the circuit names from regular human emotions); others handle **FEAR, SEEKING, LUST, PANIC/GRIEF,** and **PLAY**; and one in particular that is called the **CARE circuit**. This means that when we are having basic emotional experiences, the same parts of our brains light up that would light up if a mouse were having that same experience. We will learn more about the other circuits in other chapters, but right now we are most interested in our capacity for CARE.

When we feel emotional warmth for each other, for animals, or for ourselves, the energy and information flow in our brain in a certain pattern. This pattern runs above, around, and under the amygdala, linking the limbic system, brain stem, and body. We can notice it when we feel satisfaction when we have helped someone, or when our chests are filled with tingly sweetness when we think about someone dear to us.

Our brain connections to the CARE circuit are a gift to us from every positive relationship we have ever had, and they create associations within the fibers that become the most complex in our skull-brains, building more and more dendrites that interconnect as we age: the fibers of the PFC.[4] Together, these connections between PFC, the CARE circuit, and the body create the capacity for warm relationships with self and others. Happily, we tend to create an automatic, always running self-regulation circuit in our brains that keeps us calmer and calmer as we get older.[5]

RESONANCE SKILL 3.1:
THE NUANCES OF FEELINGS

Once again we are seeing the convergence of warmth and intention and action that characterize the resonating self-witness (RSW). This is easy enough when we are nonverbal, using affectionate eye contact or responsive touch to let others know that we care about them. But as soon as we open our mouths, we might leave behind resonant connection, because the part of the brain that "does" language is not the same part of the brain that "does" relationship.[6] If we don't know what kinds of words create connection, then we can be alienating our loved ones every time we speak without even knowing what we are doing.

One type of language that connects us with others is the naming of emotions. Sometimes people think there are just three emotions: happy, sad, and angry. But magic happens for our brains when we put precise words to what is happening for us. This section introduces you to the many tones of feeling.

You may recall from Chapter 2 that the way body-brains communicate with skull-brains is through emotions and that it soothes and regulates emotional alarm to name what is happening. Irritation, anxiety, overwhelm, bewilderment, dismay, fear, shame, grief, horror, rage, and alarm are just a few of the possibilities. Additionally, unacknowledged moments of celebration or feelings of delight, excitement, and pleasure that have not been shared by others can also lead to frozenness and disconnection from self, sometimes even to shame and hopelessness. (More on celebration in Chapter 14.) People are made to be social, to share the important experiences in their lives with others from their tribe, and to be understood.[7]

All well and good, you may be thinking, but do you actually want me to talk about my feelings? I've tried that, and it doesn't help.

It's true, when people talk about their emotions with someone who is not resonant, or who tells them that they're wrong and they don't feel that way, or who changes the subject or tries to fix, then it really doesn't help to name feelings. But when resonance enters the picture, when another body has some understanding of what feelings are at play, or when people learn to resonate with themselves, it's a different story. To counteract any belief you may have that it is not a good idea to talk about feelings, it is important to begin to understand the gifts that emotions bring.[8]

The Gifts of Emotions
- They bring a sense of aliveness, color, and nuance to our daily experiences.
- They let us know what is important.
- They help us learn and make us capable of change.
- They are signposts to what we most long for.
- Their expression improves our health and diminishes posttraumatic stress.
- They help us make decisions.
- They enrich experiences of connection and sexuality.
- They play an important role in memory.

- They allow us to enter the edge of our nonconscious world and begin to heal (more on this in Chapter 8).

Relationships that are emotionally alive feed the body and the soul. It helps so much to be able to say to someone, "My stomach hurts," and have them ask "Would it be okay if I asked you if you are you scared?" Or to tell someone you are feeling jumpy and have them wonder if the sensations are linked to excitement, delight, or worry about disappointment. The experience of being met with genuine, warm interest actually starts to build our feelings vocabulary. It is an important part of your reading experience with this book, too.

I invite you to take a look at the lists of "pleasant" and "unpleasant" feelings and see how many different emotions you are experiencing right this minute. People have "pleasant" feelings when things are going well and they have a sense of being safe and mattering. They have "unpleasant" feelings when things are not going well and they have a sense of danger and of being insignificant. You might find that you are much more complex than you expected.

"Pleasant" Feelings

affectionate	eager	giddy	open
amazed	ecstatic	glad	peaceful
amused	elated	gleeful	proud
astonished	energetic	grateful	radiant
blissful	engrossed	hopeful	rapturous
calm	enlivened	inspired	refreshed
comfortable	enthusiastic	intense	relieved
compassionate	excited	interested	satisfied
concerned	exhilarated	intrigued	secure
confident	expansive	invigorated	sensitive
contented	expectant	joyful	serene
curious	exuberant	jubilant	surprised
dazzled	fascinated	mellow	sympathetic
delighted	friendly	moved	tender

| thankful | touched | trusting |
| thrilled | tranquil | warm |

"Unpleasant" Feelings

afraid	despondent	gloomy	puzzled
aggravated	detached	grief/stricken	reluctant
agitated	disappointed	grouchy	remorseful
alarmed	disconnected	heartbroken	repugnance
angry	discouraged	helpless	repulsion
anguished	disheartened	hesitant	resentful
annoyed	disgruntled	horrified	restless
anxious	disgusted	hostile	sad
apathetic	disinterested	hurt	scared
appalled	dismayed	impatient	sensitive
apprehensive	dispirited	incredulous	shaky
ashamed	disquieted	indifferent	shock/ed
bewildered	distressed	infuriated	skeptical
bitter	disturbed	insecure	sorrow/ful
blah	downcast	irked	startled
blue	downhearted	irritated	surprised
bored	dread	jealous	suspicious
brokenhearted	edgy	lonely	terrified
cautious	embarrassed	mad	thwarted
chagrined	enraged	mean	timid
cold	envious	melancholic	tired
concerned	exasperated	miffed	troubled
confused	exhausted	mystified	uneasy
contemptuous	fatigued	nervous	unnerved
contrite	fearful	numb	unsteady
cranky	fidgety	overwhelmed	vengeful
cross	forlorn	panicky	withdrawn
dejected	frightened	pain/ed	worried
depressed	frustrated	perplexed	wretched
despairing	furious	pressured	yearning

GUIDED MEDITATION 3.1: Finding the Resonating Self-Witness

This guided meditation, where we meet our RSW, shows a new way to respond to ourselves with self-care and self-connection.

> Now, if you are listening to someone read this, close your eyes. If you are reading this to yourself, simply imagine as you read. Begin by noticing that you are breathing. See if it is possible to let your imagination start riding the stream of air in and out of your body. See what shapes your breath unfurls in your lungs as you inhale. Notice the sensation of your breath for a moment, and see if your attention is willing to stay there. If your attention wanders, now or at any point during this meditation, gently and with warmth bring it back to what you want it to focus on.
>
> Imagine that you are standing at a gate, and that you can see a path stretching in front of you, into a landscape that you love: beach, garden, rainforest, city sidewalks, desert, or mountain. Open the gate, and step onto the path and start walking. What does the surface of the path feel like under your feet? What do you smell? See? Taste? Feel on your skin? Hear? Are there any birdsongs or sounds? Can you hear the wind rustling leaves or grass?
>
> If this is a familiar place, let your imagination make it more mysterious, so that there are things you don't know about it. Up ahead there is a bend that takes you into a hidden area. As you turn the corner, there's a beautiful place to sit, a comfortable fallen log or sun-warmed boulder or bench. Sit down, and allow yourself to rest and enjoy this place.
>
> While you're resting, if it is available to you, let yourself imagine that there is a presence here, a presence that can see you and love you and that knows you deeply, that knows you intimately. This presence feels affection for you and cares about your well-being. This presence knows every part of you and why you do things. This presence sees the best in you with a very generous and open heart,

knows your best intentions and the love that lies at the heart of your actions and your plans.

What is it like to be seen by eyes of love?

If you can feel this love coming toward you, this is your resonating self-witness. This figure will be your accompaniment as you move along this journey.

If you cannot imagine this presence, then I'd like you to imagine that this book is your compassionate and resonating self-witness, and that love, acceptance, gentleness, and welcome are emanating from its pages.

This presence is curious and open, gently waiting for you to notice it. It is attuning to you, wondering about your experience, and whether it understands the meaning that you are making. As you bring your attention to it, you are able to see who this is. This presence may be your best self, or a beloved grandparent, or teacher, or spiritual figure, or animal, or friend. It does not think that it is better than you, or smarter than you, it just loves you and is focused on you.

Take a few minutes to feel how your body responds to being cared about, to having someone be interested in your experience.

When you are ready, invite your resonating self-witness to come back along the path with you.

As the two of you come near the border of your path, you see your breathing body, sitting on the other side of the gate.

Bringing your resonating self-witness with you, ride your breath back into your body, and let this presence settle within you.

Feel where your self-witness comes to rest. Is it in your heart? In your abdomen?

Notice how your body is doing. Welcome your sensations and your emotions. You may be experiencing anger, joy, heartache and sorrow, delight, or frustration. Whatever is happening for you is important and leads you to your deeper needs. You may be celebrating self-connection, or mourning self-hate or bitterness. Your experience matters.

As you work with this meditation over time, all those who have walked this path before you are holding you with understanding and resonance, lending your compassionate and resonating self-witness their strength and experience. You are not alone on this path.

Allow your eyes to open and let yourself fully return to your breathing, to your body, and to the present moment.

WHY PRACTICE THIS MEDITATION?

When we bring attention to different parts of the brain at the same time, we are strengthening the neural associations between those areas. As neuroscientist Donald Hebb said in 1949, "Neurons that fire together, wire together."[9,10] So when we use our imagination to bring our regular, everyday self and our need for care and gentleness into relationship with the part of us that is capable of warmth, we are lighting these areas up simultaneously and in this way strengthening these associations in our brain.

When we begin to embody our RSW as a particular being, one that we can easily bring to mind, we make it easier to keep firing and wiring these fibers of self-warmth. We can use this meditation both to meet our self-witness for the first time and to develop an ongoing practice of feeling warmth for ourselves. The RSW is not a particular part of the brain; it's a metaphor for a brain function that every person can foster and develop.

As we turn toward ourselves with gentleness, rather than away from ourselves in contempt, we are taking part in a radical revolution. This total change in attitude toward self transforms the basics of parenting, of being married/partnered, of friendships and employer/employee relationships. If we bring resonance to our relationships instead of evaluation, criticism, judgment, and condemnation, we change the structure of our brains, developing the neural connections that strengthen the PFC's ability to calm and soothe the amygdala and the body.[11] Empathy for self and other, including this type of guided meditation, has been found to contribute to self-regulation.

We live in a population that largely manages itself with externals, in a world where we try to take care of our problems with prisons, pills, and penalties instead of leveraging our own human capacity for relationship to make positive, sustainable change. As we shift to internal regulation, we not only benefit ourselves by gaining all of the capacity of the PFC but also take a stand for a different world.

Other Responses to the Resonating Self-Witness Meditation

This approach advocates a path of gentleness, warmth, and understanding. For some people this is like saying, "We need to get up to those clouds to heal." The idea that we can see ourselves with tenderness can be as unthinkable as being able to fly.

It may seem unthinkable at first, but as we do the basic exercises, all kinds of new options become possible. Some people have had extraordinary experiences while listening to the resonating self-witness meditation, experiencing an internalized warmth for the first time. But that is not the only thing that happens for people.

Others can become angry or despairing when they first encounter this meditation because they have never had anyone in their lives to hold them with care. Sometimes people try to follow the meditation, and instead of finding warmth they find themselves filled with mistrust for the RSW. If something like this happened to you, it is important information about how little ground for trust you may have had.

No matter what happens during a meditation, the RSW is big enough and understanding enough to respond with empathy. For example, if a person is angry at the RSW, there would be a response like, "Do you need me to understand the enormity of your rage? Have you been alone for so long that it is unimaginable that anyone could come to find you with love?" (More on this point below.)

Still others go into the guided meditation but have a sense of emptiness. They invite their RSW to come, but no one answers. If it is difficult for you to imagine turning toward yourself with gentleness, the following resonance skill introduces you to some other possible starting places from which to grow this self-witness.

RESONANCE SKILL 3.1: POSSIBLE STARTING POINTS FOR GROWING THE RSW

In Chapter 2 we started to learn different ways that the brain self-regulates: naming emotions, reframing the situation so that we feel better about it, using distraction, and grounding ourselves in warm relationship and community (accompaniment). Now we're going to build on that base by opening the door to self-warmth and by learning skills that will help integrate resonance. Each chapter of this book builds on skills that have come before to support brain health and well-being.

- If you have ever been loved by others (a parent, a grandparent, an aunt or uncle, a beloved teacher or a friend, even a companion animal), look at yourself through their eyes.
  - What happens in their heart when they look at you?

- Think of a child or an animal that you feel fondness, affection, or love for.
  - Close your eyes and imagine holding this little one. What does it feel like to care deeply about someone else's well-being?
  - If you can feel this sense of warmth, gently bring a picture of your younger self into your mind's eye, replacing the child or animal with the image of you.
  - This may seem awkward at first because the dendrites that would join your capacity for compassion and your picture of your younger self are very unused to making a connection inside your brain. It may seem almost undoable, but even just reading these words is a starting point to begin

to create bridges between our sense of self and our ability to love.

- If you have such a profound sense of a lack of self-worth that you can't believe that it would be okay for you to be loved (as many people do—you are not alone), then ask yourself whether there was any point in your life at which you were blameless.
  - Do you have a sense of having been a pure and loveable infant, toddler, young child?
  - Is there a point at which your sense of self became tainted by trauma, abuse, or pain?
  - If you have a sense that you were born "bad," can you see any imagery of your soul before you were born? Allow yourself to notice how your soul appears to you.
  - Let something greater than yourself embrace your soul and offer you understanding.
  - We don't need to change anything, but the strange thing is that when we acknowledge what's there, our experience often shifts. So we might say to this soul, "Are you exhausted from carrying this burden of pain and shame? Do you long for healing and support and to experience a world where you are welcome and where you matter and belong?"

- Sometimes when we bring the RSW into our inner world, we can feel distrust, dismay, anger, or even murderous rage. No matter what the child self's or inner self's response, we can learn to meet that response in a new way. For example, if our inner self is mistrustful, we can ask it, "Are you hopeless about ever really being seen? Is it hard to believe that you actually matter? Does it feel like if you open up to warmth there will be another crushing disappointment when it's gone?"

- If our inner self or inner child is angry, we can use metaphor guesses to try to capture the sensation of that anger: "Is it like the world is on fire and you're the only one with an asbestos suit? Is your anger like a volcano that's going to erupt and destroy the world? Is the anger so intense that you want to take a knife and cut into the world and watch it bleed?"

- These kinds of guesses can begin to capture a little bit of the enormity of our rage, disconnection, alienation, disappointment, pain, heartbreak, terror, and ultimately our love. Track your body sensations carefully as you make the guesses, and watch for small shifts that will let you guess nuances of emotion, following your body to deeper self-knowing.

- Sometimes it is startling to hear the intensity of emotion and suffering that can come from a younger self. If any emotions are frightening for you, you may need extra support to hold this part of yourself. One way to get extra support is to find a therapist or peer counselor who gives you a sense of warmth and accompaniment. Sometimes people find that friends are helpful, or partners. There is no one right way. The most important thing is that your support is not scared of emotions, and that you have a sense of being deeply understood after you have shared.

- Sometimes people are frightened to talk about anger, for fear of harming others. It may help to know that resonant empathy is not the same as agreement with or condoning violence. Resonant empathy happens when someone else, or the self, understanding why the magnitude of emotion is there and being able to say, "of course you would feel so strongly," without endorsing any particular course of action.

- And, as always, one of the most important activities that helps to strengthen the RSW is to hold our attention on our breath and bring it back with warmth when it strays.

A word of caution: If we do a meditation where a younger self appears, and that part is dead or asleep and cannot be awakened, it can be a little scary. When I first started trying to connect with my younger self, she was covered with dirt and filth and completely unresponsive. This was years before I had any understanding of responding to my inner part with empathy. I didn't know what to do, and neither did anyone else. So I just started to imagine sitting with her without words, and it took years before she began to respond, to even notice that there was a compassionate RSW there. As I learned about resonance I became able to bring a different kind of attention to this battered and broken part. When I asked her questions with empathy, she came alive, questions like, "Are you nearly dead from exhaustion and fear and other people's pain? Is it like you've been living in a sewer of neglect, or of horror and abuse? Do you need to be gently bathed in warm water so we can get all this crud off of you and find out where your injuries are and treat them? Are you horrified and shocked by the pain of the world and by the way people take it out on each other? Are you so longing for healing and transformation for yourself and everyone?"

Planting the seeds for and growing an RSW is foundational for having a brain that is capable of self-kindness. The more we awaken the brain centers that hold our sense of self, along with the pathway of attachment, the more we are able to meet ourselves with compassion. And this more than anything else is the habit that can give us a good life, where we matter and belong, can speak up for ourselves, and can care for those we love. It's not like we can't love others without loving ourselves; people can and do have deep compassion for the world even when they are mired in self-hate (see Chapter 11). But as we heal ourselves we offer a different path to everyone we come in contact with. And easy, happy breaths and a sense of grace and trust are what go with the ability to love the self.

Camilla's Story

Before I came to Sarah's class, I had no idea that it was possible to think about myself with compassion. I was eight years old when my father threw me out on the street, screaming that I was a whore. I guess I believed him. When I first heard the class talking about a resonating self-witness, I just thought that it had nothing to do with me. But I was interested in learning about the brain, so I stayed in class. At first I was so shocked that I was in prison. It took me the whole first twelve weeks to come out of shock and start listening. And then I started talking this way with my kids on the phone, and it changed things. Sometimes I can even be gentler and warmer with myself. I have become a person for myself again, with self-respect and faith and trust.

In Chapter 4, we'll begin to practice the surprising skill of meeting the vicious DMN with resonance. When we stop fighting the internal voices and start listening to them, we begin to be capable of profound change.

CHAPTER FOUR

Taming the Inner Critic:
Hearing the Attempt to Contribute

"There's something wrong with me."
(actually, "I am enough. My story matters.")

Life With the Inner Critic

As we learned in Chapter 1, if a person has lived through trauma or has never experienced resonance, then it is possible for the default mode network (DMN), dedicated to a continual review of social interactions, to turn savage. It uses as its ammunition our errors of misunderstanding, mistakes, imperfections, shortcomings, social faux pas, or moments where we feel we have not been considerate of the needs of others.

People often call the savage DMN the "inner critic" because of its negative commentary on every thought and action. This voice ranges from self-doubt to self-contempt. Chapter 11 explores self-scorn and self-hate in more detail; this chapter explores the habits of self-evaluation, self-criticism, and self-dismissal: "What's wrong with me?" "Can't I do anything right?" "How stupid could I be?" "What am I complaining about?" "What's my problem? I had a home and enough to eat in my childhood." "I'm too sensitive."

Sometimes when people start listening to the ongoing dialogue with the inner critic, they want shut it down again right away, simply out of exhaustion, overwhelm, hopelessness, or a longing for peace and ease. Some people might even ask why anyone would ever want to hear this voice. However, if the voice is never really listened to, it never really changes, and instead we have to keep moving all the time to suppress it.

There are self-help and mindfulness books that recommend people sit with the emotions they feel and really feel them, and these books say that if this is done, the emotion will last only minutes or maybe at most an hour. In my experience, this is an optimistic statement made by someone who has had no experience with a savage DMN. It is possible for people with habits of brutal self-recrimination to have no change in their emotion-connected sensations for days, weeks, or lifetimes. This may happen because if the voices of the inner critics are not met with understanding, then they may simply continue to cannibalize their host without any sign of rest for decades, stopping only temporarily when the host is able to switch brain functioning by shifting to one of the other networks, like the dorsal attention network (see Figure 1.4), as people do when they are playing video games.

Possible Layers of Inner Critic Voices

Once we start to listen for the voices of the DMN, we find that there are many layers of self-critical expression. Let's look at the levels of self-reproach that can run as a continual voice-over on daily life:

- The first voice is utterly dismissive of any need to do healing work at all, wondering why people or the self is affected by a childhood or a past in which "nothing happened."
- The second compares and evaluates self and others. ("Look, that person has been able to figure things out. What's wrong with you?")
- The third can be almost invisible, a shame, dissociation, or shrinking that happens in response to negative self-evaluation. ("I wish I were dead." "I shouldn't be here.")

- The fourth might be a voice of blame, attacking the self for shrinking and disappearing. ("What kind of an idiot are you?")
- There can be a fifth layer, trying to soften the attack by admitting fault, a continual mantra of "I'm so stupid, I'm so stupid," or "I'm overwhelmed, I'm overwhelmed," like a guilty criminal trying to stop a painful police interrogation.
- And the sixth is added once a person starts to do healing work, blaming themselves for blaming and evaluating themselves and for not being farther down the path of healing.

The first layer, self-dismissal, is often the one people have the most contact with. It can be the first line of defense to keep them from feeling. Part of living with an unintegrated brain is being unable to comprehend how bad things really are. When the resonating self-witness (RSW), a concept introduced in Chapter 3, is offline, people undercut and dismiss themselves, making it impossible to take the self seriously, let alone feel body sensations and experience healing.

When a person finally understands that the dismissing voice has no hold on reality, the work of healing can begin. Listen for the inner voice that says, "What are you complaining about? You've got it easy compared with people who are living in war zones." Bring some healthy skepticism to your own self-dismissal, shift to warm curiosity, and find out what pain, what disappointments, and what longings lurk beneath this effort to self-regulate.

Another way self-dismissal shows up is never being enough. Would this voice ever be totally satisfied with anything? Or does it always long for the highest accolades? Is it satisfied only with valedictorian, a Rhodes scholarship, a MacArthur fellowship, a *New York Times* best seller, a top modeling contract and magazine covers, an Academy Award, *and* making the *Forbes* list of wealthiest people? And if those rewards were actually achieved, would the voice then make accusations of being an imposter? Is it possible that the critical voice holds such high standards that it is actually inhuman? A person can spend a lifetime trying to win the approval of this robotic voice whose goals of perfection are unattainable.

Another type of dismissal happens when people have no idea that anything is happening for them. Even though people are actually physically reacting to their world, they may not actually "know" that they are being affected by life. This is shown in research where people are wired to record heart rate and blood pressure and shown upsetting pictures—some claim that they aren't affected, even though, in contradiction to their own beliefs about themselves, their vital signs have clearly responded.[1] As a result, when people have no consciousness of the body and emotions, they live without knowledge of the emotional consequences of their actions. Even if some perception of emotional pain arises, they can discount it. This type of self-dismissal is another way that people keep from taking themselves seriously.

A small note for those of us who have partners, bosses, or friends who are largely living without body and emotional information: when we ask them what's wrong, and they say "nothing," even though we are seeing all sorts of signs that they are having a hard time, they are telling us the truth as they know it. Sometimes they really aren't feeling anxious, sad, or angry—because the feeling part of their being is not even in the room. Sometimes they have a feeling but don't know how to verbalize it. This can help us understand any worries we may have about whether this person is crazy or lying. (A part of the brain called the anterior cingulate detects errors between what people say and what they do. When it detects a mismatch,[2] it can trigger feelings of anxiety and perceptions of danger. This area is part of the DMN introduced in Chapter 1; we learn more about it in Chapter 5, on anxiety.) Knowing that other people can be unaware of what is happening for them can be very soothing, because it creates an understanding of what might be going on and helps us move from blame to compassion.

When people are experiencing emotional upset but don't know it, pressure can gradually build over time, resulting in a sudden and seemingly inexplicable explosion into unregulated distress: unpredictable temper tantrums, black holes of despair, or uncontrollable sobbing. These people may feel like they are standing beside themselves, seeing their own desperation, and simultaneously unable to understand it.

Another experience people might have, if they are a little more integrated, is flickering self-understanding, moments of seeing the whole picture of life and then losing sight of it. Pain may come into comprehensible focus and then blur out again, as people have moments of believing themselves and believing *in* themselves and then lose faith again. People are always reaching for balance.

Once we understand this (and a person needs their RSW to help comprehend how painful it is to live with a critical voice that is never satisfied), something inside can relax. The voice of scalpel-like judgment can be heard with a bit of humor about the self's own standards being a fool's game. We may not be able to stop trying to be perfect, but we can let go of the conviction that we should succeed at perfection. We can give birth to doubt about the truth of the inner critic's voice.

Unknowingly, people may be using the voice of the inner critic to take care of the self in the vacuum created by a lack of warmth. When people try to use the voice of cold measurement and comparison to improve themselves, they are often following the modeling of their parents, grandparents, and great-grandparents. (See Chapter 11 for more on **transgenerational trauma**, when the effects of difficult historical and personal events show up in the neurobiology of the survivors' children and grandchildren.) Let's see if research into the strengths of each of the halves of the brain, called the **hemispheres**, can support more self-compassion as we connect with all of these facets of the self-critical voice in a new way.

BRAIN CONCEPT 4.1:
THE LEFT AND RIGHT HEMISPHERES

The brain is shaped like a walnut, with a left side and a right side that are almost mirror images of each other, called the **left hemisphere** and the **right hemisphere**. These hemispheres differ in structure, and those differences might help us have self-compassion.

It is tempting to fall into black-and-white thinking and separate the hemispheres in our minds, but they are never actually separated in fact. Unless one hemisphere has been destroyed by accident or disease, everyone has two hemispheres, and both are active and contributing in everything that we do. Each hemisphere specializes, while simultaneously being entirely supported by the other hemisphere. As Alan Fogel says, "A simple metaphor for this is that a person who is right handed, for example, still needs to use the left hand to hold the paper on which she is writing or the jar she is uncapping. She might use her right arm for throwing but her left arm swings for balance." (A. Fogel, personal communication, July 20, 2016)

The left and right hemispheres both contribute to the DMN, whether it is savage or warm. The left hemisphere brings us everyday language. When it is integrated with the regulated right hemisphere, it lets us use language that connects and joins us with self and other. When it is not integrated, or when it is connected with a dysregulated right hemisphere, it emphasizes language that tears down, disconnects, compares, criticizes, and dismisses.

Both hemispheres carry the heritage of trauma and its fractures. In depression these show up particularly in the right hemisphere. Both hemispheres bring us the benefit of the integrated, resilient fibers of the emotionally healthy brain. The left hemisphere may have an easier time seeing the self as being either bad or good, perfect or imperfect, valuable or worthless. And the right hemisphere may have an easier time seeing people in their full complexity and variability, as being both caring and having moments of carelessness, both complete as they are and reaching for healing and change. In addition, the integrated map of the body and the decoding of emotions both happen in the right hemisphere,[3,4] so it is primarily here that we take in and read the body's emotional experience, as well as decoding others' emotions in their speech and understanding social cues.[5]

The left hemisphere, on the other hand, is not specialized for attunement,[6] as it cannot "hear" resonance. It has a very strong bias toward action, rather than understanding, so it tries to take care of us in its own way. It doesn't really see people as infinite, interesting, unique individuals.[7] Instead, it sees people as tools and functions, as ways to get things done: wife, husband, assistant, child, teacher, carpenter, surgeon.[8] It also carries our awareness of social hierarchy, so it sees people (and the self) as more or less talented, wealthy, secure, advantaged, nice-looking, powerful, and so on, than others.[9]

Scientists have noticed these different ways of looking at the world and have investigated the structure of the brain to try to find the roots of these differences. One study shows that the left hemisphere is wired differently from the right hemisphere.[10] There are other structural variations as well, but these details are less important than understanding how to hear the voice of the brain and move toward integration.

Real-world metaphors are always inadequate to describe the quantum environment of the brain, but we could reach for understanding by saying that the feel of the interconnection of the left hemisphere is like a topsy-turvy orchard, with the leaves and branches on neighboring trees reaching out toward and touching the roots of one another. (Remember that even though scientists refer to dendrite "trees," these branches would be connecting with the neighboring tree roots, and roots to branches, etc.) In contrast, the right hemisphere is more like a jungle, with interconnections across the hemisphere, like vines running long distances and linking plants and trees that are quite far apart.[11] These structural differences mean that we measure and compare (and criticize) with the left hemisphere, while we use the right hemisphere's widely connected and associated neural networks to see the bigger picture.[12]

The hemispheres are in constant dialogue with each other. They do the same things, but they do them in different ways. This means that people have two ways they can look at themselves and at the world. As author Iain McGilchrist writes, the left hemisphere "aims to reach one correct answer ('either/or')"; while the right hemisphere "is more able to live with ambivalence and the possibility of two apparently incompatible possibilities being true ('both/and')."[13]

As we learn about the hemispheres, we start to be able to tell the difference between patterns of self-responsiveness that harm us and patterns that support us.

The Hemispheres and the Resonating Self-Witness

Both hemispheres use language, with the main speech centers for everyday life in the left hemisphere. The right hemisphere, on the other hand, hums with the language of poetry,[14] fresh metaphor,[15] emotions (even swear words),[16] familial relationships,[17] nonverbal communication,[18] and the deep values that motivate feelings[19] (all of which are listed in the introduction of this book as forms of resonant language), so this hemisphere contributes greatly to the RSW.

Each of the hemispheres contributes to our well-being, and each contributes to self-denigration. The inner critic pulls from both hemispheres to include layers of comparison, evaluation, pain, rigidity, depression, denial, and inhuman standards. The RSW brings wholeness, understanding, self-compassion, appreciation of beauty, and the power to be deeply motivated by dreams. Without an RSW, people can cut themselves to shreds at the same time that they deny they are in pain. They can continuously expect themselves to be capable of perfection, not even remembering or caring about their humanness. At worst, people are enslaved to this voice. At best, people listen with a grain of salt, not believing that the voice is telling the truth but using its brilliance, clarity, and high standards to motivate, act, achieve their goals, create exquisite balance, and keep themselves on track.

People need both hemispheres to be working at their best to have a warm DMN and an RSW, with the prefrontal cortex (PFC) linking with the limbic system to run a continual stream of warmth and regulation, and both hemispheres supporting activity and functionality. People's presence with one another comes from the aliveness of eye gaze, voice, gestures, and touch. The choice of words is important, too. When we want to capture resonance in verbal form, it can be supportive to understand the deep longings and values that help us to make sense of emotions.

RESONANCE SKILL 4.1:
LISTENING FOR PEOPLE'S DEEP LONGINGS

The students in the prisons where I taught classes on the brain and how we use language had limited contact with their families—phone calls, letters, some visits—so I didn't expect them to be able to try out their skills from our classes with their relatives. As a result, I was very surprised when one of the women spoke up about her conversations with family members. In her story you will notice that she didn't just stop with the feelings; she also asked her relatives about what might be underlying their emotions.

"My mother and her brother have not spoken in five years," she said. "We all used to have Thanksgiving together every year, but after my grandfather went into assisted living, and after my uncle's oldest daughter died, the family fell apart. Well, I decided to try out my new skills on my family. I talked to my mom on the phone, and she talked about how mad she was at her brother. I asked her, 'Mom, are you mad at Uncle? When you think about how hard you worked to keep grandpa out of assisted living, do you need acknowledgment and appreciation? And how about understanding?' And my mom said, 'Yes!' Then my uncle called, and he was talking about how mad he was at my mom. 'Uncle,' I said, 'do you feel hopeless when you think about my mom's reaction to your daughter's death? Are you worried that my mom doesn't get your grief about your daughter? Do you need understanding? And to be able to mourn?' And my uncle said, 'Yes!' And now they're having Thanksgiving together. I wish I could be a fly on the wall for that!"

This story shows us that we have feelings for a reason. We have feelings because things really matter to us—big things, like love, understanding, acknowledgment, appreciation, faith, peace, trust, and care. These are right-hemisphere concepts. The left hemisphere, our engine of doing, takes action based on what matters most to us, what we care most passionately about, the values that we set our roots into and pull our strength from. The linkage of feelings and needs was first written about extensively by Marshall Rosenberg.[20] He called this approach to connecting to one another *Nonviolent Communication*. I base my teaching about communication on Rosenberg's book *Nonviolent Communication: A Language of Life*,[21] because it gives so much clarity about what kind of language connects us and what words and habits disconnect us. An unexpected side benefit of Rosenberg's work is that it integrates the brain as well as bringing people together, awakening both the hemispheres and helping them work together.

It can be a surprise to discover that there are messages and longings behind feelings, as people often don't know that they are there. (Rosenberg uses the word *needs* to describe these deep messages, but sometimes people prefer words like *values, principles, big ideas, qualities,* or *what we hold dear*. It doesn't matter what they are called—on a brain level they all work. The only important thing is that naming them helps people attune and resonate with other human beings.)

Although people might deny that they have needs, their lives are continually woven together by their longings. People are moved by what they want, even in the most difficult of situations. And in any difficult situation there is a complex layering of what needs are or are not being met. Once people start connecting with their longings, it can be a shock to discover that they have bigger hearts than they expected and that they really want integrity, truth, or something global for everyone, such as the well-being of all children.

This complexity lies at the root of difficult decisions. For example, if adults are choosing to live in a home where there is domestic violence or emotional abuse, they may be trying to satisfy their longings for love and connection. Or it may be dangerous to leave, so they may be prioritizing survival, or financial security, or the well-being of their children. And at the same time, other needs may not be met in that situation. It might be hard for such people even to hope for respect, care, warmth, tenderness, physical safety, well-being, and mutuality. Loveless marriages can have a similar complexity. Another example is when we watch our friends pouring their life energy into a relationship where they aren't getting much back. Caring for a compromised family member or friend who is ungrateful may come from the desire to contribute and the relief when there is stability, but it may not prioritize the desire for mutuality, acknowledgment, or appreciation.

Below a list of universal human needs and values. Each need catapults us into the PFC and allows us to see the bigger picture. Identifying the deep longings that are at play moves us into the self-regulation skill of reframing. Some needs bring us more into relationship with the values of the left hemisphere, such as efficiency and optimism. Others take us into the depth of the right hemisphere, such as love and faith.

Universal Human Needs and Values
Autonomy:

Choice	Independence	Self-responsibility
Freedom	Power, agency	

Integrity:

Authenticity	Healing	Wholeness
Individuality, being a whole self	Purpose/meaning	

Appreciation:

Acknowledgment	Consideration, to matter to self	To be seen
Acceptance, self-acceptance		To be known

Self-Expression:

Creativity	Passion
Growth	Work
Purpose	Spontaneity

Interdependence:

Contribution
Community
Consideration
Cooperation
Friendship

Harmony, peace
Ease
Mutuality
The well-being of
    those we love

Preservation of life
Respect, seeing one
    another as whole
Support, help
Trust, honesty

Nurturing, Nourishment:

Affection
Resonance

Care, self-care
Comfort, warmth

Empathy
Kindness, tenderness

Survival (streams of nourishment):

Air, water, food,
    shelter
Touch

Movement
Health, well-being
Rest, sleep

Safety
Sex

Celebration:

Aliveness
Delight
Death, mourning

Fun, play
Humor
Joy

Passion
Flow

Connection:

Belonging, inclusion
Communication
Love, intimacy,
    closeness
Friendship

Companionship
Participation,
    partnership
Relationship,
    mutuality

Predictability
Dependability
Shared values
Shared history, reality,
    culture

Security

Consistency
Reliability, stability

Order, structure
Predictability

Protection
Trust
Dignity

Mental:

Understanding/clarity	Learning
Information	Stimulation

Spiritual:

Beauty	Harmony	Tranquility
Connection with life	Inspiration	Serenity
Faith, hope		Presence

The list can never be complete. Notice that these words are all abstract concepts. None of them are about anybody in particular doing anything in particular—we don't *need* our partner to agree to a vacation in Hawaii, for example, or for our children to do their chores immediately. We may *want* them to do these things, but underneath there is something more fundamental at play. When we examine the desires that underlie these actions, we may find that what we actually long for might include support, shared reality, connection, partnership, and responsibility. Happily, many different strategies, besides where we travel or how quickly someone else responds, can allow us to be in touch with our deepest values.

Looking for these values at the root of behavior is so calming and profound that its simplicity is counterintuitive. Let's bring some of this foundational understanding to the inner critic in the next guided meditation.

GUIDED MEDITATION 4.1: Empathy for the Inner Critic

What is the critic really wanting from us? What if you could tell the difference between the voice of your inner critic (which is more a left-hemisphere voice) and your RSW (which is more a right-hemisphere voice)? How would these two voices interact?

If you feel a little bewildered by the question, stop for a moment and ask yourself how you feel about yourself when you are "failing" at something. For example, "What is it like for me to meditate?" (Other questions might be, "What is it like for me to make a speech or present publicly?" "What would it be like to try something new, like writing, cooking, dancing, singing for others?") The inner critic can scream the loudest when faced with the challenge of self-expression, because it so wants invulnerability. People are at their most vulnerable when they are extending themselves into the world without knowing whether their life energy will be caught.

What if the RSW were to respond with resonance to the critic's fears? Would there be an acknowledgment of how worried this voice is? Would the critic relax a little if it heard that there was understanding for its hopelessness and exhaustion? This meditation explores more options for responding to the self-critic.

Before you begin, make a list of the judgments you have of yourself. Do you call yourself names? Do you use adjectives that imply you are wrong or bad, like *stupid, idiotic, hopeless, clumsy, or incompetent?* Do you compare yourself to others and come up wanting? Do you feel resignation, dismissal, contempt, or apathy when you think about yourself? Is there any irritation, impatience, or even rage? (You are starting to hear the voice of the left hemisphere here.)

The uncomforted right hemisphere is at play in the inner critic's experience, too. Do you feel sadness, depression, or fear about how you are in the world? Is the intensity of disgust, self-loathing, or horror part of your experience? (If this type of intensity in reaction to the self is familiar to you, make sure you also read Chapter 11 on understanding self-hate.)

Choose the judgment that packs the most punch—the statement that your body has the strongest reaction to. Now that you have a starting point for what your inner critic sounds like, let's begin.

> Begin with your body and where it is in space. Where are your shoulders in relationship to your stomach? Where are your elbows in relationship to your hips? Where are your feet and your knees, and how does your forehead relate to them?
>
> Now bring your attention to your breath. Can you feel the shape your breath makes in your lungs when you inhale? How far down into your torso does the shape go? Can you feel any changes in your abdomen as you breathe? What happens to the shape when

you exhale? Invite your attention to rest with the changing shape of your breath in your chest and your diaphragm. When your attention wanders away from your sense of the shape of your breath, gently and with warmth invite it back.

Now, invite yourself to dip back into your critic's voice. Say the words that you found aloud. What happens in your body? Do you stop breathing? Whatever sensations you find, even if there is a step into blankness or numbness, see if there is an emotion word that begins to describe what you feel. And what are the deeper longings that lie below the words?

As you slowly read the guesses in the list below, take what works for you and discard the rest. The experience of reading these possible deep motives for self-criticism can feel overwhelming. Notice your own response, and hold yourself with gentleness. If you are listening to this as a recording, pause it or stop it whenever you would like to. The purpose of this meditation is to gently inquire into how the critic is trying to contribute, and what it's like to hear the heart of the inner critic. Return to the critic's words as you read through the list, and see which questions really resonate for the deeper needs that lie beneath the criticism. If you find one that lands for you, stop reading and let it sink in. See if it offers you a different way to see this inner judge.

If nothing here really rings true for you, does the list inspire you to come up with your own questions about feelings and needs for the critic, following your body's patterns of tension and relaxation? You can use the feelings and needs lists above to support this exploration.

For now, stay with offering resonance to the critic's voice—in a moment we will come to empathy for the part receiving the judgments. These statements move from mild to intense on the spectrum of self-criticism:

- Critic, do you feel discouraged, and do you love perfection?
- Have you given up hope, and do you value accountability?

- Are you disappointed, and do you wish for fulfillment of promise?
- Is there a longing for focus, competency, and accomplishment?
- Critical self, do you feel distrustful, and do you want dependability and follow-through?
- Are you impatient, and do you long for change and transformation?
- Do you feel skeptical, and are you wishing for faith and trust?
- Inner critic, are you doubtful, and are you wanting reassurance?
- Are you irritated, and do you ache for precision?
- Are you bored, and do you want originality and authentic self-expression?
- Do you feel dismissive, and do you long for competency and mastery?
- Do you feel contemptuous, and do you ache for agency?
- Do you feel angry, and do you want success?
- Does hopelessness consume you, and do you need acknowledgment for how exhausting it is to keep trying and never hit the mark?

For the really intense inner critic:
- Do you feel enraged and furious, and would you like to destroy the earth as acknowledgment for the hugeness of your rage?
- Are there times when you'd like to obliterate the self? Do you long for peace?

Finally, and most important:
- Is this inner critic despairing and just wanting to contribute?

Do you have any more guesses for what lies beneath the inner critic's pain?

And now, shifting your focus, what happens when you bring your attention to the part of you that is receiving the judgment?

What happens in your body when you hear the words of self-criticism? Do you stop breathing when you receive them? Whatever sensations you find, even if there is a step into blankness or numbness, see if there is an emotion word that begins to describe what you feel. And what are the deeper longings that lie below the words? As you hear the guesses, take what works for you and discard the rest. If you are inspired to, come up with your own guesses, following your body's patterns of tension and relaxation.

- Self, have you become very small and ashamed, needing support and reassurance?
- Are you sad, and do you need to know that you are loved just as you are?
- Are you feeling confused, and do you need understanding?
- Are you constantly anxious, and do you need relief and hope?
- Are you hopeless and longing for acceptance?
- Do you feel exhausted and overwhelmed, and do you need acknowledgment of the heavy burden of criticism and how hard it has been to carry this load for so many years?
- Do you feel bewildered, and do you long for clarity?
- Are you scared, and do you need protection and room to breathe?
- Are you despairing and panicked, and do you need some solid ground to stand on?
- Have you shut down in order to survive the hopelessness of never being enough?
- Are you tired of trying, and do you need ease?
- Are you feeling distrustful, and do you need hope for transformation and change?
- Are you impatient with being criticized? Do you long for acceptance and support?
- Do you feel irritated at being judged, and would you like respect?
- Are you lonely, needing belonging and love?

Now, notice what has happened for both parts of you in being acknowledged for their experience. Has anything in your body changed?

As you come back to your breathing, bring your resonating self-witness's perspective up above you, so that you are looking down on yourself from the ceiling or the sky. If you change the point of view that you are using to look at yourself, does it help you shift your usual judgments? Can you see yourself with warmth and acceptance? Can you acknowledge your own accomplishments and burdens with compassion?

Allow yourself to return to the gentle and warm holding of your attention with the shape of your breath. If you have scared or alarmed yourself by letting the inner critic have a voice in the meditation, offer some empathy to the trembling, vulnerable, or angry part of you that reacted to the intrusion. This part of you may enjoy a needs guess, like "Are you longing for safe spaces and protection so that it feels good to explore and learn?" or "Are you shocked and angry, longing for respect and consideration?" Follow your body, and notice how it responds to your acknowledgment of its experience.

Now, return to your breath and the organic shape that it is making in your lungs, following the furling and unfurling movement of the air. Gradually, gently, whenever you are ready, allow yourself to return to gentleness and a relationship with the outer world.

Notice that there is a difference between looking at yourself with hard eyes and evaluating, and looking at yourself with soft eyes, seeing the interconnectedness between yourself and your community, seeing the complexity of your experience, your emotions, any anniversaries, any life-long struggles, and the values you long to be able to embody. Notice how the voice of the inner critic may not be as strong when you allow yourself to see the bigger picture of your life.

WHY PRACTICE THIS MEDITATION?

This meditation invites us to look at the relationship between the critical self and the part that is vulnerable to criticism, and it invites an understanding that people are larger than both of these parts. As people learn to identify the voice of critical self-judgment, they can start to understand its limitations, rather than trusting its evaluations, and they start to be able to look for the real voice of truth—the part of the self that is strong, resourced, and warm.

As the inner voices are heard with clarity, people begin to notice that everything they do is an attempt to meet a need. They are always trying to take care of themselves and others as best they can, sometimes with a tragic disregard of the hearts of the people involved.

As these voices are transformed by having their deepest longings heard, people get to climb out of the hamster wheel of not being enough. People get to become who they were born to be. They finally get to give birth to what lives within them, waiting to arise.

Notice whether the voice of your inner critic uses any familiar tactics or wording. If it were not you speaking to yourself, if your inner judge were actually a parent or past teacher, who would it be? Does this part of you use the words that your parents used when they were disappointed with you or with themselves? If there were deep longings that your parents had for you, or that their parents had for them, what would they be?

What We Have Learned About Responding to the Critical Inner Voice

Gradually, as we do this work, we begin to hear, identify, and call upon the different types of inner voices:

- The voice of denial, dismissal, criticism, and contempt (left hemisphere)
  - Not a trustworthy voice. If we believe it, we're in trouble. Bring in your healthy skepticism.

- Listen for the deeper message from this voice. A resonant response is to wonder about the need for acknowledgment of an underresourced world, or of exhaustion, of how many times we have tried to succeed and have fallen short of our longings. Other possibilities: "Are you longing for my well-being?" "Do you want me to survive?" "Do you believe that this world is merciless?" If we take the best from this voice, we can start to use its recommendations for change and improvement without being paralyzed or disabled by it. We access a love of balance, discernment, high standards, and intention for improvement.
- Like using a wind at our back, we can catch the energy of the critical voice to move us toward our deep longings and big-picture sense of our life to let our integrity lie at the root of our decision making and the actions that we take.
- Taking the best from this voice, we bring a balanced, integrated, and coordinated eye to our movement through the world, using both left and right hemispheres and combining integrity and organization, drive and generosity.

- The voice of pain, depression, overwhelm, hopelessness, and paralysis (right hemisphere)
  - The voice of ungrieved mourning. If we stop without looking for the root of the grief, we are in trouble. (More on this in Chapter 12 on depression.)
  - If we take the best from this voice, we acknowledge our own pain and humanness with humility, and without succumbing to paralysis and disability.
  - If we listen to this voice with strength, resilience, and self-compassion, we can find the mourning and hold it with exquisite gentleness and support, offering resonance and understanding but not losing ourselves in the process.

· If we take the best from this voice, our deepest longings are made real with integrity and power, and we start to fuel our action in the world, using our deepest dreams to move us.

Life After the Inner Judge Has Been Understood, Decoded, and Decommissioned

The following list begins to fill in what it is like to live with gentleness and self-understanding as your RSW begins to contribute to your well-being. As you read through this list, see which possibilities are within your reach, which are at your cutting edge, and which are still completely unthinkable for you:

- Starting to enjoy simply breathing
- Taking pleasure in the moments when you are alone and quiet
- Attuning to the voice of your body and hearing your own intuition
- Noticing that the people around you are interesting, that their words and their choices reveal their hearts
- Listening to all the layers of experience that people reveal when they speak
- Honoring the marks the journey of life has left in people's faces
- Taking pleasure in the invitations you receive from others to connect and spend time together
- Understanding that disconnection and the capacity to do emotional injury to others are the result of unhealed trauma or living an unaccompanied life
- Becoming willing to challenge the voices of self-denigration, self-criticism, and self-loathing
- Starting to notice what you really love and what has meaning for you

- Becoming willing to take action to create the world you want to live in
- Becoming able to describe your dreams and ask for what you're longing for
- Opening to receive what life is bringing you, finding the gifts within it
- Stopping and honoring your deep longings and loves when you are in pain
- Making sense to yourself
- Understanding and seeing the grace that has brought you to this point
- Knowing that you are a richly complex human, beautiful in your uniqueness
- Growing your capacity for awe, wonder, and curiosity
- Becoming vulnerable to both love and pain
- Choosing the way you spend your time and life energy based on what gives you joy
- Enjoying a sense of real-time relationship
- Letting your heart be broken open

Strange as it may seem, if you are just starting out on this journey, all of this sweetness lies ahead of you. As we hear the voices of fear and disconnection and feel into the underlying roots of these experiences, we are starting to calm the brain and opening the way for integration of the best of the right hemisphere (empathy, warmth, resonance, understanding) with the best of the left (clarity, action, drive).

At the same time, this can be hard to imagine. If you have a skeptical inner critic, there might be quite a backlash of disbelief against the idea that life could be better. If you are hearing this disbelieving voice, you can ask it if it is trying to save you from the pain of discouragement, and thank it for trying so hard to take care of you.

Chapter 5 looks at the physical effects of carrying the voices of our less-than-compassionate self-witnesses in our bodies—and how to bring resonance to the experience of anxiety.

CHAPTER FIVE

Calming Anxiety: Moving Toward Trust

"If I relax, all hell is going to break loose."
(actually, "I can trust myself and others.")

Anxiety is an emotion that the body interprets as a warning sign that something is wrong. It can eat a person alive. There is the gnawing sense that something is amiss, just under the surface of consciousness. It can feel like a burning, or a jangly electrical current under the skin, often in the chest. Sometimes it comes with a disquiet, tightness, or tension in the belly. It is a low-level sensation-wrapped irritation that is exhausting to live with and that some people endure for years or even decades. Once bodies are slowed down enough so that their voices can really be heard, the discovery can be made that they are trying to take care of us. Often bodies are trying to dampen the experience of anxiety with the food they get us to eat compulsively, or by drinking alcohol, smoking marijuana, or indulging in addictive activities.

Whatever the experience of anxiety, as care and attentiveness are brought to body sensations, inroads are made toward peace and well-being.

PANKSEPP'S CIRCUITS OF EMOTIONS

Circuit of Emotion	What Matters to This Circuit (needs, longings, values)	Human Emotions Involved (feelings)
CARE	Contribution, care, love, empathy, harmony, belonging, warmth, resonance, protection	Tenderness, contentment, love, protectiveness
LUST	Sexual expression, physical intimacy, partnership	Lust, desire
PLAY	Play, fun, self-expression, creativity	Amusement, delight, excitement, happiness, surprise
FEAR	Safety, predictability, calm	Anxiety, fear, terror, horror
RAGE	Advocacy, agency, effectiveness, mattering, purpose, respect, freedom	Irritation, contempt, anger, hatred, rage
PANIC/ GRIEF	Connection, love, friendship, presence	Anxiety, sadness, loneliness, grief, dismay, embarrassment, guilt, shame, pining
SEEKING	Survival, satisfaction	Satisfaction, relief, pride, excitement

BRAIN CONCEPT 5.1:
ANXIETY AND THE CIRCUITS OF EMOTION

In the best of all possible brains, the prefrontal cortex (PFC) is actively supporting emotional regulation. The less activity there is in the PFC, the more the brain suffers. This is one form of dysregulation. A brain with an inactive PFC is more likely to be an anxious brain.[1] This is why it is so important to awaken the sense of the resonating self-witness (RSW), because as we bring intentional warmth to our difficult emotional moments, we are bringing strength to the patterns of neural connection that support well-being.

In addition, neuroscientist Jaak Panksepp, the man who discovered that rats laugh like humans,[2] has spent his life researching how our emotions are hard-wired to move along particular pathways in our brains. As described in Chapter 3, Panksepp has differentiated seven distinct paths that our motivations and emotions follow, which he calls circuits of emotion.[3] We learned about the CARE circuit earlier. Here we are interested in the FEAR and PANIC/GRIEF circuits. The above below, modified from Panksepp's work, shows the seven circuits, what matters to them, and which of our human emotions each involves.

Notice that *anxiety* shows up both in connection with FEAR and with PANIC/GRIEF. When Panksepp was first discovering the PANIC/GRIEF circuit, he saw that it was most active when small mammals had been separated from their mothers. PANIC is the lonely, seeking voice of the baby seal that has been left on the beach while her mother goes out to hunt for fish. It is the mewling cry of hungry kittens when their mother has left them.

And it exists in humans: we have an entirely separate circuit that comes alive when we are separated from someone who is important to us. It's not that we are afraid of danger; it's that we have been left alone, and our full skull-body-brain knows it. This is the territory of abandonment, empty-nesting, human heartbreak, and the emotional devastation that comes with the death of loved ones, although it can also be where we feel simple sadness or loneliness.

What Panksepp realized was that the anxiety that is connected to FEAR is very different from the anxiety connected to PANIC/GRIEF, even though it feels exactly the same on the inside.[4] This is important to know because when we have a sense of which type of circuit we are experiencing, we have more of a sense of what flavor of resonance will be most helpful for us. We usually don't want safety or protection when we are anxious with loneliness. And we usually don't need intimacy when we are anxious because we are afraid for our lives or worried about the future.

It is also possible to feel FEAR anxiety and PANIC anxiety at the same time.[5] There can be worry about paying the mortgage alone and wanting a partner to share the load of life. There can be loneliness combined with the sense that there is physical danger from not being accompanied. Another mixed example is the confusing anxious pain a person can feel when a family member is in the throes of addiction. There might be fear about negative consequences and a desire to get the family member out of the home. At the same time, there might be a loneliness for that person's presence.

We can need acknowledgment of present-day loss in such situations. It is also possible for present-day experiences to be distant echoes of old, unprocessed feelings from past losses. For example, making and losing a friend in midlife can bring up the heartbreak of losing a friend in grade school. It can be calming to understand this, so that we at least check whether the past is at play when we are overcome with stress. Sometimes it can help us to see that our anxiety is ancient and that we are just trying to find present-day experiences to help us understand why we are still anxious now. If we don't look at the past, we may think that if we resolve today's problems, we will feel at peace. But instead, when peace doesn't come after taking care of that issue, we move on to the next worry, and the one after that, never finding the calm we long for, because we are looking in the wrong place. (More on resolving issues from the past in Chapter 6.)

Obviously if people are experiencing domestic violence, living in a war zone, trying to deal with the threat of impending home foreclosure, or experiencing other current trauma, then the immediacy of what's happening will create an enormous and well-grounded present-time anxiety.

If you live with blended anxiety, think about what percentage of your sensations could be connected to abandonment and what percentage of your anxiousness could be connected to fear about things that have not yet happened or about danger you are in. What is your own personal experience of this agitation? Whichever flavor your anxiety is, it makes your brain work harder and puts you under stress. If you can really get to know your own experience of anxiety, your RSW will find it easier to respond with care.

No matter what the situation is, it will be helpful in some way to name the emotional experience and awaken the RSW. The following resonance skill gives some examples of how to bring emotions and longings together when we are using language with ourselves in this new way.

RESONANCE SKILL 5.1: PUTTING WORDS TO ATTUNEMENT AND RESONANCE

One way to put emotional experience into words is to bring together your body sensations, the emotions they might be linked with, and the big ideas, or longings, that might be at the root of the sensations and feelings, all in a spirit of warm curiosity toward the self. We wonder what is most important to ourselves in this moment. Then, in the spirit of dialoguing with the self, we can ask if our felt sense of what might be happening for ourselves comes close. As we do this, we acknowledge that the RSW can't know absolutely the complexities of what we are feeling. In this way, we leave room for self-discovery.

This kind of inquiry references the idea that we most often have feelings for a reason. For example, if we are angry about a coworker taking more credit than he is due for a project that we worked on, we can stay annoyed with that person for a long time. However, if we understand our own irritation and see our own longing for some combination of acknowledgment, contribution, integrity, and partnership, we may find that the feeling of irritation melts away.

As a gesture of respect, this type of inquiry always ends with a question mark, rather than a period—for example, "Self, I wonder if you are sad today, and if you just need to mourn?" versus "I know you're sad and you need to mourn." The question that is asked is open-ended, referencing a deep value that might be important, rather than a desire to have ourselves do a particular thing, for example, "a need for acknowledgment and truth" versus "having our boss know that the coworker didn't contribute much to that project."

We can base our wonderings on body sensations and emotions that seem clear, or we can base our guesses on what we hear ourselves say. For example, I might say, "I hate her." If I, as my own RSW, am not listening closely, I might reply to myself saying, "We don't say hate, honey," missing the deeper meaning, which might be, "There is a group of girls saying things to me that hurt, and one of them used to be my best friend." This type of understanding can be so easily missed in our ordinary way of listening, but it can be revealed by a different level of wondering.

Listening deeply to ourselves has nothing to do with fixing the situation. In my classes, one of the women mentioned that she kept getting pulled into anger at a small group of ex-friends that she was spending less time with as she was becoming healthier. She was worried that she would lash out physically and lose the ground that she had gained. She looked at the list of universal human needs and values (see Chapter 4) to see what was so important to her. The words that stood out to her were *respect*, *choice*, *privacy*, *honesty*, *protection*, and *safety*. As the woman named each longing out loud, she gradually relaxed. "This is starting to make sense," she said, and she told us that she wasn't angry and afraid of getting into a fight any more. Then she said, "Now I'm just sad. I feel sad for them, and sad for myself. Change is hard. I'm not afraid that I'll fight them now." It is clear from this story that this woman's external situation didn't change. But she was able to awaken her RSW and resonate with herself.

The guessing of what might be important for ourselves or another person is a sacred, radical act. It requires faith in humanness and in the power of truth. It allows us to touch our own center. And the qualities that we find there are eternal—they are not changed by external circumstances. They have just been buried by trauma, lack of support, injury, pain, or low levels of resources (poverty, ill health, no access to nature, or too many demands on time). When we name needs and values and wonder about what is important at the deepest level, either to ourselves or to the person sitting in front of us, we reawaken these qualities, and we remind ourselves of who we really are (or the other of who they really are).

If nothing shifts when we act as our own RSW, or when someone else resonates with us, there may be old pain from childhood that is keeping us frozen. Even this experience is available to be named. As we will see in Chapter 6, if the way we felt as a child is truly known and resonated with, and if we start to know and resonate with ourselves, our body may relax and the way we think about who we are may change utterly.

And when we or others spend the time to understand us and connect with us, the message we receive is that we matter. Remember that the amygdala is asking, "Am I safe? Do I matter?" Warm attention from our own RSW or from another person answers that question with a resounding "Yes!" Our human upsets are made to be soothed by warmth and clarity, by accuracy and understanding, and by the strong sense that our message has been received.

And whether our anxiety is rooted in the past or in the present, in fear or in panic, why does it feel so unpleasant?

BRAIN CONCEPT 5.2: NEUROTRANSMITTERS AND THE "ANXIETY COCKTAIL" IN OUR BRAINS

Sometimes people are anxious all the time. These people live with an uneasy feeling in their stomach that they believe defines them. It has been part of the experience of being alive for so long that they can't imagine existing without it. As people begin to name this sensation, the word they use most often is *anxiety*. Many others have lived with anxiety for so long that they don't even know it's there. It's like an elbow or a big toe—it's just a part of them. Sometimes it takes the brand-new experience of resonance for them to really feel true relaxation in their bodies. And only then can they begin to notice that they have been carrying anxiety for as long as they can remember.

There are many ways to work with anxiety, including medication, therapy, acupuncture, and yoga. The body-based empathy approach described here can be used on its own or added to any of these.

The brain runs on a cocktail of chemicals, called **neurotransmitters**, that let the neurons communicate with one another. When a person is anxious, adrenaline[6] and cortisol[7] increase. The jittery feeling of anxiety can be hard to shift. This is partly because when cortisol stays high for a long period of time our balancing brain chemicals are depleted, including (again) adrenaline, serotonin, dopamine[8] and oxytocin.[9] (And this depletion can lead to depression.)[10]

There are also relationships between anxiety and the brain's calming chemical, gamma-aminobutyric acid (**GABA**),[11] as well as the other calming neurotransmitters, including the **endogenous opioids, endocannabinoids,** and **endogenous benzodiazepines**.[12] (Yes, the brain makes its own morphine-, marijuana-, and Valium-like substances.) When anxiety gets intense, the amygdala takes over, and production of these calming neurotransmitters declines. Suddenly there is less access to the PFC[13] and so less of an ability to regulate emotions, leading to the negativity of the unfriendly DMN. This means that a person's actions are more reactive and less considered, and the unwise decisions can cause even greater stress. This additional stress makes people even less effective, and they find themselves in a negative and self-perpetuating loop. Cortisol is a measure of our well-being, and just like Goldilocks, it likes things to be just right. Too much cortisol is harmful, and too little is hard on us, too.

As stress becomes chronic, it takes a toll on the body and brain. Cortisol levels become depleted, and fatigue can be the result, affecting sleep, functioning, memory, mood, and the immune system.[14] Rats that are under chronic stress lose their cunning and creativity and rely on old routines and automatic responses. The part of the rat's brain that makes decisions and can stay connected to its goals shrinks, and new brain territory is claimed for making habits instead of for thinking. The rat begins "going through the motions" of life and relies on doing the same things over and over again instead of trying anything new.[15] This is because stress and anxiety have shifted the rat's brain chemistry, which is very similar to what happens in human brains with anxiety. (One more thing to be anxious about!) As people heal from stress and anxiety, they find that they become more flexible and less ruled by habit. If people could see their own neurotransmitters, they would see that balance changing as well.

Whatever kinds of support work best are the most important ones to use. Many people who are on medications for conditions like anxiety and depression find that developing the RSW allows them to decrease their medications. The decrease in the power and believability of the self-critic's voice leads to increased relaxation and less struggle, so less medication is needed to keep anxiety and depression at bay.

Some people using this approach to self-care discover that they are able to reach out to the medical profession and receive support in the form of medications or therapy for the first time. The clarity offered by self-resonance lets the tumult and chaos in their brains calm enough that they can tell they need support. "I didn't even know that I was depressed or that help was possible," one person told me. "Now that I know what's happening, I know how to get help." That is the power of resonance at work. As people experience resonant warmth, they increase the natural flow of all the calming neurotransmitters, and they are able to make better self-care decisions. Follow the body wherever it leads.

The following resonance skill provides some practice with using body (or somatic) sensations, the lists of "pleasant" and "unpleasant" feelings (Chapter 3), and the list of universal human needs and values (Chapter 4) to resonate with the self. This approach is called self-empathy.

RESONANCE SKILL 5.2: PRACTICING RESONANCE FOR THE SELF (SELF-EMPATHY)

The following recipe for somatic-based empathy can be used in meditation or in journaling, and some people even record their own voices on their smartphones and then have a conversation with themselves. When we catch the essence of our experience by noticing our body sensations and understanding our emotions and longings, our inner worlds shift. Let's take a look at what this kind of experience might be like.

Recipe for Self-Empathy

1. Being as precise as you can, describe the details of what triggered you most recently. If you can name the moment that things were worst for you during the experience, what was it? If you don't know what the worst moment was, use the experience as a whole.
2. Bring your attention to your body, specifically to the inside of your stomach and abdomen, the inside of your chest with your sense of your heart and your lungs, your throat, and the muscles of your face.

3. When you think about the trigger, what happens in your body? Be as precise with the sensations as possible, for example, tight in the top of the gut, light cramping in the intestines, ribs feel stuck, diaphragm stops moving, lump in the throat, or tears pricking in the eyes.

4. Choose the body sensation that is most alive.

5. Ask yourself, if this sensation had an emotional flavor, what would it be? Is it sadness, irritation, anger, fear, shock, horror, hopelessness? Or is it something more subtle, like dismay, resignation, contempt, or shame? (You can use the feelings lists from Chapter 3.)

6. When your body says yes to one or more emotions, ask yourself, if this emotion made perfect sense, what would I be longing for? (You can use the list of universal human needs from Chapter 4 to see which things are important to you in this situation.)

7. Return to your memory of the trigger.

8. What happens in your body now?

9. Again, if these sensations were emotions, what emotions would they be?

10. And what needs lie beneath these feelings?

11. As you continue to work with these layers of sensations, feelings, and needs, your experience of irritation or other emotions may start to shift. If you are continuing to want a particular person to do a particular thing, you may have a need to mourn the difference between your dream of this relationship and what is actually present at this time.

12. Has your body sensation softened in any way? (You aren't listening in order to change your body; you are listening in order to receive the messages that your body wants you to understand. Body changes are part of the dialogue. The distinction here is similar to having a conversation with someone else, where you are listening to the other in order to really understand the other, not to make the other say the next thing, or stop talking altogether.)

13. As the conversation with your body evolves, see if any other feelings or needs rise to the surface of consciousness, wanting to be acknowledged.

We let our bodies respond with yes, no, and clarification. We are bringing the power of the simple statement "Of course" to our experience. "Of course I am sad. This is the anniversary of my mother's death, and I need time and support to mourn her." "Of course I am irritated, or even enraged, when my neighbor has cut down a tree on our property line. I loved that tree, and it provided shade and privacy. It was my old friend." "Of course I am angry and wanting choice in this world. And I need to be able to grieve the loss." "Of course I feel anxious. There has been an unending stream of requests from family and friends and work, and there is no way to get everything done. I love being able to fulfill my commitments and be in integrity with myself."

Once we start to feel this inner kindness, we are taking a giant step toward self-regulation. We get to respond to our own emotional experience in effective, calming ways, so that we are not at the mercy of our own reactivity and impulses. We start to have choice.

The body doesn't have to change for us to start to know ourselves better, but it often relaxes in the dialogue. This is a paradox, because we aren't *trying* to change anything, or to wish that we would respond differently, or to wish that we didn't have this reaction. We aren't demanding that our body immediately be quiet or happy or relaxed. We are just trying to name what's really happening, with warmth. Whatever happens, this kind of resonant self-conversation can bring our body to peace.

Anxiety: The Role of Our Parents' Past

As we make significant headway in our own healing process by clearing away past traumas and reintegrating difficult memories, we can become aware that we might be working with the multigenerational transmission of pain. The science of **epigenetics**, with research being done on the children of holocaust survivors[16] and the children of 9/11 survivors,[17] shows that the stress-related changes that parents undergo can be passed on to their unborn children and can show up in the cortisol levels of those children when they are grown.

We start to heal as we see our stories in the context of the lives of our families, through many generations. We begin to see our parents, our grandparents, and their parents before them as part of the tapestry of human history, passing down strengths through time: resilience, determination, survival, love of the arts, creativity and ingenuity, and more. Additionally, our family stories reveal the historical traumas that have touched our ancestors: poverty, war, displacement, famine, disease, financial disasters, and other horrors. Each of these traumas leaves behind its own burdens of anxiety, depression, dissociation, abuse, and/or addiction. Each one of these difficult ways of living helped someone in our family to deal with the unbearable, but left a legacy that is in its turn also hard to live with.

Because anxiety is natural when we predict that bad things will happen, and bad things have happened so often to our ancestors as they have lived through the last few centuries, our anxiety can be based on historical facts, without us even knowing it. Getting a sense of the historical traumas that have impacted our family can be very helpful in seeing the larger picture of the transmission of worry and stress from generation to generation.

Pause for a moment and think about what you know about your family's history. Have your people been land owners? What is the story of wealth or poverty in your family's past? How did your family get to the region where you were born? When did they arrive on the continent you live on? What is the history of religious, racial, national, or class discrimination that your past generations lived with? How many times did your family lose everything and have to start over? What is the history of military service, active duty, or exposure to genocide or epidemics that your forbears endured?

In the twentieth century, there were the horrors of World Wars I and II; the Korean and Vietnam Wars; the Dust Bowl and the Great Depression; residential schools for Native North Americans; the influenza pandemic of the 1910s; the genocides in Germany, Palestine, Africa, Cambodia, and Indonesia, among others; and the famines of Africa.

In the nineteenth century, we had slavery; the Civil War in North America; the dislocation, decimation, and genocide of aboriginal people all over the world as their lands were colonized; the worldwide wars of the empires: Britain, Russia, Japan, and Germany; wars throughout South America, Asia, and Africa; poverty; and starvation, including the famines in Europe that sent waves of immigrants to North America.

This is our human history, and it has affected us. Each historical event has created waves of personal traumas that are still lapping at our feet in the form of changes to how our genes help us cope with stress. It also impacts us now because, consciously or unconsciously, we use what has happened in the past to build our anticipation of the future. (A process to support this exploration is offered in Chapter 10.)

Part of why we feel anxious is that we have the ability to look forward in time to predict what will come next, as well as the ability to look backward in time to review what we have done before and see if we should do things differently now. In other words, we can and do learn from experience. In trying to help us with this, our brains become anticipation machines.

BRAIN CONCEPT 5.2: THE BRAIN'S HAMSTER WHEEL, THE ANTERIOR CINGULATE CORTEX

When we are anxious about future events, it is almost like we climb onto tiny little hamster wheels in our brain, taking ourselves through possible scenarios to resolve or prevent problems. Even when we know we can't change the past and we are aware that we keep running the same scenario for the future over and over again, with no progress being made, it can be almost impossible to get ourselves off that hamster wheel. We often need to speak directly to the guilty or scared part of ourselves to see if we can create connection and regulation with those parts.

For example, for a parent worrying about a child, it might be possible to ask oneself, "Are you running every scenario to see if you can find a better way to respond to your child? Do you feel like if you stop worrying that you would be giving up hope? Do you love your child so much that you would do anything possible to contribute to her, even to save her?

93

Are you exhausted, and do you long for support and acknowledgment and rest?" This kind of inner dialogue can sustain parents and help get them off the hamster wheel.

Another example might be worries about finances or work, like conversations you might have with yourself when awakening at three in the morning: "Are you turning over every possibility to see how to make that payment/have that conversation with your boss? Have you made your plan about how to deal with this, what you will say, and what they will say fourteen times already, and as soon as you are done, do you begin again? Is there a fear of loss so engrained that you almost can't imagine ease? Do you long for deliverance and for grace? Are you racing away from shame and regret on an eternal highway that will never let you outrun those emotions? Are you aching for self-forgiveness?"

Let's get better acquainted with the brain's hamster wheel. Its technical name is the anterior cingulate cortex (**ACC**),[18] or just the anterior cingulate. It lies between the PFC and the limbic system (Figure 5.1) and is often considered part of the limbic system, although it is structurally constructed like the rest of the cortex.[19] Some researchers consider the ACC to be a part of the DMN, and some do not. The ACC is important to understanding and transforming the unfriendly DMN because problems with its connection to the DMN are part of the picture of depression, anxiety, PTSD,[20] and addiction.[21] The ACC is one source

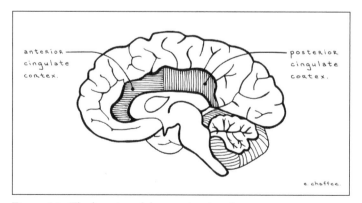

Figure 5.1. The location of the anterior cingulate cortex

of the recurrent, relentless negative thoughts that are part of the savage DMN. Once we can identify these ceaseless reruns, we can begin to see that we are not our thoughts and that they are not the voice of truth. We have one ACC in each hemisphere. They are where time, learning, and memory converge. They are where we try out all our predictions versus outcomes.[22] They try to bring past and present together for us to make our lives better. When the ACCs are not properly connected with the DMN, our ability to imagine ourselves moving easily through our lives is compromised.[23]

On a sleepless night, after you get tired of turning the same worrisome situation over and over in your mind without any new results, you might ask your ACC, "I wonder if you are trying to protect me by staying eternally vigilant? Would you be willing to acknowledge that you have already thought of every possible scenario and that sleep may serve you better right now?" Just notice how your body responds. Each of us needs to find our own humming, vibrating, connecting way of using language with ourselves to bring our RSW to life.

We don't just use our ACC to try to solve our problems; we are also always using it to see if people's insides match their outsides.[24] Does the advice that we are being given match the actions of the person giving the advice? Are unnamed motivations moving a person in one direction while he is talking about moving in another? At a higher level, are the actions that an organization, business, or corporation takes the same as its stated intentions? All of these glitches between words and actions are measured by the ACC for sincerity, congruence, authenticity, integrity, and truth. Discrepancies are another root cause of anxiety.

RESONANCE SKILL 5.2: IDENTIFYING AND ADDRESSING THE ROOT CAUSES OF ANXIETY

Let's look at what we have learned so far about some starting points for anxiety, and what other possibilities there are, both for places where anxiety begins and for ways to work with it using resonating self-warmth.

This approach to bringing resonance to anxiety is to stay with the body sensations, let them reveal the important feelings, and then guess what longings, hopes, dreams, wishes, and needs might be alive. There are many other approaches to healing, too. The most important thing is to keep exploring until the path appears that works best, so that it is possible to find out what being in a truly relaxed body feels like. Here are some questions for journaling to explore your anxiety history and possible approaches to take to integrate the skills and knowledge given in this book:

- This might be a hard question to consider, but what is it like to imagine having been inside your mother's womb when she was pregnant with you, especially at three to six months? What might her emotional state have been? Did she have warm support? Before we are born, we can experience stress and anxiety inside our mother's womb. When our mother is anxious, we are anxious. Infants born to mothers with higher levels of stress and depression (especially during the middle trimester) leave the womb less easily soothed than those born to mothers who had an easier time.[25] If this is our earliest experience, then we can be born believing that anxiety is the norm for how to be in the world.
    - *Resonance-based approach:* Work with the guided meditation offered in this chapter to bring empathy to your prenatal infant self. If you would like to, you can bring in a resonating witness to hold your pregnant mother with warmth, too. How does your body respond to this?

- After we are born, early experiences of loss, including death, adoption, unpredictability, emotional instability, and addiction in our caregivers, can give us a burden of anxiety. Were you afraid as a child? Did you have to live with abuse, neglect, financial insecurity, a violent sibling, witnessing domestic violence? What has your experience been with trauma?

Death, loss, violence, accidents, disasters, emergencies? Loss of employment security or financial well-being? Struggles with addictions or compulsions? Depression or other mental health issues? Physical health problems or diagnoses?

- *Resonance-based approach:* Bring resonance to the self that experienced the difficult moment. See if your sense of the earlier self shifts in response to that naming of body sensations, emotions, and longings.

- What did you believe about yourself when you were small? In middle school? In high school? In early adulthood? Is there a point at which you liked yourself, and then was there a point at which it changed and you became anxious? If this is so, what happened at the moment in time when things suddenly became different?

  - *Resonance-based approach:* For each memory that still has vivid body sensations attached to it, see what it is like to let your RSW meet the memory with warmth and understanding.

- Are you a member of any social or physical group that does not carry the stamp of power in your world? The experience of being dismissed or marginalized because of labels or isms impacts your health at the level of your immune system cells and creates stress and anxiety.

  - *Resonance-based approach:* Practice acknowledgment, self-expression without taking on the burden of educating the other, and allowing yourself to be held in these moments by your RSW.

- What were your parents' and grandparents' experiences of historical or family trauma? The roots of our anxiety can begin even before we are conceived, in past generations of our family. Research is starting to show that if our parents or grandparents survived traumas like famine,[26] the concentration camps of World War II,[27] or the Rwandan genocide,[28] then we see effects in the way our genes in our DNA are expressed. Links are now being discovered between these epigenetic changes and the way that we respond to stress. This means that as we develop, starting immediately after conception, we are already using a blueprint that can leave us hypersensitive and hypervigilant. This is the earliest possible starting point for our anxiety.

> • *Resonance-based approach:* See what happens in your body if you bring your RSW to hold your sense of your parent or grandparent within you, and acknowledge their worries, traumas, and deep longings.

• Which type of anxiety is more pressing for you? Does it seem more like loneliness or heartbreak? Does your body relax more when you imagine being accompanied by warm presence? This would show that you need help with being alone. Are you more reassured and relaxed by safety, protection, and the well-being of those you love? This would indicate that you need help with fear.

> • *Resonance-based approach:* Find the sensations in your body that lead you to identify the emotion of anxiety. See what happens in your body if you bring your RSW to make needs guesses about warmth and presence. Now see what happens when you offer your body guesses about how much it might be longing for certainty, security, or safety.

• What about the well-being of the people you care about? Are there any friends or family members that you worry about, that you spend sleepless nights thinking about?

> • *Resonance-based approach:* Acknowledge the depth of love and/or mourning that underlies your worry. Name the complexity of emotions, the tangle of love, warmth, fear, annoyance, resentment, bitterness, hatred, worry, con-

cern, tenderness and helplessness, and see what happens for your body when you let yourself connect these feelings with your deepest longings.

- We can feel anxious because we believe, based on early experiences of abuse or trauma, that there is something wrong with us, so that we have linked shame, fear, or self-disgust with our sense of self.
  - *Resonance-based approach:* What happens when you make guesses about needs or longings for the part of you that is being contemptuous or critical? And what happens when you do the same for the part of self that is receiving the judgment?

- Other mental health problems can contribute to anxiousness as well. For example, 50 percent of all depression is mixed with anxiety, and the two experiences can feed into one another.
  - *Resonance-based approach:* Chapters 11 and 12 contain information on adapting this approach to depression.

- We can even become anxious about our anxiety. If you have spent time being anxious, do you progressively become more anxious about your anxiety?
  - *Resonance-based approach:* Resonance, resonance, resonance for our anxious selves.

GUIDED MEDITATION 5.1: The Prenatal Self

A note of acknowledgment: If you feel any reservation or discomfort about connecting with your prenatal self, then simply skip this meditation and return to it when it calls you. If you enter the meditation and find that it is more upsetting than you had anticipated, gently stop the meditation and return to your breathing, making any feelings guesses and needs guesses that your upset self would like to receive.

Begin with your sense of existing as a physical being, as the adult that you are now. What parts of your body come to mind first? Is your stomach full? Is there pain or discomfort anywhere that draws your attention?

If you have found discomfort, acknowledge what you have found, and ask your attention, is it worried about that part of your body and longing for its well-being? Thank your attention for its care for you and for its vigilance. Ask the part that has discomfort if it is scared and needing to know that it is appreciated. If it seems sad, ask if it needs support for mourning or acknowledgment of loneliness, or if it has a longing for shared satisfaction of partnership.

Now, allow yourself to notice what your baseline level of anxiety is. What is the level of consistent tension or agitation in your chest, in your stomach? What about the large muscles in your arms or your legs, in your shoulders. Are they tight or relaxed?

And what is happening with the muscles of your face, between your eyebrows, and around your mouth?

After scanning your body, see if your attention is willing to come to your breath. Let yourself breathe for a total of ten to fifteen breaths, gently and kindly counting as high as you can, starting again at one when your attention wanders but moving on to the next part of the meditation once you've breathed ten to fifteen times.

Invite your attention to move to fuel your imagination now. Let a part of yourself slip into your past, into the tiny prenatal body that you were, inside your mother's womb. What is it like there? Are you warm or cold? Is there enough room, or is it cramped?

And what is happening for your mother? Is she anxious, tense, upset, or afraid? Or is she relaxed and at ease? Does she have support, or is she alone? Is she experiencing financial security? Or is she worried about stability? And what is it like to be the little one inside her? Can you sense how she is?

Shift your attention to the part of you that can see yourself from the outside and regard yourself with warmth inside your mother's womb. How do feel about this tiny prenatal infant? Do you feel some tenderness?

If you do, then let another part of yourself inhabit your resonant self-witness. Imagine becoming a golden light of warmth and reassurance that enters the womb space to cradle and nestle this little being with love and gentleness.

If you do not feel tenderness for the prenatal infant, see what happens if you move back further in time, to the preconception spark of your being, and see if you agree to exist on this planet. Disregard the rest of this meditation and focus on this essential spark, with guesses about how it is to enter this life.

If you have tenderness for your prenatal self, your self-witness now has an opportunity to acknowledge whatever you are sensing about the prenatal experience. Here are some possible resonant guesses for your little one. If they do not feel right, make your own guesses about what this prenatal self is experiencing and longing for.

"Are you cold and do you need warmth?"

"Do you feel cramped? Do you long for responsiveness and space to move?"

"Do you feel anxious and alone? Would it be lovely to have a sense of presence with you?"

"Are you lonely and afraid, and do you need safety and tender protection?"

"Are you worried, and do you just want your mama to be okay?"

What happens in the infant's body as you hold it with this care? Is this tiny body relaxing? If this little one begins to relax, see if he or she would like to come away with you, to be forever nestled in your heart.

Sometimes the little ones don't want to leave their mothers. If this happens for you, let the little one know that he or she has already survived this and that you are a grown-up now. Let your younger self know that he or she belongs with you. Let him or her know that your mother can come too, to be nestled and loved in the golden light of your heart, whether your mother is living or dead.

Sometimes the little ones are afraid that our heart will be no warmer than our mother's womb may have been. If this happens for you, go into your heart yourself, and tell the little one what you find there. If it is cold, tell your younger self that you will heal your heart into warmth and then come back and make the invitation again.

However the younger part responds to you, stay in a resonant, understanding place, holding onto and offering hope for healing and reunion in the future.

Whatever has happened in the meditation, as you begin to come to a transitional place, make sure you have given the infant self as much care and support as this little one will accept.

Now begin to reconnect with your present-time adult body, with your breath, your lungs, your ribs, the small movements that you make with your breathing.

Before you fully reenter your present life, in your own time, notice what has happened in your body overall with the anxiety that you were noticing in the beginning of this meditation. Is it the same? Is it slightly different? Whatever you notice, appreciate yourself for your presence, your commitment to healing, and your care. With gentleness, reenter your regular life.

WHY PRACTICE THIS MEDITATION?

Anxiety affects us deeply. It affects heart rate and **heart rate variability**[29,30] (the varying tempo at which our heart beats); blood pressure;[31] immune system function;[32] the way we digest food;[33] attention, learning, focus, and memory;[34] and mood, perception, relaxation, alertness, and sleep.[35] When people don't have enough support or sense that they are alone and abandoned or that the world is a dangerous place, then brain and body become disconnected. We are made to flourish in supportive and warm communities.[36] We do best if we have a sense that, even if the world is dangerous, there are parts of it that are good and that sometimes we can be safe. We all need to know that we can look into the future and have some probability that it will be good, that some people will be supportive, and that we matter.

Words of hope: You may be reading these words and thinking that this is impossible. The world that you live in may include daily violence inside or outside your home. You may have felt alone as long as you can remember. It is important to acknowledge that the world can be far less supportive, fun, safe, and warm than anyone would like. Even if that is the case, as we work to develop self-compassion and understanding, we are better able to recognize people who are kind and funny and warm. We are better able to make decisions about how to be safe and connected while still staying in integrity with our hearts. Even just reading this book is creating significant brain change and making more of a foundation for self-warmth.

Just as this meditation invites, we can always time travel through our lives with the help of our RSW. We will learn more about why this is effective and possible and how it contributes to our well-being in Chapter 6. In the meantime, what is important to know is that warmth is always our most important ingredient in healing. With it, we shift into the ever-changing, fluid, and responsive attachment circuits linking the PFC to the limbic system, where movement and self-understanding are possible. With it, we calm the hamster wheel of our ACC. Without it, we are cold wanderers in the unchanging world, forever stuck in our pain. There are no wrong answers. The most important thing is our own individual journey. The next section will give you a general idea of what our journey might look like.

The Path of Transforming Anxiety Into Dynamic Peace

As we practice self-resonance, or are held with resonance by others, we see the following changes that help anxiety decrease:

1. We develop the soothing nest of neurons that holds and reassures our anciently or presently anxious self.

2. Resonance helps balance our brain chemicals.

3. We see our actions and behaviors coming into balance.

4. We start to notice that there are warm, stable, and reliable people in the world.

5. We experience an increased ability to trust and an increased willingness to reach out to others for support and to make friends.

6. Our body starts to feel better, our immune system improves, and we start to have access to inner peace and aliveness.

Check in with your own hamster wheel, the part of you that longs so desperately for everything to turn out well. Is this part of you willing to stop running for a moment? How did it like receiving the questions and information in this chapter? Are there any feelings guesses and needs guesses that have been helpful?

Chapter 6 looks at the nuts and bolts of time and trauma and helps us build understanding and compassion for the times when things that happen in the present take us into states of fear, anger, or hopelessness due to events from our past. It also provides solid tools for the return to a fully resourced present.

CHAPTER SIX

Time Traveling With Resonance: Healing Old Hurts

————————

"I can't get away from my past; I'm stuck."
(actually, *"Resonance brings me to the present."*)

A Special Note About Trauma From a Reader

"I'd like a neon sign that says, 'Hey folks, we're venturing into the land of trauma. Make sure you've got support!' and 'Go at your own pace—go super-slow if you have to. Don't open Pandora's box all by yourself.' The traumatized parts stay frozen in time for a reason, right?"

This reader is correct; our traumatized parts have good grounds for staying frozen in time. In this chapter we'll learn about how disconnected memories protect us, and as you read, be very gentle with yourself. Close the book if you want to, give yourself long breaks, and feel free to skip this chapter if your body relaxes when you imagine doing that.

Old Hurts Can Be Land Mines in the Brain

Have you ever been having an ordinary conversation with someone new, with a sense that friendship is starting, when all of a sudden they come out with a pronouncement or with advice, and your heart suddenly has a sense that it has shriveled, and you don't care if you ever see this person again? Or have you ever had to turn off a song playing on the radio because it brings up old memories that you don't want to revisit? Or smelled a familiar perfume or cologne that makes you want to leave the room? Chapter 2 described the amygdala filtering everything coming in to check for danger, but we haven't yet examined in detail the amygdala's role as a collector of memories. Whether you know it or not, your amygdala has been saving the sensory impressions that have come with difficult or painful experiences since before your birth, and creating a catalog of predictions that give your brain and body the sense of whether or not the present moment is safe.

Viveca's Story

"I'm so stupid! I can't remember anything!" Viveca said. This was her third time through our class at the women's prison, and whenever Viveca tried to speak, she turned red and could not remember what she wanted to say, crippled by shame. So I started talking with the class about the way that stress will prevent our brains from working and leave us unable to learn anything at school. Then we believe we are stupid when it is not true. Viveca began to cry.

"What made you think you were stupid?" I asked.

"In first grade the teacher made me read in front of the class, and I was so nervous I couldn't even see the letters on the page. She told me I was stupid."

"Are you willing to connect with this little first grader?" I asked. When she said it was okay, I asked her to imagine stepping into that classroom and freezing that teacher and all the children to stone. The little girl that she had been was glad to see her.

"How is she?" I asked. "What's happening in her body?"

"She feels hot and red, and she can't think."

"Ask her if she feels embarrassed and humiliated," I said quietly. "Is she longing for gentleness and support?"

"Yes—now her chest is caving in, and her shoulders are slumping," said Viveca.

"I wonder if she is exhausted and overwhelmed, and if she needs protection and safety?"

"Yes. She wants me to pick her up. I'm reaching out for her."

"Is she relaxing into you? Can you feel that sweet heaviness in your arms?"

"Yes," Viveca said. "But now my heart is burning."

"Are you angry and sad for all the little kids of this world who aren't met with care?"

"Yes, and I'm angry and sad and all mixed up. I want responsibility and understanding, and for all kids to be seen, and for me in particular to have been seen."

Viveca's story is an example of how trauma prevents self-warmth. As this woman followed her body sensations and received feelings and needs guesses, she started to relax. "Do you mean I've hated myself for all these years for nothing? That I've believed I'm stupid and I've been wrong, when really I was just scared and embarassed?" Her features lightened, with a funny mix of relief and irritation. After this day she began to speak more often in class and was surprised to find it easier to learn, once that terrified and paralyzed little one within her was able to move and think again.

This story gives us a glimpse of the way that powerful but unnamed emotions can freeze us in place and prevent forward movement. If we were being affected by difficult events from our past, how can we know? Here are some of the signs and symptoms that the aftereffects of trauma are at play:

Signs of Past Trauma

- Inappropriate reactivity (becoming more angry or scared than the situation calls for)
- Intrusive memories (having a memory replay over and over again without choice)

- Nightmares and night terrors
- The sudden, unpredictable drop into tears, sobbing, or irritation
- Dislike of the self
- Groundless dislike of others
- The sense of being incapable of love
- A consistent feeling of shame
- A sudden need to control the environment or another's actions
- Ongoing exhaustion, fatigue, overwhelm, or the inability to concentrate
- Emotional numbness, loss of pleasure and meaning
- Hypervigilance
- Obsession with death

These signs and symptoms start to make sense once we learn how the brain classifies traumatic experience and we understand the two different kinds of memory.

BRAIN CONCEPT 6.1: TWO WAYS TO REMEMBER—IMPLICIT AND EXPLICIT MEMORY

You may remember from Chapter 1 that the inner part of your brain is called the limbic system (the thumb in the palm-of-the-hand brain model). The limbic system is a key player in feeling, learning, and remembering. Our brain's primary purpose is to support life, and to do that we need to remember what is most important to us. The more intensely we feel about something, the more important the brain thinks that something is, and the easier it is to remember (learn) it. The amygdala is made to write memory into our brain with just one exposure.[1] So after just one bite from a scary dog, our heart rate may increase around dogs for the rest of our lives. Our amygdala-centered memories are not time-stamped— our amygdala holds everything in present time. Emotional memories can be just as intense now as they were when they originally happened. This information also helps us understand the real-life quality of flashbacks in posttraumatic stress. The "as-if-it-happened-just-now" quality of these memories sends ex-soldiers flying for cover when there is a loud bang. This is also the reason that old shames are often all-consuming. These memories can be so persistent that we may start to believe that they are permanently installed inside our skulls and that we will never be free from being ambushed by old pain. But their vividness is exactly what makes them available for healing.

The amygdala writes into memory every sensation connected with any significant difficult experience. For example, in an automobile accident, it might record the smell of diesel fuel and blood; the look of crumpled metal, torn flesh, a stunned facial expression; the sound of screeching brakes, a gasp, the creak of a stuck door hinge; a crumpled body position; or the feel of the unrelenting seat belt across the chest.

(If you have been in a car accident and these words have stimulated the memory, then you are experiencing exactly what we're talking about. Emotions may have arisen for you in connection with this memory: old shock, horror, confusion, worry, or fear. Don't move too quickly—take a moment to acknowledge what is there and to bring gentleness and warmth to the part of you that experienced this accident. Just say, "Of course you felt this way—humans need safety, predictability, and survival," and see what your body does with this acknowledgment.)

Other traumatic memories would have other sensory elements, all of which the amygdala would also file away as indicating life-threatening danger. These memories are actually stored in the sensory cortex and indexed significantly to the amygdala, as long as the amygdala continues to link them with unprocessed trauma.[2] These sensory elements are not necessarily available to conscious knowing, and they may arise when some similar sensation or perception occurs.

Amygdala-based learning is one very important kind of nonconscious memory. Scientists call all nonconscious memory **implicit memory**. To put this in different words, nonconscious memory consists of networks of perception that are written into the neurons without conscious attention. Just one exposure to a stimulus can "set" masses of brain associations between neurons, so that they are linked together to form a vivid memory of the event.[3] Added together, the millions upon millions of emotionally significant seconds throughout people's lifetimes create a glacier of implicit experience. The force of this glacier is impossible to stop. Sometimes the glacier lurches forward with sudden rages, unexpected storms of tears, or the out-of-nowhere feeling that a person is absolutely unable to endure a relationship any more. At other times the glacier of implicit memories moves so slowly that people don't even notice the drift, but they are still being pushed. It is possible to see the nonconscious results of this pushing in paralysis, resistance, self-sabotage, quarrels and rage, unnoticed judgments, dissociation, racism and other forms of prejudice, discounting and contempt, apathy, and even depression. Unlike a glacier, however, this enormous force of unknown memory is entirely responsive to whatever is happening in people's lives, fluidly bringing forward the anxiety, worry, fear, irritation, panic, rage, grief, delight, and joy that are its language. When people begin to notice, understand, and respond to that language, they change their lives.

The face of this glacier is always interacting with present-time experience. This can be seen clearly with flashbacks and shame spirals. Both are the intrusion of past moments into the present with no clear sense that the memory is over. These loads of implicit pain can keep bodies and immune systems continually activated, with chronic conditions being a kind of extended flashback. So the face of this glacier is really the only part of the implicit that people can know, the liminal space of the intersection between the emotional world and the conscious world, which has its own flavor, and which we will explore next, beginning by contrasting it with known or **explicit memory**.

In preparation for understanding the second, conscious way that we remember things, let me introduce the star of explicit memory, the **hippocampus** (Figure 6.1). The hippocampus is part of the limbic system and shares a lot of neural interconnections with the amygdala (our emotional alarm). The hippocampus remembers things the way we usually think of

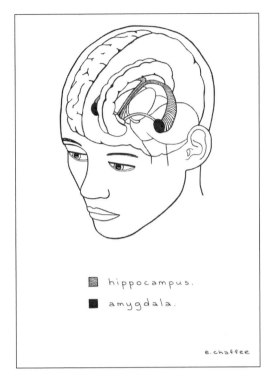

hippocampus.
amygdala.

e.chaffee

Figure 6.1. Location of the hippocampus

our memory working. We use it to put stuff into our brain and pull it out when we need it.

Additionally, the hippocampus organizes our map of our outer world, holding everything from how to get to the grocery store to what countries border Argentina. The hippocampus files and supports what we remember about our world and the stories of our own lives.[4] And, very important for our healing work, this is the part of us that time-stamps our memory, so that we know that we fell yesterday but we're steady on our feet today. In contrast, for the amygdala, we're still falling, terrified, and we never hit bottom.

The hippocampus is not powered by emotion, so, unlike the amygdala, it doesn't have the weight of significance and survival helping it to write in its information. This means that people have to work harder to learn conscious knowledge with no emotional significance, like multiplication tables. The amygdala is like a rough-and-tumble memory cowboy, getting the job done fast, as opposed to the diligent librarian that is the hippocampus. People can use repetition and practice to memorize, or they can hitch a ride on the amygdala's ease of remembering by connecting any new learning with something that has emotional content: a feeling, a story, a passion, an intensity, or a hunger. This hitching of memory-rides and the way these two memory organs work together mean that, if people's brains work the way rats' brains work, people have explicit memories, primarily stored in the hippocampus but connected to the amygdala, that are given aliveness by their connection to the emotional world.[5]

RESONANCE SKILL 6.1: ACCOMPANYING OUR PAST SELVES TO HEAL TRAUMA

Since the amygdala, the organ of emotional alarm, keeps emotional memories forever in the present,[6] time doesn't do a lot to heal trauma. Posttraumatic stress can persist for decades without much change.[7] For healing to happen, it helps for both the amygdala and the hippocampus, the time stamper, to be involved, so that there can be a change in how people remember their past. It is possible for there to be an actual memory transfer with the resolution of trauma.[8]

In other words, when people can hold ourselves with warmth by bringing their compassionate resonating self-witness (RSW) to visit the pain that's locked up in the unintegrated memory, it is possible for the pain to be resolved, and then the memory becomes integrated and known within the chronology of the person's life. To go back to the glacier metaphor, when a chunk of previously unknown memory becomes known and understood, it is like the glacier calving a piece of ice off into the sea of consciousness. The stimulus that used to hook into implicit pain is now fully understood, time-stamped, and integrated, rather than remaining a trigger.

Three major brain networks, the central executive network (which helps us plan and take action), the network that discerns importance (which tells us what has meaning), and our old friend the default mode network (DMN), have to be restored to heal posttraumatic stress disorder (PTSD).[9] (All three networks are shown in Figure 1.4.) When we see the pain dissolve from our old memories, we start to realize that we are changing the associative patterns of our brain. We begin to understand that memory is not solid, unchangeable granite that we return to again and again, finding it the same every time. We start to understand that we are continually growing our own autobiography, making meaning and changing the ground of being. Memories do not form and then last forever, as neuroscientists used to think. On the contrary, we rewire our memories every time we remember them. The brain doesn't need to have a perfect set of memories of the past. Instead, memory naturally updates whenever it is accessed, which might make memories less accurate, but probably also makes them more relevant to the future.[10]

Let's look at how this process occurs and how we can support positive change in relationship to our past. As we become familiar with the movement of memory within us, it helps us to chart our progress. Additionally, knowing what is possible lets us map out what we are working toward. We can look at the road ahead and gauge whether or not we want to proceed.

A note of caution: When we are working with old and painful memories, we don't want to retraumatize ourselves. If a person is not currently experiencing any intrusion of past pain, there is no need to time travel. And if there is something we want to resolve, we don't need to relive the whole incident. We can work with the most difficult instant, make sure that that particular moment is fully resonated with until our body in the memory relaxes completely, and bring that part of ourselves back to present time and safety. Additionally, there is no hurry to do this work. We have already been surviving for however many decades since the trauma happened.

Bodies dissociate in order to survive, and difficult memories stay disconnected to protect from overwhelm. If you know that as soon as your brain touches a certain memory, the whole thing will replay from start to finish and compromise your ability to function, don't do this alone. If you have any doubts or worries, work with a therapist so that you have the support you need to be fully held with warmth and understanding.

If this process seems to make sense, and your trauma is not overwhelming, consider a regular practice of self-connection. Doing this helps us make decisions based on conscious choice and frees up our capacity to think more clearly. Let's take a look at the way that healing unfolds:

The Progression of Memory Transfer and Healing

1. *The nonconscious stage:* We live at the mercy of the unknown past or of unknown depths of feeling within known memories that ghost along, directing us without our knowledge.

2. *The dawning of consciousness:* We experience a confusing or disturbing trigger and realize that the depth of our reactivity is inappropriate to the present-day experience.

3. *Implementing the tools of healing:* We scan our body to see where our sensations are. We ask ourselves, "If this sensation were an emotion, what would it be?" And we ask ourselves if the sensations and the emotions are familiar, if we've ever felt them before. This helps us ask the question, is this experience guiding us to a memory, age, or old feeling that needs to be known and understood? If we find a memory to work with, we bring our RSW back in time (the time traveling mentioned above) so that the self that experienced the trauma is no longer alone. (See this chapter's guided meditation for an example of this process.) If we don't find a memory to work with, we see if we sense that a particular age is connected with the physical state of being that comes with this reactivity. And then we work with whatever imagery comes with the physical sensations, whether there is a particular age of self or not, making resonance guesses and following the way the image or the body sensations change or shift and making more guesses until there is relaxation. This step lets us be sure that all the messages that the amygdala is holding in the form of body sensations and emotions have been received. We let the trau-

matized self know that we have actually survived this experience, and we invite it to come back to present time with us.

A note of caution: Don't be in a rush to tell the traumatized self it's all over and in the past—that's one way people dismiss pain. Sometimes as an empathizer we can be overanxious and want healing for our wounded parts so badly that we will try and yank them out of the past and into the present without fully capturing their overwhelm and frozenness. They may need quite a bit of time to thaw out. Please take time to attune to the wounded one. This process doesn't have to be done all at once—we can visit ourselves multiple times. This step invites the hippocampus to start to time-stamp this memory.

Also, please remember that one way that we have warmth for ourselves is to ask for help when we need it. For people who have been badly hurt, it can be too much to ask to do this on their own. There are sweet discoveries to be made by asking for and receiving help. Therapists have the training and experience to be excellent guides on this journey. In choosing a therapist, look for a sense of warmth, presence, and accompaniment. Your journey is worth having a responsive and empathetic guide.

Upon reunion with the present-day self, the traumatized self sometimes melts into our present-day body and sometimes stays separate and enjoys life in present time. Either way, the present-day self is invited to fully experience feelings of warmth, relief, and care for the younger self. As this integration happens, there may be an integration of the memory. People who explore making sure that they have fully understood their younger self and addressing all body sensations before bringing the previously traumatized self to present time certainly experience contextualization of the memory, placing it into the larger life story, with a new, clear sense of chronology.

See if there is any reframing or new understanding of the original situation, now that the self is safe. (This is shown in the guided meditation below.) Check in with the confusing or disturbing trigger. Is there a different perception of this experience now?

BRAIN CONCEPT 6.2: MEET YOUR VENTROMEDIAL PREFRONTAL CORTEX

Of all the parts of the prefrontal cortex (PFC), the area that is most important for our purposes is called the **ventromedial PFC** (Figure 6.2). It links into the neural networks that connect the body and emotional awareness, which together calm the amygdala, and brings in the warmth from the amygdala's connections with parts of the brain that control the nervous system, the hormone flows, and the neurotransmitters to create feelings of safety and warmth.[11] It is considered to be a part of the DMN and is negatively impacted by trauma, and without its integrative qualities the tone of the DMN can be shifted in the direction of painful experiences, such as occurs with depression or PTSD.[12]

For those of you who love the brain, the research that comes closest to explaining why these changes happen is that being done with fear extinction, which reveals that the healing of PTSD involves interactions and feedback between the amygdala, the hippocampus, and our new friend the ventromedial PFC.[13] As the connections between these areas are balanced and restored, the previously traumatized self can be

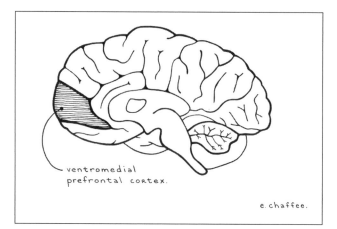

Figure 6.2. The location of the ventromedial prefrontal cortex

reintegrated with more pleasant emotions, and the memory can be time-stamped. For those of you who want to heal your trauma, know that there is a part of your brain that holds the convergence of intentionality for self-warmth, and that the learning you are doing as you read this book is activating it.

Betrayal of Trust After Trauma

Trauma by itself is difficult enough to survive, but the response we receive is almost as important. Among my clients it is often not the trauma they have experienced that is most painful—instead, it is the way they were received when they tried to share their experience. It can be harder to be ridiculed for sadness at losing a pet than it is to lose the pet. It can be harder for children to be told they are a liar than it is to be abused. It can be harder for people to be told they deserve it than it was to be assaulted or raped. Working from such experiences, it is possible to say that trauma is the moments that still live within us that have never been resonated with. While this book is a useful start toward self-connection, it is also important to begin to imagine that you will be able to reach out to others to affirm, guide, and support healing even though it was not available at the time of the traumatic events.

The importance of the way that we are received after trauma is born out by the 2010 research into Nepalese boy soldiers. The boys who went off to the civil war and came back to a welcome from their communities ended up with fewer signs of posttraumatic stress. But the boys who went off to the same war, fought shoulder to shoulder with those other boys, and came back to communities that turned their backs on them had much higher levels of posttraumatic stress.[14] This research helps us to understand that trauma is less defined by what happens to us than it is by how we are received afterward. (The exception in this research was the children who were tortured—anyone who has been tortured needs special healing support.)

RESONANCE SKILL 6.1: WORKING ONLY WITH ONE MOMENT WHEN TIME TRAVELING

Think very briefly of your traumatic memory. Notice whether or not you are completely overwhelmed and taken off-line by even imagining touching the memory. If this is your experience, then you will need accompaniment by someone else. You may want to work with a therapist who understands healing from trauma, or a body-centered practitioner who does something like somatic experiencing, Hakomi, or the Rosen method to support your healing (see Appendix 2 for online resources). This kind of body-savvy support can speed your healing process, because it can take some time to develop such a strong sense of your RSW that you move effortlessly to hold your past self with care, all by yourself and without support.

How do we know when we need external support? The sign that I use to tell when I am over my head in the emotional past and I need someone to help me is when I think of the event and I can't find my own RSW anywhere, or when I don't like the part of myself that experienced the trauma. That is when I reach out. Other people may have other cues, like a persistent emotional stomach ache, an inability to breathe low into the belly, or cycling thoughts that just don't shift with resonance.

However, if you'd like to see what it would sound like to bring this support to yourself, the first question you might ask yourself is, what was the most important moment? Over and over again, when I'm doing empathy work with people who have lived through trauma, and I ask them what the most important moment was, there can be two answers: the greatest moment of fear (sometimes the greatest moment of fear mixed with clarity) or the moment when they were discounted or dismissed—this is not to downplay the need for acknowledgment, care, and healing for the shock and injury of receiving all kinds of violence, but often it is the experience of being ignored, dismissed, not believed, or told we were lying that leave the strongest mark. When painful things happen, the most significant question often seems to be, does anyone believe, notice, or care?

This has very interesting implications for time travel work. In these cases, the memory work must begin with the moment of disbelief by a trusted and loved person. Often, once this rescue is done, it is followed by a rescue of the self during the actual trauma. Sometimes after this sense of betrayal has been acknowledged and resonated with, the brain doesn't even go back to the actual trauma. How do people know what path to follow through our memories? By staying connected with and following the revelations of body sensations.

Major injuries to body and heart are not the only kinds of trauma. Anything that has happened in the past that hurts us now is trauma, and we are the only ones who get to say whether or not something was traumatic. Nobody else can tell you that your pain isn't real. It can happen that a support person, a friend, or a therapist can see that someone has really lived through something horrible and help that person to name events as traumatic, and this can be a huge relief. But the people who lived through it are the ones who get to tell their own life story and decide what is true for them. Sometimes people will try to minimize others' pain. Often they don't even think the others are wrong—they just can't bear it that they have pain, and they are trying to manage their own panic and overwhelm by making the other people's emotions disappear.

If this happens to you, I recommend that you see your friends' love, but don't believe their words. (This may not seem possible, and you may need to take some resonant care with the part of you that shuts down in response to dismissal, but I have noticed that, after a lot of emotional support, this is where I end up.)

Your pain is valid and true, and if someone had been there to share it with you, it would not hurt you as much as it does now. Neural networks that hold pain persist because we didn't get any support to help us connect them back up to the rest of our brain and make sense of them. This support can be as simple as the welcome and acknowledgment provided by warm community. As we have seen over and over again in this chapter, there is a surprising link between how we are received after suffering a trauma and what kind of a burden we carry in the years following the event.

Now that we've explored some background, the following guided meditation lets us give time travel a try.

GUIDED MEDITATION 6.1: The Time Travel Process

Begin by thinking about (rather than sinking into) the memory you would like to work with. As you think about it, what was the most intense moment during the whole of this memory? The starting point for this work is your body sensations. In memory rescues, the body is most often agitated, and while it is important to have live sensations to work with, because this means the brain is neuroplastic and ready to be changed, it is also important not to be overwhelmed by emotions. If a person is flooded (sobbing, crying uncontrollably, enraged, terrified, or dissociated), the triggering can be decreased by imagining moving into a safe environment, away from the memory. Here, work with feelings guesses and needs guesses until the body calms. If this has been your experience, it is best to skip the rest of this chapter and do this work with a support person, like a therapist or counselor.

The next step is to visit the most intense moment of the memory only long enough to find out the first edge of what is happening with the body, and then step out of the memory again, into the felt sense of being the RSW. While there, notice the sensations that this memory brings. Where is it most intense, and where are there just shadows of tension? Make a mental note of this pattern of sensations.

If you appreciate using a physical anchor in working with different parts of yourself, one option is to choose one hand to represent the part of yourself that is still embedded in the memory of the trauma. The other will represent the RSW. Another possibility is to use two chairs, one for the memory part and one for the RSW, and move between them as you shift your attentional focus. Yet another possibility is to do the process while journaling, using different colored inks or dominant and nondominant hands to write the different parts.

Now we will awaken the RSW. Invite the part of you that has the ability to see yourself with gentleness, welcome, and warm acceptance.

This is the part of you that can say, "Of course this was difficult," and make needs guesses for you. If you don't have warmth for this former self, see if you can bring someone else to mind who would have warmth for you and carry them with you in your imagination.

(I strongly advise you not to embark on a memory journey without warmth for your traumatized former self. If you would like to build the warmth, reread the earlier chapters of this book. Another option is to do this work in session with a therapist who understands resonance, if you aren't able to carry it for yourself and you don't want to wait for your self-warmth to develop.)

> Allow yourself to sink into your breathing. See if you can feel the breath coming into you and going out of you.
>
> It may be that, in preparation for the memory work, your breath has stopped almost completely. Where is that sensation most alive, even if it's very slight? Is it in your lungs? In your ribs? In your nose, your upper sinuses, your mouth, your throat? Wherever the sensation has the most intensity, invite your attention to rest there.
>
> When your attention wanders, as attention does, gently and with warmth invite it to come back to your breath. Thank your attention for its commitment to keeping you going with its alertness to importance, and see if it is willing to come back to the sensation of breathing.
>
> Now, bring to mind the memory or bewildering stimulus you wish to work with. Allow yourself to feel the body sensations connected either with the memory or with the confusing experience of having been triggered. A possible question to ask yourself is, have I ever had this set of body sensations before? If so, what is the earliest memory that arises with this set of body sensations? Or, if there is a sense of familiarity, but no clear memory, ask yourself, how old do I feel?
>
> If you know what memory you are working with, let yourself see what it is like to shift your consciousness between the sensations that are alive in this traumatized part, and your consciousness of

your resonating self-witness, anchoring this self in the warmth that you had for your attention and that you are feeling for the younger part that experienced the difficult memory.

If you don't know what memory you are working with, ask yourself how old this triggered self feels. What do you know about your life at this age? Have you seen a photograph of yourself at this age that you can bring to mind? If you don't have a specific memory emerging, simply continue this rescue using the general memory of yourself at this age.

Shifting your attention into the point of view of your resonating self-witness, come into relationship with your younger self. As you look back through time at your younger self, do you feel tenderness and warmth for this part of you?

If you do not, try a few empathy guesses for the self that may feel impatience: As you look at this younger self, are you irritated and angry, longing for strength, maybe even superhuman strength? Are you aching for this younger part to feel fully separate from this experience, to be completely free of his or her emotional burdens? See if any other body sensations can receive needs guesses to bring you more relaxation and let you move into a self-compassionate point of view. Now shift back into your resonating self-witness. Can you feel tenderness for this younger part now? If no, please stop this guided meditation here, work with the previous meditations in this book for a few months, and then return here.

If you do feel tenderness, take a long step through time and space to enter the room or the area where your younger self is, freezing everyone else so that the environment becomes safe. Can your younger self see your self-witness? If no, then make empathy guesses based on your younger self's experience, either what you can feel when you step into that part of you or what you can see from looking at that part, until your younger self can see this older part. Your guesses might sound like this: Are you overwhelmed and frozen, and do you long for a world where safety is possible? Are you worried about the other people in this situation, and do you need everyone to be okay? Do you need acknowledgment that this was really hard? As your younger self starts to realize someone is there, you can see if this part knows who you are. If your supportive presence brings bewilderment, then introduce yourself, using words like "I am the older you. I have come back to be with you, since this situation was too hard for anyone to be alone in."

Come as close to your younger self as seems comfortable. Based on what you can feel or see in your younger self's body, acknowledge your self's truth using metaphors and reflections. Track what is happening in this younger body, either by shifting your perspective or by watching changes in posture or movement, and let your guesses reflect these observations.

Guesses might include, "Are you stunned and paralyzed, and do you need acknowledgment of your grief and your loss?"

"Are you terrified, and do you long for protection and a sense of safety?"

"Do you need to survive?"

"Does the rage make you shake as if you were touching a high-voltage wire?"

"Are you bewildered about how to feel so much rage and still let the world survive?"

"Are you worried about the people you love, and do you need them to be okay?"

"Was this moment so horrifying, or terrifying, that you thought you actually died? Is it a surprise to find yourself alive?"

As your younger self's body relaxes, gently offer physical contact. If this contact is welcome, shift into your younger self's physical being and experience receiving this surprising support and warmth. Shifting back to the resonating self-witness, if an embrace is welcome, see if you can feel the warm heaviness of your younger body in your arms. Once the younger self relaxes, let that part of you know that you have survived this and that you need the energy and gifts that have been frozen at this point in time. Invite your younger self to come back to the present time with you.

Sometimes these parts dissolve into us and find their place in our heart. Sometimes they are so happy to have a safe environment that they just want to play or explore near us. It doesn't matter which they choose—just enjoy it. Notice what it is like for you to have this part with you safe now, beloved. Do you feel delight? If you feel warmth, love, or delight, let yourself close your eyes and feel the sensations of these emotions until they come to a peak and start to ebb.

And now, return to your breathing and your warm self-connection practice until you are ready to reenter the world.

WHY PRACTICE THIS MEDITATION?

This meditation is a key process in clearing our implicit minefields, getting to know ourselves intimately, and transforming the painful patterns that prevent the closeness that we long for. It helps us take advantage of the brain's natural capacity to learn with ease when emotions are involved, as well as the incredible healing power of resonance. When we start with and follow our body sensations, letting our bodies relax as they are heard, we are supporting our continuing relaxation and moving toward living in the present-day world instead of in the past.

We can tell what needs to be done in time travel work by reading our body as we touch on the memory in our minds. Sometimes an intrusive memory can feel like a live electrical wire when our thoughts flick across it. Sometimes we feel our face suddenly turn to heavy clay and our body stops having any impulse to move at all. We start to realize that if our body responds, either with sensation or with sudden deadness in response to a past event, it is something we can work with.

The understanding that traumatized parts of us continue to live in the past and never quite come to present time has profound implications for understanding all the incomprehensible things that we and the people we love do. It explains the sudden blankness that comes over people, the inexplicable cruelties, the incomprehensible rages or black holes of tears and despair. The responsibility that we have tried to take for others' pain starts to lift as we see how much we all live in the grip of events that happened long ago. To understand this more fully, let's take a look at some different definitions of trauma.

Trauma and Health

Why is it important to know about and heal past traumas? Because trauma can worsen health and stop people from being who they are supposed to be. The Adverse Childhood Experiences study (**ACE study**), a huge study with 17,000 participants, correlated experiences of trauma with ill health, addiction, and early death. It found that the more different kinds of trauma we experience, the higher our chances of suffering poor quality of life as adults.[15]

The types of trauma that the original ACE study measured were childhood experiences of[16]

- Living with an alcoholic or problem drinker as a child
- Living with a drug addict, or substance abuser, including abuse of prescription medications
- Parents separated or divorced
- Family member with depression, mental illness, or suicide (attempts or completion)
- Family member incarcerated or sentenced to serve time
- Witnessing or receiving domestic violence
- Verbal abuse (being sworn at, insulted, put down)
- Sexual abuse including sexual touching or being forced to touch sexually

The more of these traumas that are experienced, the higher the likelihood that a person will suffer from[17] (This is not a complete list. There are more than 40 researched negative outcomes of adverse childhood experiences.)

- Diminished quality of life due to health issues
- Early initiation of smoking
- Early initiation of sexual activity
- Adolescent pregnancy
- Unintended pregnancies
- Multiple sexual partners
- Sexually transmitted diseases (STDs)
- Alcoholism and alcohol abuse
- Illicit drug use
- Other addictions
- Depression
- Risk for intimate partner violence
- Lifetime smoking
- Fetal death
- Suicide attempts
- Ischemic heart disease
- Liver disease
- Chronic obstructive pulmonary disease

People can counteract the negative effect of the traumas they experienced when they were small. Profound changes in self-regulation and attachment style can happen throughout life.[18] Healing brings brain integration and changes the way we hold memory. As people start to hold themselves with compassion and allow themselves to be accompanied, everything becomes easier. Brains change in large and small ways. Researchers studying mindfulness practices and resonant attention, similar to the resonance and mindfulness practices taught here, have found that healing can create changes in the way genes are expressed (epigenetic changes) that can have a positive impact on health and possibly the health of subsequent generations.[19] Additionally, when people do the work of moving toward earned secure attachment (see Chapters 10 and 14), they create a positive flow of attachment patterns for subsequent generations.[20]

A More Expansive List of Traumas Shown to Have Health Impacts

There are five main categories of trauma. There is *present-time trauma*, or ongoing experiences of distress, such as a disaster that has just happened, living with domestic violence, or workplace bullying. And there is *single-incident trauma* from the past, for example, a car accident, an earthquake, or a single sexual assault. Then there is repeated and compiled *complex trauma*: many different kinds and repetitions of trauma. We can be affected by *attachment trauma* from early experiences of being parented. Finally, there is *transgenerational trauma*, which can include experiences as diverse as famine, war, extreme weather events, and the attachment trauma of previous generations, which change parents and grandparents epigenetically. When this happens, people can be born with those epigenetic changes already integrated into their own biology and their own immune and stress responses.[21]

Here is a (necessarily incomplete) list of possible traumas, all of which research has shown have negative effects on people who have survived them. How many of these have you lived through?

- Verbal abuse (name-calling, being ridiculed, made fun of, or dismissed)—both peer verbal abuse and parental verbal abuse show aftereffects in the brain[22]
- Receiving bullying or social exclusion[23]
- Neglect (no one talking to you; no one looking at you; being left alone for twenty minutes or more below the age of nine, eight hours or more below the age of thirteen, more than two days below the age of eighteen—especially without notice or prior arrangement)[24]
- Homelessness, dislocation, emigration[25,26]
- Car or other accident[27]
- A parent's suicide[28]
- Seeing someone be killed or die suddenly[29]
- Losing someone to violence, suicide, or sudden death[30]

- Losing anyone to death as a child[31]
- Witnessing violence on television as a child[32]
- Experiencing or witnessing domestic violence[33]
- Sexual assault, attempted sexual assault, or attempted murder[34]
- Hearing about others' traumatic deaths[35]
- Earthquake, flood, or other natural disaster[36]
- Robbery, burglary, or other home or vehicle invasion[37]
- Discrimination, racism, exclusion, bias, or microaggressions[38]
- Poverty[39]
- Community trauma (coming from a difficult neighborhood)[40]
- Your addiction, or the addiction of a parent when you were a child[41]
- Diagnosis with a life-threatening or chronic illness[42]
- Awakening during a surgery or medical procedure when you were supposed to be unconscious[43]
- Complicated births (for fathers, too[44])
- Experiencing or participating in wars, military interventions, or active military service[45]
- Being a police officer[46]
- Having a rescue/recovery occupation[47]
- Having a mental illness or having a parent who is mentally ill[48]
- Being kidnapped, confined, or tortured[49]
- Disappearance of a parent or caretaker due to death or abandonment[50]
- Sexual abuse[51]
- Physical abuse[52]

Different types of trauma leave different traces in the brain. Some affect the cerebellum, some the way neurons connect, some the amygdala and the hippocampus. The more different kinds of traumas a person has experienced, the more profoundly the nervous system, tendencies toward addiction, and even health are affected.[53] Traumas fracture people, dividing their life energy into frozen parcels. As we have seen, this discon-nection from the life force has an impact on integration at the level of epigenetics and the way that cells respond to stress, as well as on people's ability to make decisions to choose self-care.

Let's look at what it is like to live with islands of known self and islands of frozenness. Part of the healing process involves reconnecting to old neural nets of memory that hold disruptive pain and acknowledging the depths of feeling that we lived through during the traumatic events. As mentioned earlier, three major brain function networks need to be reintegrated in the healing journey (see Figure 1.4). We need to restore the network for decision making and acting, link the meaning-making network back in, and reclaim a positive sense of self, which means bring-ing the DMN back toward self-warmth.[54]

As we bring resonance to traumatic memories, the hurt dissolves, as pain always does when someone is there to comfort us, and the previously disconnected net of memory becomes interconnected with the rest of the brain the way it is supposed to be.

The tricky thing is the word *hurt*. When is a present-day difficult situation the result of present-day events, and when is it the result of old, unprocessed trauma? How do we tell the difference? By following the trail of body sensations. If the sensations signaled by the body are observed and felt, it is possible to find out what the cue was that moved us from the regular, ordinary coping self into the neural network of pain. If we talk only about present-day events, and those events are held with resonance, and then we relax, with no tension left in the body, then there's no need to ask about the past. If talking about present-day events doesn't result in bodily relaxation, then it may be worth looking at whether the body remembers similar events from when we were younger.

The price that is paid if we never look at the past is bewilderment. If we don't look backward, then once we stop crying or floating and come back to ourselves, there is no way to get back to that disconnected net, and we live bewildered lives, not knowing when the next unexpected meltdown will happen. So as we begin to track and pay attention, we start to collect the information we need to change our brains. Let's look at one important way to work with traumatic experience that may make healing more doable.

As We Heal, We Reclaim Our Lives

Over and over again, as people do this memory rescue work, they are able to make new sense from old memories. A man who was trapped in a car wreck for several hours, waiting for help, believed that he had been waiting alone, but after doing the process work and understanding how frozen he had been after the wreck, he realized that a passing motorist had stopped and waited with him and that he had forgotten the man's presence entirely. A woman who was raped but spent years being bewildered about how it happened finally understood how the rapist had ambushed her. A man who knew he had been sexually abused but didn't know who had done it realized it was his older cousin. He had the sense that he had always known, even though at the beginning of the process he could not have said it. A woman who nearly died during childbirth three years before her rescue process realized that a part of her had believed that she died, and that this part of her that had been frozen in time was surprised to learn that she and her child had survived. In all of these cases, the people had a new sense of wholeness and confidence, a new capacity for intimacy that came with the reclamation of self.

Sometimes during this reclamation process, as people are coming back to life, there can be a tremendous surge of rage or anger, or even just unusual levels of crankiness, so it is good to have the ability to see the life energy that lies within anger. It is also possible to live for years in an extended state of anger, arising from unresolved experiences of trauma. Chapter 7 explores what is possible when we bring compassion and resonance to experiences of being angry.

CHAPTER SEVEN

Claiming Anger's Creative and Protective Gifts

"Anger is bad," or "I am an angry person."
(actually, "My anger can be a force for good," and
"I am a complex person who sometimes gets angry.")

Anger's Gifts and Burdens: Harnessing the Power of the Amygdala

The need to fight danger (of loss of life, resources, or important people) is the force that fuels anger and rage. People are driven to take action to protect themselves, their resources, and the people they care about, and this shows up in the impulse to lash out. In and of itself, there is nothing wrong with anger.

It is the angry actions that people take and the angry words that they express in blame that create difficulty. Anger that is expressed in physical violence, acts of revenge, punishment, insults, or invective, and even its quieter cousin, contempt, leaves a trail of trauma. Anger and contempt affect other people's health and well-being. And the continual experience of being in the cortisol-driven fight response takes a huge toll on the angry person's body as well.

On the other hand, people don't advocate for themselves or others very effectively if they have no access to their life energy and to their fight response. When people can harness their energy and express it in meaningful, intense ways that simultaneously hold others with care, they achieve the maximum effect. But without access to a robust capacity for self-regulation, people are at the mercy of their amygdala.

When I say "at the mercy of our amygdala," I really mean it. When the amygdala finds something worrisome, it responds as fast as fifty milliseconds.[1] And if the neural fibers that run from the prefrontal cortex (PFC) to the amygdala aren't solid and aren't accustomed to regulating high intensity with grace and self-connection, then reactivity can take over. This is why people can do things that aren't very smart when they are really angry and not well regulated. Without solid emotional self-regulation, the part of the brain that has common sense, the PFC, isn't available once people get mad. With a lot of integrated emotional support, people can be really angry, feel it, choose to speak about it or not, and not hurt themselves or anyone else.

Recall the image of the brain in the palm of your hand (Figure 2.1). A regulated brain is like a closed fist, with the middle fingers (the PFC) wrapped around your thumb (the limbic system), regulating its effects. Now open your fingers. This movement represents what happens when the amygdala is the dominant force (although in actual fact, of course, the PFC doesn't move; it just goes dark on brain images).[2] Without self-regulation, the PFC is off-line. It's like you have flipped your lid, and then you end up reacting blindly, instead of choosing your actions with care.

For those of you who love science and precision, the part of the PFC that can be helpful to awaken here appears to be the right **ventrolateral PFC** and its ties to the medial PFC. Both of these areas become active when people begin to name emotions, as we do when we move into verbal resonance, and as is modeled in the guided meditations. As you may recall from Chapter 2, naming calms the amygdala.[3]

For those of you more interested in understanding the healing process in general terms, the network that we are strengthening and making more resilient is the PFC-amygdala-emotion network, rather than any one location "doing" something. What is important is that we can all learn to regulate these intense feelings and that neuroscience supports an understanding that this is possible.

When the PFC is off-line, people yell at family or friends, or say cutting and dismissive things. They damage relationships, break trust, and inflict pain. Without regulation, people get angry and hit others, or smash their own tender hands or feet into walls, hurting themselves and even breaking their own bones. They drive their cars without regard for human life. They take out their pain on pets, partners, or children. They make unfortunate unilateral decisions. And then there is the flood of pain, regret, and remorse for having "lost it," and the hopelessness and despair that follow, since this is not the first time they've seen themselves behave in ways they don't enjoy.

Many of the students in my prison classes said that they walked into their first class without a clue that they had any emotion besides anger and that it ruled them. There are some good reasons for this:

- Anger is a solid fallback if no one is supporting us. It is a fairly safe and self-protective resource. It cuts short vulnerability and creates boundaries, facilitating survival in difficult situations.
- Anger is what we may really feel if we've had a lot of experience of no one listening to us, closely followed by hopelessness.
- Anger brings a dopamine flow (the feel-good brain chemical that has a role in addictions) to the brains of mice, so it may well give people a rush of well-being, too.[4]
- The more trauma we have experienced, the trickier it is to build solid neural connections running from the PFC to the amygdala. This makes it more likely that anger will take control. Life without an active PFC is emotionally painful, and its absence makes it more likely that our actions will be antisocial.

People without robust contributions from their PFC can be at the mercy of their amygdala, which can show up in compulsive or addictive patterns or in knee-jerk emotional reactions.[5,6] So people learn to compensate for not having an active and warm inner parent to take care of themselves by self-managing. As we have explored before, compensations may include reacting with anger, responding with contempt, retreating in fear and isolating, eating for comfort, drinking alcohol, engaging in risky behaviors and sports activities, domestic violence, taking drugs, smoking cigarettes, gambling compulsively, shopping or spending compulsively, needing home or work environments to be particularly neat or ordered, getting in fights to blow off tension, workaholism, acting out sexually, or being addicted to sex, strip clubs, or pornography. The way we can tell whether what we are doing is to compensate for (manage) an incapacity for inner self-regulation is by asking, what has to keep being done to maintain or return to calm?

Anger is about what is at stake and what is being threatened in the moment. It can be a spark that starts in the nervous system and roars into flame, and it can burn down the emotional house. It has a bad reputation because people have received so much harm from angry people misusing their power: domestic violence, bullying, and abusive or scary parents, teachers, religious figures, and supervisors. Despite anger's destructive power, it is meant to help us survive, as part of the fight response. We are fighting for what the brain and body believe is a good reason, often based on staving off grief or fear. When we find out what that reason is, the anger becomes less intense. Sometimes it is even possible to defuse the anger by asking, what is frightening me or making me sad?

The least helpful manifestation of anger arises when people seem to believe that if they can figure out who to blame, they can make things turn out differently next time ("You'll think twice about that in the future!"), and then things will be better. People will often try this tactic with themselves, calling themselves "stupid" or "idiot" in the hope of self-improvement.

But blame-fueled anger can create a negative response in the self, the family, or the social circle. At best, people can have hurt feelings, and at worst, there can be a trail of broken relationships and terrified family members, and even physical injury and death.

As we begin to notice and strip away blame, we can move toward using the energy of anger without wreaking social and emotional havoc. There is a purity in the intensity of expression that anger brings when it is cleaned of blame. Let's take a look at the way anger moves in the skull-brain and the body-brain.

BRAIN CONCEPT 7.1: UNDERSTANDING ANGER IN THE BODY AND THE BRAIN

The amygdala doesn't just send its alarm message to the skull-brain; it also sends urgent chemical alarm signals to the rest of the body-brain. It shifts the system's gears in response to whether the environment seems safe. The brain chemicals of alarm (cortisol and adrenaline) speed up heart rate and increase blood pressure, make us breathe more quickly and higher in the chest, and move the flow of energy from small muscles to big muscles so that we can fight the danger or run away from it (fight or flight),[7] and then, if that is hopeless, we begin to shut down or become immobile.[8]

To understand this, it is helpful to know a little about the three physical responses to levels of safety: social engagement, mobilization (fight/flight), and what has traditionally been called "freeze," but now is referred to by researchers as "**immobilization.**" (The word "freeze" implies a sense of tension that is missing once we have given up hope, so scientists have moved away from its use.) The body shifts the way it uses energy and how it relates to the outer world in complete dependence on how safe we believe the environment is. This shift happens with the help of the **vagus nerve**,[9] a little-known nerve bundle that runs up from the inside of the body, between spinal column and heart, to the skull-brain and back, mostly carrying information from all of the organs and digestive system. (About 80 percent of the fibers of the vagus nerve run up to the brain, and about 20 percent run down to the body.)

Neurobiologist Stephen Porges, who has most fully recognized the importance of this nerve for the understanding of our sympathetic and parasympathetic nervous systems, calls the forwardmost lane of this highway the **ventral vagal complex**. When people are relaxed and at ease, their systems automatically run in these fast, **myelinated** (insulated) lanes of the vagus nerve. When people are feeling safe, when their very nerves have a sense that the world is a good place to be (Porges calls this a "**neuroception of safety**") their systems are set for growth and restoration. They have exquisite mastery of their social interaction, which is why Porges sometimes refers to this state as **social engagement**. In this state, the fine muscles of the face are in a dance of responsiveness with the other faces in their world, the focus of the eyes tightens to the human face, and along with it, the muscles of the middle ear tighten to the sound range of the human voice.[10] (More about the way humans respond to a neuroception of safety in Chapter 14.)

As alarm mounts, the sense of safety falls, and the body's gears shift into the full-body **sympathetic activation** of the stress response,[11] which people usually call fight or flight. Anger, of course, takes people into fight mode, and fear takes people into flight mode. This chapter is about the sympathetic activation of the fight mode, or anger. There are sympathetic fibers both inside and outside the ventral channels of the vagus nerve that carry the fight-or-flight message to the heart, while the entire human body responds to the chemical messengers of stress. Once this flood of chemical messages hits the body, people can no longer really engage with others at the complex level that is possible when things are calm. The part of the brain that reads faces is even affected, interpreting neutral facial expressions as hostile, even causing parents to think more negatively about what their children are doing.[12]

And then, if people's fight-or-flight response doesn't get them to safety, and they start to feel hopeless, or if there is a sudden shock and they are trapped in some way, they move into the immobilized state, activated by the **dorsal vagal complex,**[13] the rearmost, slow channel of the vagus nerve. The dorsal vagus mostly carries information from our intestines, liver, kidneys, and other organs below the diaphragm up to the brain. It is a slow lane because the fibers of this part of the vagus nerve are **unmyelinated**, which means that they do not have the insulating layer of **myelin** that makes energy and information travel quickly along nerve and neuron pathways. (More on the dorsal vagal complex, the immobilized state, and the dissociation that comes with it in Chapter 9.)

The sudden rush of emotions that comes with fight-or-flight doesn't stop with just one person. As social animals, people get caught up in one another's cascading nervous systems.[14] This means that the movement into the fight response can create mounting and seemingly unstoppable flows of energy in relationships (quarrels and fights), as people ricochet off one another's anger.

So if people want to become less reactive and improve their response to getting angry, including the possibility of utilizing its power for good, they're up against this neurobiological avalanche of cortisol and increased heart rate. As we create an ongoing sense of being accompanied and being held by our own resonating self-witness, we are aiming to shift our neurobiological response so that we stay in the social engagement state more easily rather than shifting into anger, reach out for the support of others more automatically, and demonstrate more flexibility and resiliency, the way that infants do who have more support from their parents.[15]

To understand anger in the entire body-brain even more clearly, we can return to Jaak Panksepp's work with the circuits of emotion.

BRAIN CONCEPT 7.2:
UNDERSTANDING THE RAGE IN ANGER

One of the circuits of emotion that people share with animals is RAGE. Anger increases in direct correlation with what we sense as being blocked or under siege. The larger the number of things that are under question, the bigger the anger. When just one or two questions are in play, a person will be peeved or a little irritated. When there are many, the person's emotions will reach the boiling point (for some of us, perhaps right before the collapse into helplessness). When people are in a rage, they don't believe that they matter to anyone else. In the brain and body, as the level of intensity of activation of the RAGE circuit increases, adrenaline starts pumping, and heart rate and blood pressure increase.[16] If things continue, tunnel vision and tunnel hearing can begin, and the blood supply to the face, hands, and feet can be lost. The point of greatest anger is murderous rage, where people might cause great harm and may not even remember what was done. The more that issues are acknowledged, the more people have a sense of mattering, and the less angry they become.

The anger continuum is a possible way to look at the words we use as we have less and less of a sense of mattering. The list starts with words of mild dissatisfaction and builds in intensity of emotion up to lividity, the experience of being so angry that blood actually leaves the extremities. Different people have different ways of ordering this list. Feel free to change the order to reflect the level of intensity that you feel with these words.

The Anger Continuum
Dissatisfied
Piqued
Displeased
Vexed
Peeved
Indignant
Irritated
Exasperated
Resentful
Aggravated
Mad
Angry
Outraged
Irate
Fuming
Seething
Infuriated, furious
Incensed
Enraged
Livid

Dismayed by Ongoing Reactivity? Working With Irritation

It is confusing to be human. People can swear to themselves that they will never snap at their partner or child again, and still, the next time the milk is left out or someone makes an accusation of dishonesty, or the next time "that tone" shows up in the other person's voice, a switch gets flipped. In response, people can find themselves being sarcastic, or losing their temper, or completely turning off and withdrawing from relationship, before they even know they have done it. This bewildering state of affairs is entirely due to the amygdala and its automatic reactions.

When the individual has had many experiences of not being heard, broken trust, lack of safety, lack of predictability, discomfort, or trauma, this can oversensitize the amygdala to the point that it reacts to even ordinary alarms in daily life.[17] And these experiences mount up. Once the body reaches a certain level of ongoing stress, then little things like drawers that won't open, fingernails that catch, changes in plans, or small disagreements can be the matches that light a fire leading to emotional explosions.

Whether people's experience is of one particular irritation or of many, the way to create sustainable change for the nervous system is to bring resonant empathy to experience. The next guided meditation goes through a **posthearsal** process that, when practiced regularly, can clear the presence of outdated alarms and decrease reactivity and irritation.

GUIDED MEDITATION 7.1: Posthearsals

A **posthearsal** is an intentional rerun of an experience that we feel triggered by or regret about, or both, to bring resonance to the part of the self that was overwhelmed and unaccompanied in that moment. As the previous self receives warmth and understanding, the body relaxes and new choices become possible for the next time such an event occurs.

Note of acknowledgment: It can be hard to have warmth for yourself when you have a sense that (or know that) you have either lost control or harmed others. So reassure yourself that finding and growing the part of you that has generous acceptance for your past can take a long time. There is a reason we keep punishing ourselves. When the brain reruns shameful memories of anger and punitive behavior, the evaluating self may not you hold yourself with tenderness, because there can be an ongoing hope that self-punishment will help stop this from ever happening again. With this in mind, try this guided meditation, and see how far you get with it. Stop whenever it is uncomfortable, stay with your body, and listen to your heart.

> Begin with your breathing. Let yourself find the place of live sensation in your breathing, and invite your attention to rest there. Continue to breathe and offer yourself warmth. After ten to twenty breaths, let your attention go back to the memory of the difficult incident. As you replay it in your mind, let yourself notice your body sensations. At what moment in the replay does your body tell you that your anger began? What were the words, gestures, facial expressions, or thoughts that were the trigger for this anger? Stop the memory right at this moment, freezing everyone else who is involved.
>
> Shift your attention away from this scene to your sense of a loving presence who wants only the best for you. As you look back through time at your starting-to-get-angry self, do you have a sense of warmth and understanding? Or are you upset with yourself and worried? If you don't have a feeling of warmth for yourself, you have not fully located your resonating self-witness.
>
> Once you have connected with a resonating self-witness who has compassion for your angry self, continue on with the next paragraph. If you haven't found one, simply skip this meditation and continue on with this book to see if you begin to build this compassionate inner part, and return to this meditation after you complete the book to see if there is more solid ground for this act of self-connection.
>
> With resonance, first make some empathy guesses for the present-day worried or regretful self. (Maybe he or she is needing

hope, faith, or trust? Or maybe some acknowledgment that he or she is worried about the other people in this scenario, or about whether you will ever learn or heal?)

Now, activating your resonating self-witness, look back at yourself with warmth. Take a time-travel step back to yourself, so that you are not alone. Can your angry self feel this accepting, reassuring presence? Switch your consciousness between your angry self and your more resourced self-witness. Let your self-witness acknowledge the body sensations and the intensity of the emotions, and make some feelings guesses and needs guesses based on the body sensations you find.

If your stomach is clenched, are you feeling dread and overwhelm? Do you worry that stability, predictability, and respect are slipping away? Do you want to hang on as tightly as possible to some solid ground, some truth in everything that is going on? Are you afraid that the other person has given up, and are you lashing out against hopelessness? Are you exhausted and needing support, and do you feel hopeless about ever receiving it?

Check in with your body sensations again. If the new or slightly different sensations were an emotion, which emotion would they be? Let your resonating self-witness make more feelings and needs guesses until your body relaxes in the memory of the trigger. Let yourself imagine behaving differently, taking a different action, saying different words. And now, let yourself relax and come back to your breathing. You have just done a complete posthearsal.

WHY PRACTICE THIS MEDITATION?

Several things about this meditation are helpful. The first is that as we identify and work with our triggers on a daily, or at least weekly, basis, we are developing a practice of self-noticing that is foundational for any type of change. Second, we can use posthearsals to clear the unexploded mines from our past. In doing this, we are leveraging the learning about time travel for healing from Chapter 6. The third benefit is that, whenever we link our resonating self-witness with places of pain, offering ourselves comfort and soothing, we are strengthening our capacity for self-regulation.

And as we become better able to regulate ourselves, we become more resilient, less reactive, and more stable. At the level of our body, we begin to stay more grounded, easily experiencing what used to upset us without losing our neuroception of safety.[18] As we gain ground in this way, we become more predictably able to stay in the social engagement state, and we are less at the mercy of fight-or-flight and immobilization responses. We grow more capacity for space, contemplation, and choice before action.

In the face of all this moving energy, what kinds of power and groundedness help transform life-destructive rage into life-serving self-care, self-expression, and advocacy for self and others? If we allow ourselves to make positive attributions about people's motivations, rather than assuming the worst about them, it will decrease our angry response to their behavior. Here is a way to begin to find the positive motivation in the other by turning your new resonance capabilities outward.

RESONANCE SKILL 7.1: RESONANCE FOR BOTH PARTIES

First, let yourself bring one of your most challenging relationships to mind. Choose a relationship or a moment in time where you are fairly certain that the other person has meant to hurt you.

Fold a piece of paper lengthwise, open it up again, and write one main problem from that relationship at the top of the page, something that you have anger about, for example, "My partner rarely calls me when he/she is away from home." Underneath those words, note the body sensations you have when you think about this situation. For example, "tight gut, constricted breathing, corners of mouth pulled down."

Now look at the lists of negative feelings in Chapter 3 and

use the left-hand side of the piece of paper to write down every emotion you have about this experience.

After you list your feelings, turn to the list of universal human needs and values in Chapter 4. For each feeling, write down the values that are important to you when you think about this behavior: in this example, the feelings might be sadness, loneliness, irritation, and impatience. If you take each of these feelings and you say to yourself, "Of course I feel _____, because I so long for _____," you will find the underlying needs for your feelings. For the feelings in the example shown above, the values might be connection, warmth, acknowledgment, and partnership.

Now check back in with your body sensations. Have they shifted at all? If this exercise lets you relax a little, turn the page over to imagine and write down what the other person's body sensations, feelings, and needs might be.

In the case of not calling when away from home, the other person may be struck with sadness and unable to imagine continuing to function well after he or she has checked in. Or perhaps worried and hopeless about the situation at home and trying to conserve energy and strength. He or she might have body sensations of constriction and feelings of irritation and might be longing for independence, ease, freedom, or other needs that you see on the list.

Now bring the situation you have chosen to mind, and allow yourself to be generous in your wondering, both for yourself and for your partner, child, friend, coworker, employer, or neighbor.

It is important to do this in a spirit of generosity. If you still feel bitter when you think about the other person, spend more time with your own body sensations, asking what emotions these sensations might represent and what needs might underlie them, before checking back in with your bitterness. Sometimes, when things are really tough for me, I end up listing most of the needs on the list on the left side of my paper. It is important for our body to relax before we ask ourselves to think about things from the other person's perspective.

We can practice this exercise in various ways. Sometimes simply taking ourselves seriously and taking the other person in our relationship seriously opens our heart to that person. Sometimes it can be the basis for a new kind of discussion about an old problem. Sometimes looking at all the needs that are not met for us in a given situation can support us in letting our lives develop in new ways. The important thing is that we start to see and believe that how we feel and what we long for all make sense.

As people begin to get used to the idea that feelings are important and that they point to valuable messages about what is vital to their well-being, they find that often the root of difficulties in relationships come down to the same need being expressed in different ways. For example, in the situation explored in the resonance skill exercise above about travel and communication, the partner left behind has a longing for intimacy. And the partner who is traveling and not calling may also, oddly, be longing for intimacy and feel hopeless about being able to access any place of depth and connection on the telephone.

We never know until we start to explore these questions with the people in our lives, bringing our curiosity and generosity to the discussion. If we have long-term, important relationships with people who are not willing or able to have these conversations, we may find that making silent and open-hearted guesses to ourselves about what is happening for the other shifts things enough to provide a little more room to breathe for both partners. And as we begin to realize the delight we feel in mutuality and intimacy, we might find that we start looking for opportunities to add other warm friendships to our lives that will complement those we already have.

It is almost like there's an ancient lost secret about being human, that we were made to be calmed by being deeply understood by one another, but we have forgotten how to do it. As we open this door, we start to get closer to people. Now that we know what it's like to have someone be warmly curious about our experience, we start to miss that response when it's not available. And at the same time, we get better at responding to ourselves with resonance. We get better at noticing when we are lonely, and paradoxically, we get better at being alone.

The Honorable Expression of Anger

A nonharming regulated expression of anger takes practice. It necessitates staying closely connected with your body sensations and speaking them aloud, and combining them with your deepest values. For example, imagine your partner tells you he or she thinks you are lying or that you are hiding something. You do not have the sense that this is true, and you are feeling very angry. You might say, "I notice that I'm breathing very heavily, and that I have literally started to see red at the corners of my vision. My fists are clenched, and my toes are curling, and my chest is heaving. I'm having a hard time thinking at all, and I can hear the tension in my voice. It is so important to me to be seen for my intentions. Honesty and clarity are the most essential things for me. I want to be known, and I want shared reality with you."

Notice that in the aftermath of this expression, no matter how loud your voice became, there is nothing that has to be cleaned up. You have not insulted your partner or said how your partner feels or what he or she was thinking or was doing to you. You stayed with your own experience. You remained open and vulnerable. Your partner could hear both your intensity and your truth.

However, this clean expression of anger may not yet be very available to you. If you have integrated blame, contempt, threats, or actual violence in your expressions of anger, you have the responsibility to clean it up. Blame, contempt, threats, and violence are harmful to the brains, bodies, and immune systems of the people around you, and it is important to realize this.

When Anger Leaves Scars

When we have frightened or shamed people in our expression of anger, we need to take responsibility for this. It doesn't matter how justified we feel, how much we believe that someone else has done something wrong—contempt and fear leave scars and wounds on the people we have relationships with.

Even when someone isn't in a rage, anger can be scary for the people nearby. It is a powerful energy, and when children are the focus or even just the witness of adult anger, it can be frightening and disturbing. (Witnessing domestic violence is one of the forms of trauma that leaves aftereffects in the brain.)

When this happens to children and people who have less power in relationships, they may end up having little to no access to their own protective energy. They may have made a vow never to be angry themselves because of their awareness of the harm that could be done. It is also possible that their nervous system will shut down completely in the presence of any anger because that was the way they survived their childhood (or adult) terror. This leaves them without resource when other people are angry or shaming with them. With our behavior, we may have stripped them of their own protective and self-protective energies.

An essential part of the journey to the whole self is learning to express anger in ways that honor it, the self, and the beings around us. When we know we have not been able to do this with our partners, family, and friends, we may want to reach out to acknowledge the impact our anger had on them. Here is one way to do this, called making a repair.

RESONANCE SKILL 7.2: MAKING REPAIRS

An effective repair has five steps:

1. Make sure that you have received enough emotional support that you are no longer angry at yourself for what you have done, or at the other person for whatever you think that person has done. You may need to do a posthearsal before you can even begin to think about making a repair (see above). If

you are blaming the other person or thinking about what that person did to cause your outburst, or you want that person to acknowledge his or her part in the event, then you are not yet at a point where repair is possible. Certainly a dialogue is possible in such cases, but not a repair. (If you want to blame, you need to get more support and empathy!)

2. Ask the other person if he or she is willing to receive a repair. Here is one example of how you might ask this: "I don't feel good about something I said or how I acted. Are you willing to have me tell you about what I regret?"

3. State what you did that you regret, as briefly as possible.

4. Ask the other person what he or she would like you to hear about how it was to receive your original outburst.

5. Let that person know that you heard what it was like, and how that knowledge impacts you. You can do this by reflecting verbally, using gestures, or with silent, full presence. With the silent, full presence, people may not actually have a sense of being heard, so it is always possible to check at the end and ask if the person feels heard, or complete, or whatever words you like to use to ask about his or her experience.

You may never have heard someone make a repair in this way. It is certainly very rare in our North American and European social worlds. Mostly people get apologies over with as quickly as possible, using words like, "My bad," or "I'm sorry." They never inquire about the other person's experience, and instead they tell the other person why they did it, saying things like, "You made me so mad when you . . . ," or "I was really upset about this other thing. . . . " Repairs are hard, but they are worth every ounce of effort, and they often take us a long way toward a full sense of restoration of relationship.

A particularly difficult kind of repair is bringing healing to the harm that parents did to children while they were small. This kind of harm can hang in the air for decades, preventing family warmth and closeness.

In honor of this difficulty, here is some specific support for making this type of repair.

Making Repairs With Grown Children

If you are experiencing any shared mourning here, it might be a relief to know that no matter how old our children are, repairs are what distinguish healthy and close relationships from distant and unhealthy relationships. If you would like to speak with a grown child about your realizations about your parenting, it might sound like this:

> Choose an incident that your child might remember that illustrates your point.
>
> Ask, "Do you remember the time when I . . . and you . . . ?"
>
> If your child says yes, then proceed. If your child says no, then say that you remember it, and ask if you can say something about it. If your child says yes, then proceed. If your child says no, please respect this refusal. Let your child know if he or she is ever willing to talk about it, you would like to have the conversation. Ask if you can check in about a year from now, and if the child says yes, put a note in your calendar so that you remember.
>
> If your child says yes, then say something like, "When I think about that incident, I realize that I was so lost in my own pain, I was unable to tell what was happening for you. It seems characteristic of a larger pattern between us, where you were not seen or known in your childhood by me. What was it like for you?"
>
> Now, if your child speaks, it is your job to listen without defensiveness. If you can, repeat what seems most important to your child, or say the words, "It's true." Try to refrain from apologizing during the flow of the response until the very end, unless your child asks for an apology. At the end, if it seems like something you would like to do, your apology might sound something like this:

"I'm so sorry. I regret that I wasn't able to give you the care and emotional responsiveness that I would have liked any child, especially you, to have had. As I think about it now, I feel _____ (name your body sensations), and I know how much I wish I could have been there for you."

If you find that you want to defend yourself, or blame your child for being difficult, or for not taking responsibility, hold yourself with care and breathe, and try to stay as close to the script as possible. This experience is in service of your child, not of you. Get your support for your pain from another source besides your child.

Note for resonance beginners: You may not have this kind of flow of words with yourself when you are starting out. Even the *intention* to be compassionate toward yourself, just in silence, can make a big difference. Remember the assumption of innocence. This is the principle that everything you do, even yelling at your kids or your partner, is an attempt to serve life. Just remembering this, without being able to remember what resonant language is, let alone make guesses for yourself, can help enormously.

This type of repair is part of a larger conversation, a healing exchange that happens over years of small repairs. In other conversations over the years the child may bring up this or similar experiences and relay more about their emotional impact. What is important is that the parent stay resourced enough to be able to hear whatever the child wants to say. This practice of staying open to making repairs lets children, as well as partners and friends, know they matter. Sharing our vulnerability increases trust and everyone's willingness to say what's really true.

These four important skills can change our relationship with anger:

- *Learning to do posthearsals:* Each time you become angry and behave in a way that you do not enjoy, follow the guided meditation in this chapter to start to create new levels of self-compassion, self-understanding, and self-regulation, until you can do this process easily on your own.

- *Self-empathy during an episode of anger:* (See Resonance Skill 5.1, in Chapter 5.) In the beginning of this work, you may not be able to do more than remember, for a few seconds before the avalanche takes over, that you would like to respond differently this time. Then, as you continue to hold your intention for self-connection and follow through with these exercises, you will find that you can keep your attention on your breath for a little longer, keeping the avalanche at bay. Finally, you will find your resonating self-witness standing beside you as you remain calm in situations that used to trigger you.

- *Learning to express anger cleanly, without blame:* This means referencing our deep values in life in tough situations (see Chapter 4). It is helpful to name body sensations as well as emotions and needs, since the discipline of staying grounded in our body with our prefrontal cortex online, while letting intensity blow through us without causing us or anyone else harm, is an art form. This is the most difficult skill of all, because the body sensations of anger can be so distressing that, even if people have mastered the other skills, they may still tend to suppress them. Or they may blow up and then apologize and repair. It is important to have warmth toward the self for any missteps if this seems unmanageable in the moments of intensity. For example, where we used to say, "You idiot, why would you do something like this?," we learn to say, "I feel so angry! My fists are clenched, my heart is pounding, and I really want accountability and care! I'm terrified for you, for us, and for this family!"

- *Learning to make effective repairs:* This is one of the most important skills we can practice while we are learning to control our anger. It involves learning to make effective repairs with people after we have lost control, used violent and blam-

(DMN), as both states are too focused externally to easily permit the DMN to swing into action.[2] But negative thoughts that have angry and fearful components can be part of the shame and rumination cycles of the DMN. These thoughts can arise in the aftermath of active anger and fear, unless some kind of comfort, understanding, and warmth can soothe the previous state of upset.

Because fear takes people out of presence and into vigilance, it also moves them out of being able to pay attention to the nuances of what is happening for someone else. Instead they try to manage, control, and limit the environment to make things safe, or they are forced to live with an inner disruption of terror that can be almost unbearable. This is because a neuroception of safety (a sense of safety so complete that the nerves themselves know that there is nothing to fear) is the body's primary need. Our bodies will not relax if we have a sense that we are in danger.

Part of the neuroception of safety comes from a predictable certainty that there is no physical danger. And since people are such social beings, another part of this sense of being safe comes from what is happening in the social environment. Do we belong to the people we are with? Do we matter? If we speak, do they listen?

The next very important question is about how power is held in groups. If someone else has the decision-making power (for example, if we are a student in any way, or a client, a patient, a child, a dependent, a parishioner, an inmate, or an employee), then someone else has power over us. Does that someone play favorites? Or is he or she fair? Does that someone disclose his or her own humanness? Is that someone modeling warmth, so that the members of the family or community can also have warmth for one another?

Some Qualities That Contribute to Bodies Having a Sense of Safety

- Belonging
- Mattering
- Security

- Respect
- Care
- Consideration
- Being heard
- Predictability
- Trust
- Dignity
- Acknowledgment
- Transparency
- Accountability
- Self-responsibility

Some Qualities That Take Us Into Creativity, Relaxation, and Play

- Warmth
- Delight and curiosity
- Welcome
- Appreciation
- Tenderness
- Presence

Would you like to add any qualities to either list that are particularly important for you to have a neuroception of safety and a relaxed sense of creativity?

How Safe Was Your World When You Were Small? How Safe Is It Now?

Take a moment to review the lists of qualities that generate a sense of safety and relaxation, thinking about the ways that your parents or other responsible adults behaved in your world from when you were first born to eighteen years of age. Which of these qualities were a part of your life as a child? Did the environment change when you were alone with either of your parents? Did it change when they were together? Was it different before or after a sibling was born or moved out of the house? Did it change when your parents had work or didn't have work? Was it different on weekends or holidays?

Take a moment to consider your early school environment. Were your early teachers warm and encouraging, and did they have faith in your abilities as a learner?

You may recall from Chapter 6 how, when we learned about trauma, we learned that the hippocampus is the memory organ that time stamps our experiences,[3] while the amygdala has no sense of time connected to the memories that it stores. If we lived in a world that did not provide much support or encouragement when we were small, the memory networks connected with our amygdala may still believe that we live in that world now, even if the people we are with now are very different from our family of origin.

Take a moment to connect with resonance with the little one that you were. Use some of the skills of acknowledgment, respect, tenderness, and warmth to be present to that small person, who survived moments that may have felt very unsafe. It is possible that that child had a lot of reason to be afraid. If there was fear there, how intense was it? Let's explore.

The Fear Continuum

Often when people think of fear and how it grows, they stop short with the words "scared" and "afraid." They don't remember that there is an entire shading of gradually growing anxiety that people can move through as things become more intense. This chapter is about living with the levels of fear between anxiety and frozen terror, the livable levels that impact the nervous system and shift us into the brain and body's flight response, without actually taking us into terror and then immobility. Have a look at the words used to describe the gradual increase of fear in human bodies, the emotion words that make up the fear continuum. As you read through this list, see which states of fear are most familiar to you. Again, there will be individual nuances of ordering—place the words in any order of intensity that works for you.

The Fear Continuum

- Disquiet
- Discomfort
- Unease
- Wariness
- Concern
- Nervousness
- Trepidation
- Worry
- Anxiety (a different flavor of this can show up in the grief continuum)
- Apprehension
- Agitation
- Dismay
- Alarm
- Fright
- Fear
- Dread
- Panic
- Horror (can also encompass disgust and revulsion)
- Phobias
- Terror
- Frozen immobility

Think about which states of fear are most familiar to you. What are the body sensations that you feel when you are in these states? And what are you longing for? Safety? Or acknowledgment for the enormity of your experience and that safety seems impossible? Do you need protection? Tenderness and gentle warmth? To be sure that you can take your own time with things? Is there a longing to be able to watch people from an invulnerable or invisible place until you are sure it's safe to come out?

To understand the physical effects of fear on us, the next section explores the effects of fear on the brain and the body.

BRAIN CONCEPT 8.1: FLIGHT—UNDERSTANDING FEAR IN THE BODY AND THE BRAIN

As signs of danger start to mount, the amygdala becomes steadily more activated. The brain's primary purpose is to keep us alive and safe. As you remember, between 12 and 100 times a second our amygdala is scanning all our incoming information to see if we are noticing anything alarming or otherwise emotionally important.[4,5] When it does, it sends messages of alarm to the body through the brainstem and the part of the brain that produces the body symptoms of danger described above. And working in the other direction, it decodes the brainstem's language of body activation, changes it into raw emotion, and passes this information on to the part of the brain that helps give words to our emotional world.

As alarm mounts, and the body symptoms of danger spread, the nervous system shifts gears, from a state of feeling safe to a fight-or-flight state. During this process, a person might feel the increasing signs of fear shown in the list below. Which of the following experiences are familiar?

- Increased heartbeat
- Increased blood pressure
- Shallow breathing, with chest only
- Increased rate of breathing
- Dry mouth
- Heart palpitations
- Increased startle response
- Lower skin temperature overall
- Higher leg skin temperature
- Sweaty palms
- Upset stomach and intestines
- Lessened fine motor control, such as inability to put a key into a lock
- Pounding heart
- Running away or cutting off contact

Integrating Panksepp's FEAR Circuit

Just as there are CARE and RAGE circuits, we all also have a FEAR circuit. Inside the brain the flow of energy and information focuses into the FEAR circuit, running up and down from the central part of the amygdala to the hypothalamus, which sends out the chemical flow of danger signals, and then down through the brainstem to the body, as our whole beings get involved in the flight state that arises from fear.

We are not supposed to live without fear. It keeps us safe and alerts our system to be watchful and get out of the way of danger. We don't want to obliterate our capacity for vigilance; we want to have flexibility, resilience, and easy recovery from moments of alarm.

Fear, Attention, and Intelligence

When we do not have flexibility, things are more difficult. The state of hypervigilant awareness, with its lack of ability to settle and focus, can sometimes bear an uncanny resemblance to attention deficit hyperactivity disorder. When people have had a hard time learning, often they believe they are stupid or that their intellectual capacities are limited, when the root cause of the difficulty integrating new information is that they have lived in a dangerous world and their brain has been using all its resources to make sure that they survive, rather than helping them learn arithmetic, spelling, or history facts. People who have been under terrible stress have never had a chance to know how smart they actually are because their brains have endured years of disabling stress chemicals.[6]

While some people are actual geniuses, with an easy capacity to hold multiple bits of knowledge in their brain at the same time and manipulate them, most people are simply normally intelligent. Having the ability to assess your full intelligence involves the following:

- Feeling safe enough to explore the world with the mind, play with information, and become curious about knowledge

- Feeling safe enough to be able to focus on what you want to learn
- Being in an enriched environment which has things to explore in it
- Receiving support and mentoring from the community

RESONANCE SKILL 8.1: BRINGING WARM CURIOSITY AND RESONANCE TO THE SCARED SELF

If a person has lived in environments that were short on predictability, security, and respect, then it might be difficult to imagine anywhere being safe. At the same time, rest and the neuroception of safety are so supportive that it is worth spending some time imagining an environment of trust, warmth, and freedom from abuse and neglect. If people can conjure such a safe place, they can travel there in their thoughts and experience small amounts of relaxation and small moments when their body might start to function the way it would if they actually lived in a world that felt safe.

Not everyone's safe space is the same. Some people add an imaginary room to their homes and fill it with whatever their younger self would like. Some people build enormous concrete walls enclosing acres of forest with soft, green moss, and wild animals. Some people create a house in a world that isn't this one, since this one could never be safe. Some people need to put their younger self on a planet far, far away. Some people need a house made of glass on the side of a mountain so that they can see people coming for miles. Some people bring their younger selves into their hearts forever. There is no wrong way to make a safe space. Everyone's safe space is exactly right for them.

The following guided meditation is an invitation to create a place that feels completely safe within you, a place in your imagination or your heart where all the parts of you are welcome and can find refuge.

GUIDED MEDITATION 8.1: Finding Your Safe Place

Take a breath. How far into your lungs can you breathe with absolute ease? If you have spent any time being on guard or vigilant, you may not breathe in very far before you feel a constriction. If you feel any limitation, allow your resonant self-witness to turn into a gentle light that visits the cells of your lungs, at the area of the constriction. Ask your cells if they were once so frightened that they stopped breathing. Ask them if they long to know that things are safe, that you survived, and that you are well.

Continue to breathe, following your breath wherever it moves with ease, not forcing it, just bringing gentle, warm attention to the shape that your breath naturally makes in your lungs.

As you breathe, you may find that your attention is drawn to other things, like worrying about sudden noises, feeling an anxiety about social balance, remembering things you should have done, or making plans. Gently and with warmth, invite your attention back to your breath whenever you notice that it has strayed. Your attention is supposed to wander everywhere, making you safe, so let your attention feel your gratitude and your warmth, gently inviting it back to your breath.

Now invite yourself into your imagination, and let yourself see a place that you love. It can be a real place in nature, a particular house, or a made-up dreamscape. Allow yourself to make this place unreachable by ordinary means. Let it be surrounded by an unpassable moat, or a forest that makes anyone who enters it or flies over it get lost, or let it be high in the mountains or in an unknown valley. Make sure that only you and people you invite can come to visit or live in this place.

What does this place look like? If it is inside, what are the furnishings like? What is your sense of beauty? This is your safe place, and it gets to be as beautiful, comfortable, and nourishing as you can imagine. What are the smells here? What sounds do you hear?

What does it feel like under your feet? When you sit down, what does that feel like?

What is the weather like, the temperature? Is there wind? Mist? Sun? Are there clouds?

What are your favorite foods, books, music, films? What will you bring to this place to make you feel happy?

Who do you feel comfortable having here? People you love? Animals?

What does your body do in this place? Does your stomach relax? What happens with your heartbeat and your breathing?

Allow yourself to enjoy this place for a few moments with your eyes closed, introducing this place of safety and comfort to the parts of you that need a secure place to rest. Let these parts of yourself know that they get to decide who comes here and who has to stay away. How does it feel to have choice?

Let these parts of yourself know that they get to choose exactly what they want to do and when they want to do it. How does it feel to have freedom?

Whenever you are ready, bring your attention back to your breath and the shape that it makes in your lungs. Come back to the warm connection with your attention, and gently bring yourself back to the present moment.

Open your eyes. What do you see around you? Is it possible that, just for this moment, you are actually safe here and now? If it is possible, give yourself another minute to enjoy this unusual sensation. If it isn't possible, remind yourself that your safe place exists within you, ready to hold you at a moment's notice.

WHY PRACTICE THIS MEDITATION

When people have never had a safe place, the body has no idea how to relax into comfort, connection, play, ease, or flow. Even the birthright of existing, of being the self, is tentative and comes in snatches, rather than being a solid, self-knowing person. If people never fully relax into social engagement, when they can read the fine muscle movements in their own and others' faces, they don't know what their social gifts are. They don't know how they play, or even what kinds of things they find spontaneously funny or delightful. If they are always in a fight-or-flight state, it can be difficult to read their own bodily input to know what decisions to make, what their integrity is, how they want to contribute, and where their natural boundaries are.

When we are doing personal work to rescue our inner parts, we need a place to bring our memory-selves. Sometimes present-day life doesn't feel safe, and a person's own heart doesn't feel safe. This can be because a sense of safety has never really been felt before and isn't yet part of the person's feeling vocabulary. Especially if people have never or rarely experienced safety and a full-on feeling of belonging and being wanted and welcome, it is important to create this safe place inside, to begin to know what it really feels like to be themselves. As people do this more and more often, they are giving birth to a new collection of neural connections that create a sense of "home" within them.

It is not just the brain that is affected and needs support for healing. The regular life-serving body processes also slow and stop when people are afraid. This includes the digestive system, in part because it has its own brain.

BRAIN CONCEPT 8.2: THE ENTERIC NERVOUS SYSTEM—THE "GUT BRAIN"

Not many people know about the second brain, called the **enteric nervous system**, even though everyone is continually informed by their "gut instincts." This second brain, also called the gut brain, contains around 500 million neurons that are embedded in the walls of the digestive system, from esophagus to anus.[7] These neurons manage the complex process of keeping us balanced and alive in relationship to what we take into our bodies.

The enteric nervous system responds to messages of safety and danger. Here are all the things the gut stops doing when the world is not safe:

- Moving food and drink through the digestive system[8]
- Sending messages to the brain about how well digestion is going[9]
- Taking in nourishment and hydration[10]
- Creating digestive enzymes[11]
- Balancing the intestines' hormones[12]
- Supporting the immune system's defense of health[13]

An unsafe world makes life literally indigestible. Stress and danger make the digestive system stop working, resulting in either constipation or diarrhea. Ongoing fear stops the immune system from refreshing the cells of our stomach lining, which can result in stomach ulcers.[14]

Fear is not the only thing that stops our gut from working. Anger and pain, as well as life learning or social learning connected with traumatic experiences, take a toll on our body and digestive functioning. There is a two-way interchange of information and energy between the gut brain and the skull-brain. Illnesses like functional dyspepsia, gastroesophageal reflux disease, IBS, and peptic ulcer disease all begin with stress.[15]

The stomach and intestines do their best when people feel secure and free of danger. People cannot relax until they know with their gut that they are safe. Empathy and resonance help with that knowing, but neither is effective until the environment is free of danger, which is why the guided meditation in this chapter invites you to find your own safe place. It is also why Chapter 6 recommended freezing everyone in the memory environment when time traveling, to make the environment of the memory safe and let the traumatized self relax enough to be able to take in the presence of the resonating self-witness.

What About Panic Attacks?

When people get panic attacks, they might believe they are dealing with intense fear, since physically that is what panic attacks feel like, especially the frightening experience of not being able to breathe. But some research suggests that panic attacks are activations of the grief and abandonment network. Jaak Panksepp's research shows that panic attacks are accompanied by a fall in endogenous opioids (and thus come from the PANIC circuit), rather than being related to benzodiazepines (the Valium-like neurotransmitters) and thus involving the FEAR circuit.[16] These attacks seem to be the felt experience of the ground—the ground of relationship, the ground of being—suddenly falling away without a trace. As people grow and nourish their relationship with their abandoned self, panic attacks become less intense, and they learn how to hold their grief-stricken and panicked small selves with infinite warmth and care.

What About Phobias?

Phobias and persistent fears differ in their capacity to be transformed by deep, comforting self-connection. One man doing this work found that his paralysis about crossing running water was helped by connecting with the memory of the little boy he had been, who was trying to keep up with a bigger brother and fell into a stream. People trying to live with phobias or persistent fears may need to try multiple approaches, and try combining all their attempts to find support with warmth for the self. Whatever happens, what is important is being gentle with ourselves and creating an ongoing sweet self-acceptance.

Here is a list of fears that might bring shared reality to the experience of persistent immobility in the face of stimuli, submitted by fellow readers (this is an incomplete list, provided to give you a sense of the vast number of things people can be afraid of):

- heights
- deep sea

- slugs
- dirt
- mess
- being a hoarder
- not hoarding
- germs
- snakes
- spiders
- mice or rats
- birds
- bats
- swarms of insects
- cockroaches
- maggots
- homework and expectations
- Possessive love without understanding
- The future—I can't project myself forward in my imagination beyond six months.
- Deadlines and the consequences of punishment if I don't perform to task (this often paralyzes me or drives me into distraction).
- Commitments and being held accountable (one of my biggest triggers).
- Intimacy—to know and be deeply known might be equal (in my mind) to being engulfed and disappearing.
- Success, because it will separate me from my "tribe" (my immigrant family; my working-class roots; my band of sweet, funny, and underachieving friends; even my country as a whole). If I succeed or exceed the norm, then I will perish, especially since I didn't grow up with role models that I could identify with.
- War, mass violence, the anarchy and chaos of places that have experienced mass violence and war, because my brain doesn't know if that's survivable.

Whatever the fears you may live with, you can explore the possibility of warmth for your frightened, afraid, or even terrified self. If the body and its memories are tracked with resonance in a spirit of warm curiosity, you will find that the body's fears make sense. Follow the unfolding sensations and memories with the time-travel process (see Chapter 6) to see what makes sense for your body.

Chapter 9 discusses what happens in the body when neither fight nor flight can help us, the collapse into immobility and dissociation, which can be very important to explicitly acknowledge and to learn to respond to with resonance—it is often the first body state we meet if we are time traveling to rescue a traumatized past self.

CHAPTER NINE

Returning From Dissociation

"I'm not really here," or "I don't know what I want."
(actually, "I'm really here, and I matter.")

When Staying Present Is Too Hard

Dissociation, as it is most commonly understood, means no longer being connected with the body—a disconnection between the felt sense of being in the body and the sense of self. Being present is simultaneously the simplest and the most complicated experience of being human. It sounds so easy: just breathe, and notice, and be. At the same time, our skull-brain and body-brain are engaged in anticipating what's coming, reacting to what's happening, and attending to what we are supposed to learn from the past. When we feel we are not completely safe, it takes a skilled and gentle sense of a larger self to hold ourselves with warmth in our alarm and defensiveness and stay connected to this moment, right now. Entire spiritual practices are built around creating answers to the riddle of how to be present in the external world and inside ourselves at the same time.

There are ordinary ways to be distracted from existing and noticing our body: any shift of focus to external attention tends to take us out of self-connection, as do some internal foci, like intense thinking about issues, questions, or problems. In some of these states people are in "flow," when the experience of time and self seamlessly merges with what is happening. In some of these states people are just "getting things done," working hard, thinking about what's next, and not paying attention to their bodies or their relational connections. Sometimes I find this happens when I'm writing: I'm trying so hard to get the footnotes into some semblance of order after the rewrites that my back aches and I haven't moved for three hours, or three days go by before I realize that I failed to respond to a friend's bid for connection.

When people are in this common form of dissociation, they don't even know that they are being affected emotionally by their world. They can live like robots and get through their day. At the same time, they can be very smart and very articulate. They can accomplish a lot and be perceived positively in school or in their professions. But they may sacrifice their connection to their bodies and to satisfying relationships, and they may sacrifice their sense of meaning (more on this style of living in Chapter 10).

In common language, we can refer to these disconnected states as *being dissociated*. Reawakening the body is just as effective for these minor states of disconnection as it is for healing traumatic dissociation, so this chapter focuses on the more severe experiences of dissociation, letting you remember that the same invitations to self-connection and self-gentleness made in this chapter also hold true if we are disconnected from ourselves while "doing."

BRAIN CONCEPT 9.1: THE EMBODIED SELF-AWARENESS NETWORK AND THE INSULA

The sense of self is said to be founded, at least partially, on experiences of existing as a physical, embodied being in space and of being reflected relationally.[1,2] One prerequisite for being able to fully embrace having a sense of self is a neuroception of safety linked with body awareness. The habit of not noticing the body can begin very early, with our earliest relational patterning (more on this in Chapter 10).

The brain network that lets people read their own body is what Alan

Fogel calls the **embodied self-awareness network**.[3] This network takes all the sensory information from where our body is in space, its boundaries, and interoceptive information (sensory input coming from inside the body, such as the gut, the heart, and the lungs), runs it up through the brain stem to the limbic system, and then lets it link in to the skull-brain associations that let us read and understand this information to decipher our relationship to the world. This sensory input begins in the **ergoreceptors**, nerve endings that sense pressure, tension, fatigue, temperature, pain, and all the other sensations coming from inside our bodies. These ergoreceptors connect to slow, unmyelinated fibers at the back of the spinal cord and make their way through the brain stem and then into different parts of the brain associated with sensing the inside of the body and knowing where we are in space.

To fully understand how we make sense of ourselves, we need to meet a new part of the brain called the **insula**.[4]

The insula is located in an inner layer of cortex and works closely with the anterior cingulate cortex (ACC), the major player in anxiety (see Chapter 5), to put words to emotional experience. The insula takes the raw emotional charge coming from the amygdala and helps us name what we are feeling. One set of sensations might be given the words *hopeless anger*; another might be named *shocked grief*. People can also live

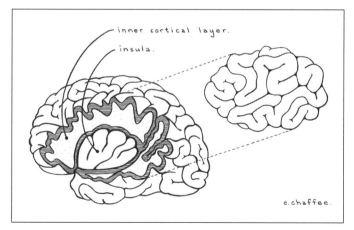

Figure 9.1. Location of the insula

without giving words to what's going on. Using functional magnetic resonance imaging to look into the brains of dissociated people, we see that the insula is inactive.[5] People can live with a consistently dark insula, such that they never know what's happening in their body.[6] Or they can just darken the insula when they are asked to remember trauma. The greater the tendency to darken the insula, or to dissociate, in the face of trauma, the trickier it is to heal.[7]

The embodied self-awareness network runs through the insula and also the ventromedial prefrontal cortex (PFC; see Chapter 6), which in turn regulates the amygdala, which then regulates the brainstem and the body, creating the circuit of self-knowing and self-understanding that supports well-being.

One of the most important messages of this book is that *if we can feel it we can heal it*, so the transformation of dissociation and awakening the insula (so that we can feel and give words to what is going on) are essential for healthy living. (More on awakening the voice of the body in Chapter 10.) When people either have had experiences of never being anchored in their body through relational connection (a kind of attachment trauma) or have been so helpless, terrorized, horrified, or overwhelmed that they have gone into long-term collapse, they can develop consistent habits of traumatic dissociation, often without even knowing it.

Defining Traumatic Dissociation

Traumatic dissociation is the name for the state of being where connection between the inner world and the outer world and the sense of self and the sense of body become fractured. The leaving of the body is a shock response. It is what a deer experiences if it has been caught by a pack of wolves. The endogenous opioids (the brain's own version of morphine) flow so freely that people are literally stoned on their own brain chemicals,[8] so that they don't have to feel the pain of being torn apart. When this happens, the parts of the brain that help integrate experience into explicit memory work less effectively.[9]

This may be part of why when bad things happen, people may not consciously remember the events until something reawakens the memory, creating the flashback experience. When people dissociate around the time of trauma, they are much more likely to end up with persistent posttraumatic stress disorder. The less that we remember about an experience, the more complicated it is (but not impossible!) to heal from it.[10] Another form of dissociation is when people are in a traumatic situation and, in order to survive it, they float out of their bodies and watch things happen from outside themselves.

Dissociation might happen if someone partially awakens during a medical procedure when they are supposed to be unconscious,[11] or if they witness or experience violence or abuse, bullying, rape or sexual assault, physical beatings, or excruciating humiliation, or even receive a life-threatening health diagnosis—all experiences that are overwhelming.

The original event doesn't have to seem traumatic to others. We are the only possible judges for ourselves. For example, dissociation can happen with something so apparently minor as when a person is socially trapped, for example, at a dinner party when another guest makes a remark that makes the person want to scream but the person refrains to honor social niceties, or it could be major, such as surviving an explosion and being physically injured. It is an entirely individual experience. No one else can know what might be "enough" to make people leave their bodies entirely or disconnect brain parts. Dissociation can even happen from terror that might arise from eye contact with someone who is enraged or themselves terrified.

Dissociation, Immobility, and the Vagus Nerve Complex

Let's look at disassociation through the lens of the vagus nerve complex. Traumatic dissociation is what happens to people when they are in physical or social danger[12], and their brain and body stop believing that fight or flight will help. Then there is the move into dorsal vagal "**immobilization.**"[13] You may recall from Chapter 7 that when we shift into the fight response, we change vagal gears into the sympathetic branch of the nervous system. This is true for the flight response as well, when fear or terror take over. In both of these cases, the amygdala sends urgent chemical alarm signals to the rest of the body to speed up heart rate and increase blood pressure, to increase breathing, and to divert the flow of energy from small muscles to big muscles so that it is possible to lash out or run away: to fight or flee. Meanwhile, the brain watches to see how effective fight and flight responses are. If we are helpless, hopeless, cornered, overpowered, or outnumbered, or if we are seriously injured, then the brain tries to preserve energy and life by downshifting into the dorsal vagal complex, or the immobilization response.[14]

The moments that are most likely to lead to traumatic dissociation are when people feel helpless or trapped, either physically or socially, because movement would result in danger. When people are dissociated, their heart rate can fall fifteen beats per minute.[15] This slowing and the probable decrease in speed in thought and action are partly because most of the nerves in the dorsal channel are slow, like a bumpy dirt road, rather than fast, like a smoothly paved freeway. The fibers in the dorsal vagal complex are mostly unmyelinated[16]—they don't have the white coating that makes energy and information travel quickly. When people feel safe (ventral vagal activation) or angry/afraid (sympathetic activation), they're on the paved superhighway of myelinated nerve tissue. Thought and action are fast. In fight, flight, and social engagement, people respond really quickly, with energy and information traveling at up to 120 meters per second.[17] When people are overwhelmed, trapped, helpless, or in shock, the energy and information travel in the unpaved lanes of unmyelinated fibers, at less than 1 meter per second.[18]

Identifying Traumatic Dissociation

Self-identifying dissociation can be almost impossible, because part of the brain is offline, which prevents people from seeing the full picture of themselves. The cues that a person might be experiencing dissociation without noticing it include not having any idea what is happening in the body; breathing quite shallowly; having a sense that the self is inanimate—made of wood, cloth, or metal (a puppet, a doll, or a robot); having a sense that the world is not real—that other people are aliens, robots, or insects; feeling numb, bewildered, and out of synch during social interactions; experiencing unexpected or cued intrusions of past memory; losing time; hearing voices; not understanding what people are asking, or feeling ashamed when asked, "What's happening in your body?"; or finding it hard to remember events or timing of events that happened with family or friends (not having relational memory). People in dissociative states are unable to learn from experience, so they keep making the same mistakes over and over again. They get involved in painful relationships with people who are not able to see them, or they remain in addictive relationships with substances or activities.

Signs of Traumatic Dissociation

- A feeling that you are an imposter or that the world is not real[19]
- Depression[20]
- An inability to sense the body's messages[21]
- Consideration of suicide[22]
- Feelings of helplessness, confusion, dread, horror, or sadness[23]
- Numbness to pain[24]
- Absence of voice inflection—having a flat voice[25]
- A heavy and immobile face[26]
- Very large and nonreactive pupils[27]
- Difficulty tracking what other people are saying[28]
- Loss of the sense of the small details or social details about what is happening for other people[29]
- Very shallow breathing[30]
- Low heart rate and blood pressure[31]

Since humans are so complex, people can be functioning perfectly normally one minute, and then almost without warning, the next minute they can find themselves unable to cope or function. Sometimes there is a slip into dissociation, floating spaciness, and disconnection. Sometimes there can be a descent into crying that makes the body shake with sobs. The suddenness of the shift can be shocking all by itself. A person is going along living their lives and boom, the bottom falls out of the world. Body-shaking grief takes over, often as a result of pain that has never been recognized.

BRAIN CONCEPT 9.2: THE DISCONNECTED NEURAL NETWORKS OF TRAUMA

You may recall from Chapter 6 how a person experiencing trauma can form long-lasting, lifelike memories that are wired to the amygdala, with its emphasis on vivid.[32] These amygdala-centered memories of previous experiences (some of which are unprocessed trauma) can lie like unexpected triggers or trip wires of association below conscious awareness, and people may know they've been tripped only when they notice they've gone into immobilization (and this noticing can take days, weeks, or years). The vivid memories of trauma float in the brain in unintegrated memory networks that are anchored by the amygdala.[33] The more we consciously know about the memories, and the more we can talk about them, the more they are consciously available.

People plunge out of their regular brain into their emotional pain or into dissociation when there is a rough match between some stimulus in present time and the stored association of the cue with past danger. In dissociation during an original trauma experience, even if a person is dissociated, the memory of the event is actually still being stored in neural networks that are under the sway of the amygdala (which tracks every emotionally significant experience). The more complete the disassociation, the less access we have to the experience, and the more difficult it is to heal.[34] The more integrated a person's brain is, the fewer hiccups there are in memory to take a person offline.

RESONANCE SKILL 9.1: EXQUISITE GENTLENESS FOR THE TRAUMATICALLY DISSOCIATED SELF

In bringing resonance to the traumatically dissociated self, the main quality that seems to be needed is an exquisite gentleness and slowness. The state of traumatic dissociation has been brought about by some kind of cruelty, overwhelm, harshness, or helplessness, so it is very important to move slowly, without any desire other than acknowledgment and accompaniment. The asking of consent supports reconnection, for example, "Dissociated self, are you willing for me to talk with you?" or "Dissociated self, would you enjoy some company? Would you like to know that you don't have to come back if you don't want to? Would it be a relief to know that your timing is what is most important to me?"

If we are working with a persistent experience of dissociation, we might have a sense that a part of us is often located some distance away from ourselves. Sometimes it can be helpful to know where the dissociated self has gone. We can make the inquiry with warm curiosity: "Dissociated self, where are you?" Is it ten feet away to the left? Is it on a mountain peak, a cloud, or another planet? Is it lying behind us on the ground, as if "dead" from the helplessness, stress, and overwhelm?

The following guided meditation, for those who are not fully in their bodies, may help grow a connection between the speaking self and the self that has gone away.

GUIDED MEDITATION 9.1: Inviting the Dissociated Self to Come Home

Before you begin, notice what your attitude is toward your dissociated self. If you are irritated with this self, you have not yet picked up your resonating self-witness. If this is so, then empathy guesses for your irritated part are important. Maybe the part of you that is irritated is concerned for your well-being and viability and is longing for some sign that there is hope? If you notice self-loathing, and this meditation feels impossible to you, please don't force yourself to embrace the dissociated one until the evaluating self gets more resonant acknowledgment. Refer to Chapter 11 for more information on working with self-hate.

See if you can feel your breathing. Spend some moments gently inviting your attention to stay with the place where your breath is most alive. If you can't feel your breathing, simply move to the next paragraph.

If there were a part of you that was not in your body, where would that part be? You may have a sense that this part of you is here in the same room with you, only five or ten feet away. Or you may have a sense that this part of you is stuck in the past somewhere, or in some simple unidentified space that is not connected to your past but is entirely separate from you. Locate this self, and see if you can shift your perception, from being in your actual body, with your resonating self-witness present and available to you, to being the dissociated self, and then back again.

Let yourself pause here, and imagine freezing anyone else who is in the space, especially if it is a space of memory, so that your dissociated part is safe. Now, with great gentleness, allow your resonating self-witness to travel to where your dissociated place was, whether it is five feet away, half a lifetime away, or half a world away. As your resonating self-witness arrives, see what distance is most comfortable for the dissociated self. Let yourself see the dissociated part with tenderness and warmth.

As your resonating self-witness looks with soft eyes at the dissociated part, check to see whether the dissociated part has any idea who the self-witness is. If introductions are necessary, go ahead— something like, "I am the best and warmest part of you, come to be with you so that you are not alone."

Let the self-witness express a little longer. Acknowledge the wisdom of this part in choosing to be apart from you when your body seemed like a dangerous or uncomfortable place to be.

Acknowledge its need for safety, acknowledge what you both have lived through. (In most of our meditations we work with body sensations, but in the beginning of this meditation we rarely have body sensations to work with.) The most important thing to remember is that the self-witness is offering gentle, acknowledging contact, without any expectation of change or movement. There may be words; there may be an embrace or gentle touch. It may be important for the self-witness to stand some distance away, even in another room or outside the space. See how much contact or connection your dissociated part is willing to receive.

Here are some possible resonant empathy guesses from your self-witness to your dissociated self:

- Are you fairly certain that being in a physical body isn't safe? Would you like some acknowledgment of how unsafe bodies have been? Are you worried about your body and about how it's getting on without you?
- Do you feel hopeless, and do you long to be able to feel warmth, welcome, and belonging from the earth itself?
- Are you confused and bewildered? Do you wish you remembered or knew what clarity felt like?
- Do you feel a distrust so deep that you would need a trust transplant in order to ever feel faith in anything again?
- Do you need acknowledgment of the enormity of the original shock that blew you apart? Was it like an atom bomb that destroyed the earth and all of humanity in that instant?
- Do you feel lost? Are you unsure how to return home? Do you need absolute guarantees of protection, simplicity, and ease?

After making these guesses, see where your dissociated self is. Is it still the same distance away as when you started the meditation? Is it farther away? Closer? Wherever it is, ask if it is willing to rejoin your body. Or to go to the safe space that you created in the meditation from Chapter 8. Whatever response comes, receive it with warmth, acceptance, and understanding.

Sometimes as the self is acknowledged and seen with respect and gentleness, it comes back and rejoins the body with a kind of shift of energy; a click; or a small, silent thud. Wherever this self is, as you near the end of this meditation, let it know that you see that it is trying its best to ensure your survival. Ask it if it would like some acknowledgment or appreciation for that. And now invite your attention to return to your physical body. See if you can catch any whisper or sensation of breath, and acknowledge your toes, the bones of your heels, the skin over your knees, your belly button, your collarbone, your right little fingernail, the very top of your head, and your body as a whole. When you are ready, gently bring your attention all the way back to your present-day life.

As the dissociated part has a sense of being seen, known, or held, perhaps over the course of several weeks or months of meditations, it will often start to relax, bringing some access to body sensations. Sometimes images of self will come that are inanimate, as if this part were a doll. And sometimes, with resonance, the disconnected part merges back into the body. (This is directly attributable to what we have learned about the vagal nerve: when we feel completely safe, the nervous system returns like a homing pigeon to social engagement.) As the body comes back to consciousness, and sensations arise, remember to guess about possible feelings and needs that they may be connected to.

If you have an image of yourself as inanimate, take a look at the next section on how to make empathy and metaphor guesses to support the reassuring understanding of self, no matter how odd the perception may be.

WHY PRACTICE THIS MEDITATION?

This is a meditation you can use as a daily practice as you are working with your dissociation. You are working on the practice of accompanying yourself without an agenda except for self-love and understanding. You can ask the dissociated part if he or she is willing to come back to your body. You may receive a yes or a no. No matter what answer you receive, the most important thing is to remain gentle, warm, and accepting with this part. This approach builds neural associations between the right orbitofrontal cortex (containing our sense of self), the PFC (with a sense of warmth), and the disconnected neural network of memory that causes your dissociation. When we start to heal, we can find that we have been on pause (dissociated) for a very long time and that the effects have been much greater than we realized.

Once people recognize what it means to live partly removed from reality, they can look back on their lives and see that much of what used to be confusing now makes perfect sense. The trail of bad decisions, partners who didn't really know how to love, an inability to be present to children, the movement into careers or professions that weren't satisfying, being at the mercy of their addictions or compulsions—all of these experiences make sense when people realize their life energy was on "pause," waiting for the world to become safe again.

The irony is that, while people are dissociated, they are actually less safe than they would be if they had access to the signals from their body that can indicate something is amiss. The system's attempt to stay safe (in its dissociation) actually decreases access to information that could be useful to helping get to a safer environment.[35] For example, if people have access to body cues, they may know that someone is acting in an unsafe way and leave. If they are out of touch with their body, they might not be able to process that information, and they might stay too long. Or they might not have the kind of energy they would otherwise have to mobilize a response when a present-moment danger arises. Awareness about dissociation in general and specific body cues in particular can help people know that they are perceiving danger. So bringing back the dissociated parts is very practical for physical safety, as well as for spiritual communion and a sense of wholeness and integration.

Once people move to presence, they really do have the capacity to make the world safe for themselves and for everyone within their sphere.

And as soon as it's safe, the little disconnected selves come peeking out, available for integration and reunion. They bring the hope and possibility of discovering the self and connecting with truth and can teach the language of true souls. Presence also provides very down-to-earth strategies for physical and emotional self-protection and self-care.

Working With the Strange Ways a Person Can Perceive Themselves While Dissociated

If, when looking for body sensations, you discover that you have an inanimate body image, like a doll, a lump of stone, or mud, it is just as important to bring your resonating self-witness to acknowledge and support this aspect of yourself. Again, you will offer reassuring welcome to this incarnation of your experience. Ask questions like, "Would you like some acknowledgment of what it was like to live without real human interaction? To be treated like an object, rather than like a human? Did you have to be what others wanted you to be, rather than yourself? Did you try so hard to be good that you simply disappeared? Were you so lonely that you stopped being alive? Are you exhausted beyond belief?" It is also possible for body parts, like your heart or your stomach, to feel like inanimate matter as well. The empathy and metaphor guesses for these parts will be similar: acknowledgment, reflection, warm acceptance. All of them convey the understanding that there is wisdom in your body holding itself in this way—for now.

When Sexuality and Dissociation Are Confused, and When Dissociation Is Contagious

Once people start coming alive again, they start to inhabit their bodies more fully, which means that their capacities for emotional intimacy and for sexual intimacy start to awaken. Once they feel safe and connected, people use the dorsal vagal complex for something entirely different from shock and dissociation.[36] Mother and child move into dorsal vagal states when they are deep in the bonding experience and **oxytocin** (a bonding hormone) is flowing, especially during nursing. And between sexual partners, the experience of languid sexual connection also moves through the dorsal channels of the vagus nerve when there is an abundance of oxytocin.

The neurophysiological similarity between dissociation and languid sexuality can result in deep confusion when experiences of sexuality, trauma, and bonding merge (and this is only one part of the complex neurophysiological tragedy that sexual abuse inflicts on us!).

To integrate what we have been learning about Jaak Panksepp's circuits of emotion, in sexual abuse there is a confusion among circuits, where the LUST circuit gets linked with RAGE, with FEAR, or with PANIC/GRIEF. Part of the healing involves disentangling these circuits with resonance. Follow the body sensations and name experiences to untie the knots that came from sexual trauma. It is very important to receive help to disentangle these circuits. If you would like to do this work, please consider interviewing somatic-based therapists to find one that you consider warm and with whom you have a neuroception of safety.

Sometimes during sexual abuse abusers themselves are in a dissociative trance when they are carrying out the damaging acts.[37] They are only partially present themselves, unable to see their victims as human, caught up in a disconnected neural network that they themselves do not understand and in which they may feel simultaneously ashamed, helpless, and excited, or they may not consciously know what they are doing. Because people are made to be social animals and to entrain with one another's brains and nervous systems, victims of trance-state abuse may end up internalizing both the trauma of their own helplessness, terror, and overwhelm, and the dissociated state that the abuser is in.

Let's say this using different words. Because we are social animals whose brains and nervous systems entrain with one another, when we interact with someone who is in a dissociated state, the likelihood is high that our brains will entrain with that state. That means that if we have been victimized by someone who is in a trance-like, dissociated state, our brains are coping with (a) the trauma of our own helplessness, terror, and overwhelm, and (b) the dissociation inside us that matches the dissociation of the other person. This is part of the generational aspect of the transmission of trauma—the cycle of dissociation breeding dissociation may have gone on for centuries. Tools of self-warmth and mindfulness can break this cycle.

As people begin to heal, resonant empathy and reflection help them reclaim and disentangle their sexuality and their full selves from previous experiences of trauma and bewilderment, even from the entanglement of dissociated states that can be carried for decades or that individuals have have been carrying for many generations.

Having a Relationship With a Dissociated Partner

What is it like to be in relationship with someone who is disassociating or who easily goes into immobilization? It can be very hard on the nervous system, because people are made to be in relationships—people are made to be social. When someone collapses into immobilization, it is almost like their humanity is erased. They really do disappear while they are disassociating. Their faces become immobile, their voices become flat, they lose their capacity for alive gestures, and, depending on a person's past history with dissociated people, their own nervous system can react with alarm. It is very distressing for infants or children when they have a dissociative parent. When this is part of the parent's history, the parent will go into alarm; anger; despair; or their own fight, flight, or immobilization reactions—possibly even reacting with more terror, rage, or intensity than is warranted by present-day experience due to the original, implicit trauma.

Additionally, due to the influence of mirror neurons in the motor cortex, which help us understand the actions of others (more on this in Chapter 11), people may to some degree even experience the other person's dissociation as if it were their own. Mirror neurons are the brain's basis for learning by imitation. This means that people can "learn" dissociation when someone else who is close to them is experiencing it.

We can become angry or despairing when our significant other dissociates. When someone "disappears" for us, our levels of endogenous opioids in the brain fall, our heart rate increases, and the experience is—for brain, heart, and stomach—just like what baby mammals experience when they are lost and cannot find their mother—the PANIC/ GRIEF circuit is activated (see Chapter 5). So we protest this disappearance. We may become angry, despairing, or hopeless. We may believe that the other person is doing this on purpose to punish or to be mean, but, in fact, people do not have control over their own disassociation. It takes healing to begin to expand the window of welcome for emotion and remain present. This is the root of many persistent arguments and cycles of pain and violence for couples and families.

Everyone can learn to cope with and transform these patterns. The tools of resonant witnessing and compassionate, gentle presence offered here provide compassion for the self when dissociating, compassion for others when they are dissociating, and compassion for all the poor humans bumbling around trying to cope with all the trauma that they have experienced and that they may be triggering in others.

It is important to note the distinction between cause and stimulus here. Person 1 can be speaking in a voice that seems normal, but the partner, Person 2, could shift into a sense of danger and all of a sudden perceive this voice as yelling. It's very difficult to tell what is happening between two people. The perceived shift could be entirely due to Person 2's nervous system state, with defensiveness leading to Person 1's neutrality being perceived as hostile. This is what happens when there is a shift to the fight-or-flight state—danger is perceived everywhere. The perceived shift could also be due to Person 1 leaving relational space and addressing Person 2 as a to-do list, rather than as an infinite essence with his or her own path and unfolding journey. Other possibilities include that the perceived shift could be a result of Person 1 becoming insistent, trying to prove something, or losing hope of connection with Person 2 and becoming disengaged. Another possibility is that Person 1 doesn't have much of a read on his or her own emotional world and so uses a voice that really has increased in volume and tempo, but Person 1 can't tell that it has happened. And of course, past trauma could be disrupting connection for either Person 1 or Person 2.

Most of the arguments that couples have are about these kinds of nuanced slippages between nervous system states. Everyone wants to be seen. Everyone needs their best intentions for connection and care to be known. But once nervous systems start to change states, it becomes a wild ride that we usually don't have many words for.

The most important action is to bring the resonant self-witness to the situation so that both people can hold a generous space for each other, with gentleness for all the different levels of dissociation, fear, and anger that show up in the connection. It is also necessary to acknowledge how hard it is when another person disappears into dissociation. The emotional absence can feel like physical abandonment, with an accompanying plunge in endogenous opioids for the person who remains behind. It takes a lot of effort to be present for the self when the brain's levels of feel-good chemicals are falling. External emotional support can be very helpful. Once people are okay—no matter whether the other person can be there or not—and can bring their constant warmth and care to hold themselves and the other with gentleness and tenderness, a climate of safety is created that invites the other's return much more quickly and effectively than confrontation or withdrawal ever can.

The Gradual Return From Dissociation, and Its Path Through Fight or Flight

1. We are dissociated. Our heart rate is slow, and we are breathing very shallowly.
2. We learn that dissociation exists.
3. We begin to notice our disconnection from self—that we can't perceive our body, that we can't breathe deeply—and we start to wonder if maybe we are dissociated.
4. We start to hold our dissociated self with gentle warmth.
5. Body sensations begin to return.
6. Emotions come back, too. Along with body sensations, intense emotion can arise.

7. Body memories can also show up, bringing surprising, unexpected, and unwanted physical sensations. As these experiences are held with resonance and named, they subside, and the body is claimed as a part of our wholeness and health.

8. We use the processes offered here to take small, safe steps of warmth that transform our brains from war zones with hidden land mines into a welcoming home.

9. Other capabilities return, including new curiosities, new decisions, new intentions, and a connection to our larger selves, including contribution and spirituality.

It takes time to move out of dissociation and answer the questions, what is happening in my body, and why would I want to know? Gradually, people start to become clear that when they are living without their body, they are not fully connected with the human race. When they are receiving their body's messages, they are alive and vital, and they can feel the life force in their body and their connection to all things. It becomes possible to appreciate and enjoy the gift of life.

The only problem with reentering the body is that, as it starts to awaken, any trauma that was frozen in time and inaccessible starts to awaken as well. There can be flashbacks of physical, emotional, and sexual abuse. It is no wonder that people who have no emotional support might want to continue to turn off the voice of the body in every way possible. People will find that this kind of surfacing of old memory happens as they do any healing work that links up body awareness and physical sensation, such as somatic empathy, systemic or family constellation work, massage therapy or bodywork of any kind (particularly Rosen method bodywork), or Hakomi or movement therapy. Neuroscience education seems to also invite people to hear the voice of the body.

However, the more warmth that accompanies the resurfacing, the easier these changes are to integrate, even when they are accompanied by flashbacks of painful memories and mourning. If we move with care and resonance, the gentle possibility can arise of doing the welcoming work that lets body sensations be felt and understood.

The understanding of neurobiology gives people solid ground to stand on to reach for this new experience. Chapter 10 looks at how learning about and bringing warmth to lifelong patterns of relationship can support a new access to capacity for intimacy with self and others.

CHAPTER TEN

Attachment: How Brains Respond to Accompaniment

"Nobody understands me," or "I am alone."
(actually, "As I heal I see that I am profoundly interconnected.")

We Love in the Way We Were Loved (and We Can Change)

As humans and social animals, we all pattern our brains on the brains that are closest to us when we are tiny. Infancy is the time when our neurons are developing and figuring out where to connect and how to grow. We learn about relationship, what it means, and how to do it from the way that we are loved or not loved, responded to or ignored. We love back the way that we are loved. We internalize the way our parents' bodies respond to stress and the way they are or are not able to depend on others for help and nurturing. Our hearts actually beat differently in response to the world, depending on how much we have a sense we can rely on others to help us.[1] And we tend to grow up to care about ourselves and others the same way we were first cared for. Researchers call this learning about how to bond and what to expect from relationships **attachment**.

Happily, wherever we begin, our brains are not cast in plaster—we are changeable, we continue to learn from significant relationships, we learn from being loved and letting ourselves be loved, and our healing journey creates more integration and more ease in our connections with ourselves and others. The work of this book is the work of healing attachment wounds. It is the work of bringing a resonant voice to our experience and rewiring our brains with tenderness, so that we can experience real mutuality and give and receive warmth. Wherever we start, we can make ourselves more resilient, healthier, and more connected in our world. This is the journey of becoming "securely" attached to ourselves and others. The next section introduces what resonance can contribute to helping our brains move into more supportive attachment patterns.

Attachment and Self-Regulation

Because the brain learns so easily when something has emotional importance to us, it is probable that everyone who has been essential to us (whether they have been kind or cruel) leaves behind some trace of their relationship with us in our brains, not just emotionally but as actual physical neural connections and neuron growth in our relational memories. (Recall Moshe Szyf's quote from Chapter 2: "Our mother is in every cell of our prefrontal cortex."[2]) This leaving behind of traces appears to be particularly true when we are talking about first relationships: mother, father, or grandparent. It is interesting to realize that what kind of brains have loved us matters. The more we have been loved by integrated and healthy brains, the easier it is for us to thrive in our day-to-day lives. Adults pass on their health and stress regulation (or lack of health and dysregulation) to the children they love. This is the essence of the science of attachment research: the study of the effects of parents on their children.

BRAIN CONCEPT 10.1:
ATTACHMENT CHANGES OUR HEART RATES

We all think of the heart as a symbol of love, but on a physical level the heart and the way it responds to stress are linked with the way that we have been treated in our important relationships. It turns out that the more stable, warm, and responsive our parents were to us, the healthier and more resilient our heart is.[3]

Researchers are able to tell this from something called **heart rate variability**. Think of your heartbeat. It beats a certain number of times per minute, usually between sixty and eighty beats per minute when you are at rest. When you run, it beats faster. You might think that the more regularly your heart beats, the better your health, but that is not true. Your heart rate is actually an average number of beats per minute, rather than an exact number. Your heart is supposed to change its rate from beat to beat, slowing with exhales and quickening with inhales, so, for example, for two beats it's at sixty-six beats per minute, then for three beats it's at sixty-two. Your body is supposed to be able to mobilize your heart in small emergencies, making it beat faster and slower to deal with stress, instead of having to generate cortisol and the fight-or-flight response.

The way we were parented has a profound effect on the way our heart responds to the world and to others. And the foundation of the changes in the way the heart beats is our old friend the vagus nerve complex. Researchers have discovered that bodies can respond to stress and to relationship in four main ways: secure attachment, avoidant attachment, ambivalent attachment, and disorganized attachment. Let's take a look at each of these strategies for survival and how the vagus nerve responds in each case.

Style 1: Secure and earned secure attachment
Both we and other people exist, and we have a sense of warm curiosity about them and about ourselves.

When children experience **secure attachment**,[4] they are able to depend on the parent for predicable warmth, responsiveness, and reso-nance. As a result, they experience less stress over their entire life. Their hearts mostly dance in relationship with life (this is one way of saying they have high heart rate variability), and instead of having to mobi-lize fight-or-flight responses when something goes wrong, their heart shifts from dancing to walking (slightly lower heart rate variability—still socially engaged) when there is moderate stress.[5] These children have internalized their parents, and their hearts perform differently from those of insecurely attached children, even when their parents are gone. These children always seem to be accompanied, even when they are alone. This style is particularly characterized by warmth.

When we are securely attached as adults, we have the ability to understand intensity, to see long-term and global consequences, and to have a balanced, realistic view of the world. We are realists, not idealists, and we carry an internalized strong, calm, loving presence within us. This presence is the resonating self-witness, and when it is awake and active, then the brain, heart, body, and relationships work better.

People can come out of childhood with this secure brain pattern in place, or they can heal their way into it as they move through their lives. The movement out of insecure attachment into more balance and an anticipation of warmth from others and for ourselves as a result of healing work or supportive relationships is called **earned secure attachment**.[6,7]

Once people have either secure or earned secure attachment, they have trusting, lasting relationships. They feel good about themselves and have good self-esteem. They feel good about sharing their feelings, their longings, and their lives with friends and partners. They are able to seek out social support. And when people have someone they care about with them, hills actually seem less steep and pain is less intense.[8] (More on secure and earned secure attachment in Chapter 14.)

Style 2: Avoidant attachment
We can depend only on ourselves.

The bodies of toddlers who have received a dismissing response to their emotions react differently than do secure children.[9] They have an **avoidant attachment** style, which means that they have learned to take care of themselves, because they don't have the sense that their parent's body is a resource for them. Their hearts work just a bit harder all the time to stay regulated, like hikers carrying a backpack. (They stay in social engagement, but with the lowest possible amount of heart rate variability, which still lets them use the heart for stress management.) Their hearts tend not to dance in these situations, nor do they walk— they just keep hiking along.[10]

When avoidantly attached children become adults, their main pattern for managing life is internal self-reliance and a resultant unlikelihood of trusting easily. There is little connection with the body awareness network, as this kind of linkage with self is fostered by emotionally connected relationships.[11] These people, with their heart's limited capacity to dance, can be a little baffled by other people's intense emotional experiences. It is possible to be completely blind to one's own and others' pain when the heart is only hiking alone, rather than dancing with others. People who have grown up with avoidant attachment do not expect to be accompanied, so they take care of themselves on their own.

Style 3: Ambivalent attachment
As soon as there is any stress, self-regulation disappears.

In **ambivalent attachment**, the child is parented by a mother (or father) who immediately moves to alarm under stress. Following this pattern, the child is trying to manage his or her system in a fight-or-flight state and sending behavioral signals of distress. No one is easily soothed. The child's (and the parent's) heart dances as a general rule, but as soon as there is even moderate stress, there is a full-body cortisol response accompanied by behavioral cries for help rather than any shifting of the heart to support stress regulation. There is no walking; there is no hiking. The ambivalent heart is crying out for support, which the ambivalently attached vagus nerve complex does not know how to give.[12] The child is crying out for support, which the parent does not know how to give. It is stunning, how completely our bodies mirror our experiences of relationship.

An ambivalent attachment style does not mean that people don't want their children—they love them very much. At the same time, they are unable to see their children or their partners clearly because they lose self-connection as soon as there is even moderate stress. Parents who are ambivalently attached find it difficult to tell what is really happening with their children because the parents are ruled by alarm, depression, or painful rumination. These mothers and fathers are either living in the past or anticipating the future. Because of this, sometimes this attachment style is called anxious or intrusive attachment. When people are ambivalently attached, they are so anxious about what is happening with their children, the world, or other relationships that they can't stop and breathe and enjoy their children for who they are.

The same thing happens in adult relationships. There can be continual worry about whether ambivalently attached partners really love them or will leave them. If people are living in their uncomforted emotions in this style of attachment (that is, if their amygdala has never received adequate soothing), then they are more chaotic. They are regularly overrun by emotions—their own or those of others. When people are not really regulated, but still functional, they might find themselves continually upset with friends and partners, continually longing for proof of love. Never sure that they matter, never sure that they are loved or belong, they are always trying to find external reassurance.

Dissatisfaction is a key emotional experience for ambivalently attached people. If people have never been satisfied with the response they get from the world, if there is an ache for words and experiences to land perfectly, and they rarely do, these people may be working with very early experiences of never quite being seen and known by those taking care of them.

Style 4: Disorganized attachment
The world of intimacy is made of pain.

The more that people have had experiences of not mattering, not being heard, being frightened or hurt, or no one understanding their pain, the weaker the brain connections are that are supposed to support well-being, and the more these people will suffer from depression, overriding anxiety, addiction, mental illness, violence, abuse, neglect, outbursts of temper, and feelings of shame.[13] Children with terrifying or terrified parents will often need intimacy desperately but find it alarming and respond to it unpredictably. Their bodies will react strangely to relationships. This is called **disorganized attachment**. It is the precursor to grown-up experiences like domestic violence and the transgenerational transmission of abuse.

The brain is vulnerable to being fractured by difficult things that happen: the deaths of beloved people, or having lived in homes where people were hit, punched, or pushed; where sexual abuse happened; where people were called names; or where emotions were not welcome. Hearts that have lived through these dangerous moments believe that intimacy is dangerous, which makes for very confusing and painful adult experiences. (More on healing from disorganized attachment in Chapter 11.)

People don't even need to have experienced trauma directly for their brain to be changed in this way. Brains and bodies are affected by the difficult things that happened to past generations: parents, grandparents,[14] and probably ancestors. It can be that parents were terrified themselves when they were small, which disorganized their brains, and as a result they do not have much solid ground to give their children, although they might love them very much.

It is important to remember that the presence of just one empathetic and caring witness helps people to survive and to have reserves of self-regard to call upon for the rest of their lives. Warm grandparents can be particularly important,[15] but this witness can even be a neighbor, a teacher, or a police officer who shows up during a trauma.

As you think about your life, I invite you to remember the people who have been resources and who have loved you or shown you respect and care. These people live on within us, as we live on within the brains of the people we have loved and supported. I also invite you to think about the children you have treated with kindness, understanding, and respect, so that you can see your own part in bringing healing and hope to this world.

Being disorganized is not the final word for the brain. Healing is still at hand. Every time there are meaningful experiences of warmth and being understood, brains are reaching to build new, healthier connections in the fibers of attachment that run from the prefrontal cortex (PFC) to the amygdala and on to regulating the body.

There is no substitute for human-to-human warmth, but we all have different roads to healing. If reading is giving you any aha moments or helping you feel compassion for yourself, you are creating new connections in your brain that support increased well-being.

Doing and Being in Attachment

Humans at their best live integrated lives, both being able to take action (doing) and being able to exist relationally (being). Humans at their worst come out of difficult early attachment experiences into rigidity (doing without being—avoidant attachment), or chaos, existing in a world of feeling without the capacity to act calmly in the face of stress (being without doing—ambivalent attachment). These patterns show up most clearly later in life in parenting and love relationships. When people are parented by doers who are not being, their needs for soothing and emotional security in the relationship are not totally met. When they are parented those who are being but not doing, they are left in a state of hair-trigger alarm in response to relational stress.

A lot of literature links attachment and dominance of left versus right brain hemispheres (for a review of the brain hemispheres, see Chapter 4). This makes sense if we characterize the left hemisphere (the doer) as being essentially nonrelational (avoidant attachment), and the unstructured right hemisphere as being vulnerable to dysregulation. We can also characterize the structured right hemisphere as being essentially relational (the be-er), integrating the left hemisphere and thus supporting secure attachment. The research that supports this linkage between attachment style and how our brain use is structured is less easy to quote than the heart rate variability, so I have focused on heart rate variability as the basic determinant of attachment style, but I deeply enjoyed Iain McGilchrist's *The Master and His Emissary*, a book on how our world is affected by the fact that we have two hemispheres.

I recommend it to you highly, and it is included in the book list at the end of this book.

As you read through the section on attachment styles, did you notice that when the (sometimes devastating) impact of intergenerational patterns is acknowledged, the blame comes off the individual and space is created for forgiveness, breathing room, and choice? What is it like to learn about these attachment styles? What do you notice in your body? Sometimes when I am sharing this information in a workshop there's a hush in the room, and we need to take a pause because a lot of synapses are firing, both in mourning and in celebration, as people allow themselves to track these attachment patterns back through the generations.

Identifying Your Own Attachment Style(s)

The way we use our brains to be in relationships is reflected in the stories that we tell about ourselves and the world.[16] Notice how your body responds when you read through the four descriptions below. The information in parentheses includes the name that researchers give attachment patterns when they are talking about adults (called **adult attachment styles**). They are not exactly the same categories as infant attachment styles: avoidant attachment is split into fearful avoidant and dismissive avoidant, and disorganized attachment is dropped off the list altogether.

> **A.** It is easy for me to become emotionally close to others. I am comfortable depending on them and having them depend on me. I don't worry about being alone or having others not accept me. (adult: secure or earned secure attachment; infant: secure attachment)
>
> **B.** I am uncomfortable getting close to others. I want emotionally close relationships, but I find it difficult to trust others completely or to depend on them. I worry that I will be hurt if I allow myself to become too close to others. (adult: **fearful avoidant attachment**; infant: avoidant attachment)

C. I am comfortable without close emotional relationships. It is very important to me to feel independent and self-sufficient, and I prefer not to depend on others or have others depend on me. (adult: **dismissive avoidant attachment**; infant: avoidant attachment)

D. I want to be completely emotionally intimate with others, but I often find that others are reluctant to get as close as I would like. I am uncomfortable being without close relationships, but I sometimes worry that others don't value me as much as I value them. (adult: **anxious-preoccupied attachment**; infant: ambivalent, anxious, or intrusive attachment)

There is no easy set of ideas that indicates disorganized attachment. People are in their disorganized places whenever they are terrified, terrifying, harming one another, not acknowledging the harm they are doing, caught in addictions, mentally ill, or dissociated.

RESONANCE SKILL 10.1: SUPPORTING THE HEALING OF OLD ATTACHMENT WOUNDS

Approaches to healing avoidant attachment patterns

If you suspect that you are avoidantly attached, have little to no connection to your body, and are puzzled rather than panicked by the thought of intimacy, you may enjoy getting to know your physical and emotional being in order to bring a greater sense of meaning in living and to enhance connection with others:

- Make the request of yourself to begin to invite your body's experience into your use of language. Make this body scan a daily practice: Put a hand on your stomach, and see if you are getting any information. If you feel safe, this area will feel relaxed, open, and gently pulsing. Any areas that feel constricted, cold, tight, closed, rigid, or motionless have information for you. Now put a hand on your chest. Can you feel your heart rate? If you feel safe, there will be a dance of responsiveness between your heart rate and life. If your heart is racing or feels slow and dead or encased in a binding, then it has emotional information for you. Now touch your throat. Now your face. Can you feel any tightness, tension, pain, or constriction? Can you feel any tingling or discomfort? Can you feel a collapse, a catch, or a stuckness?

- Try to reference your physical experience at least once in every nonbusiness interaction you have, for example,
    - "Funny, as I hear you talk about _____, I can feel myself wanting to take a step back."
    - "When I saw _____, my heart started racing."
- Ask your closest friends to bring you back to your body if you speak for long without referencing it. That might sound something like this:
    - "Hey there, I'm curious what you're noticing in your body as you talk about how much money your brother owes you."
- Set a timer and do a body scan regularly throughout the day, focusing on stomach and intestines, heart and lungs, throat and face.
- Work with someone who offers resonant empathy sessions or therapy professionally one on one. Talk about your thoughts, and get help tracing your thoughts back to feelings, needs, and physical experience.

Approaches to healing ambivalent attachment patterns

In everyday life, you might have heard this referred to as enmeshment between parent and child, or as codependency between adults.

- Think about the people you are closest to. If you drew a diagram with each of them and yourself as circles, showing how close you are to one another, would your circle overlap with anyone else's? Slightly? Entirely? Is your circle completely inside other people's circles? Completely disconnected?

- Try saying "I am (your name). I am not (their name)." Does this feel true? If it does not feel true, what happens in your body? Bring your resonant self-witness in to make feelings guesses and needs guesses based on your body sensations. Repeat the phrase with your names until it feels true.

- Think about the habit, compulsion, behavior pattern, or addiction that bothers you most in another person. What happens in your body when you think about this trigger? See if you can tell what is happening with your facial muscles. Do you feel contemptuous and impatient? Are you longing for presence and self-responsibility? Do you feel doubt about this person surviving? Are you wishing for this person's well-being? Do you need faith and trust that the process this person is choosing is right, even if the path diverges from yours? Are you terrified about your family making it? Are you longing for partnership and shared responsibility? Do you feel grief and loneliness? Would you so love connection and intimacy? How is it to shift the focus to self-support and self-acknowledgment, rather than being focused on managing someone else? Is it peculiar that you actually exist and matter?

Working with the aftereffects of
disorganized attachment

If whenever you dip into the idea of having a body, or being in a relationship with someone else, you are filled with horror, disgust, shame, or dismay (more on healing self-hate in Chapter 11):

- Approach your body slowly, acknowledging the possibility of emotional overwhelm and being gentle with yourself.
- See how many layers—of self-disgust, disgust for yourself for having self-disgust, disgust for yourself for having disgust, and

so on—you need to go out before you can hold your whole being with warmth.

- The most important thing is to respond to yourself with empathy (feelings and needs guesses) for any panic and fear of overwhelm you might have. Bring yourself resonance as often as possible, and notice that when you include body sensations you may have more of a sense of physical and emotional shifts.
- If it is helpful, work with Chapter 9 on dissociation so that your disconnection from self makes sense to you and you can have warm self-acknowledgment about how you have survived emotional overwhelm.
- You are doing the best you can to survive, living on the self-management strategies that you have built over dysregulated emotional hell. Continue to bring self-regulation to life with your practices and guided meditations.

Healing Toward Earned Secure Attachment, No Matter Where We Start

People need to know themselves and their bodies in order to have easy, flowing relationships. And yet it can be bewildering to even try to begin. What are some possible starting points? We are building our sense of self whenever we have experiences of

- Being seen
- Being known
- Being heard
- Being accurately reflected
- Being attuned with
- Having someone be curious about our experience
- Having our intentions seen

It can be hard to find places and people that provide warm understanding without advice or fixing, but this is very important for healing.

This quality is one of the unexpected benefits of really good Nonviolent Communication practice groups, 12-step meetings, group therapy, warm church communities, and support groups that create the conditions where this can happen.

As you do this work, allow yourself to remember the times when you have been deeply loved, or sweet moments when you had a sense of belonging. These are moments of secure attachment in your life.

What Can We Do to Help Our Children Be Securely Attached?

Changing entrenched patterns of difficult attachment, both for ourselves and with our children, is tough. Over and over again the transformative force is warmth and acceptance. Paradoxically, the most effective route to change is not wanting change at all but instead moving into full relaxation and self-love as our neurobiology tries to use its old habits to survive interpersonal acceptance.

The way we talk with our children is important. It is essential to be curious about our children's

- Thoughts
- Memories
- Experiences
- Body sensations
- Emotions
- Longings
- Passions
- Dreams

When we talk about these things with our children, we awaken and nourish their sense of self. As we help them to lay down tracks of memory of their own lives, we help them develop their sense of self and their grasp on their own autobiography. We used to think that people without much memory of their childhood had been abused and were repressing what had happened, but now we know that it is completely possible that no one ever expressed interest. We can be very responsible parents who happily teach our children algebra and how to drive, but we may not know how to have curiosity and be personal with children.

The more we have been met with kindness and understanding in our lives, the more resilient we are. And the more stories that our family tells about itself, the better we know ourselves, the more we feel connected to the world, and the more resilient we are. For example, Drs. Marshall Duke, Amber Lazarus, and Robyn Fivush showed that in the families who survived the World Trade Center disaster in New York City, the children from families who told stories about their experiences and their family history did better than those whose families did not tell stories.[17]

GUIDED MEDITATION 10.1: Attachment in Community

Begin with your sense of your body. What does the space that your body takes up feel like? Is there an emotional tone that you live in? When you simply let yourself breathe and exist, do you feel calm and happy to be yourself? If not, are you numb, or frozen and needing acknowledgment of shock or exhaustion? Or is there any dominant sense of fear, loneliness, or anxiety? Do you long for certain safety? For the well-being of those you love? Or is there ongoing irritation and a need for effectiveness? Or sadness and a need for supported mourning? Simply notice what you find, and meet it with gentleness.

Now let your attention come to your breath. As you breathe, see if you can feel your breath go in and out, moving your ribs. As you ask your attention to stay with that place of alive sensation in your ribs, hold it with warmth and acceptance. If your attention is drawn to other parts of your body, or to other thoughts, gently and with kindness ask it to return to your breath.

Now close your eyes and let yourself imagine your community

and your family members spread out around you like an interconnected web. How close are the people who are most important to you? Is their distance from you a comfortable one? Turn your attention to the person who is standing closest to you in your imagination. If this person is very close, or merged with you, have him or her take a step back. If this person is quite far away from you, let him or her take a step closer to you. Either way, with this change in proximity, what happens in your body? If that sensation were an emotion, what emotion would it be? And what deep longing, what kind of integrity, or love, or longing for freedom and autonomy, lies beneath that emotion?

As your body relaxes, notice what meaning you make of the movement. And in your mind's eye, if someone comes closer to you, does it create a sense of overwhelm? If someone moves away, are you being abandoned? Allow your resonating self-witness to stand with you, at the comfortable distance or closeness of your choice, to provide an anchor of empathy and support for you. Invite another movement toward you or away from you, and see what happens in your body this time. What are the emotions that arise for you? And what are your deep longings? See if there is any exhaustion, and if you have needs for hope, for meaning, or for trust. Would it be sweet to know that you are exactly right, just as you are? And that you get to move or heal at your own speed? Would you like to be able to rely on everyone else in your community and your family to each be on his or her own healing journey, and to know the feeling of being held with warmth by the universe, no matter what you do or don't do? Continue to follow your body sensations, emotions, and needs, and let your body lead you.

When you are ready, allow your attention to come back to your breathing and to the space that your body takes up. Check back in with the emotional tone of your body, its space, and your world. And finally, for a last moment, please allow yourself to breathe in the wondering that maybe you are beloved, just as you are, and that you get to heal the way a flower unfolds or a healthy baby grows, organically and perfectly.

WHY PRACTICE THIS MEDITATION?

Every adult lies somewhere in this picture of attachment styles. A recent compilation of the results of 10,000 attachment interviews showed a worldwide picture of 24 percent dismissing (avoidant), 50 percent securely attached, 9 percent with anxious attachment, and 16 percent unresolved, possibly disorganized.[18] Seventy-eighty percent of humans stay the same over their lifetimes. Twenty to thirty percent experience changes in their attachment style, which can happen relatively quickly, over periods of weeks or months.[19] Patterns can change for the worse in response to trauma, and they can change for the better in response to healing.

These figures are another way to prove that healing is possible and that brains can change. The more people feel warmth for themselves exactly as they are, with their own attachment style, whatever it may be, the more they move themselves toward earned secure attachment. When people are securely attached, they tend to have longer lasting relationships, probably because they are better able to be committed and are more likely to be able to be satisfied.

Long-lasting relationships can also be insecure. It can be very stable for anxious people to be in relationships with avoidant people, but these relationships are not as happy or satisfying as those where the people are more secure or grow together into earned secure connection. Relationships between two anxious people usually don't last long, as they tend to be volatile and unstable. With two avoidant people, the relationship can either dissolve quickly due to lack of connection, or last forever in parallel, nonintimate partnership.

Many life patterns and choices are affected by attachment styles. One interesting illustration of this is the experience of jealousy. People who are avoidantly attached are more likely to be jealous if they think their loved one has a *sexual* connection with someone else. People who are securely attached or have earned their security are more likely to be jealous if they think their loved one has a *strong emotional* connection with someone else.[20]

Chapter 11 takes us into a deeper exploration of how the effects of disorganized attachment can be expressed as self-hate and offers some possible ways to work with the aftereffects of childhood trauma.

CHAPTER ELEVEN

Healing Self-Hate and Disorganized Attachment

———

"I hate myself," or "I shouldn't be alive."
(actually, "Self-love is within reach.")

Self-Hate and the Savage Default Mode Network

The mystery of self-hate is that from the outside it makes no sense. Why would a perfectly good brain attack itself? What possible purpose could self-hate serve? What is the point of having a savage default mode network (DMN)? We have learned that trauma can lie at the root of unkindness to self, but is there more to self-hate? Many people carry the capacity for momentary cruelty to or judgment of the self, or don't have a sense of warmth for themselves, without taking the further step into actual self-hate or self-loathing. And some people live with the constant sense of self-revulsion that makes being alive consistently agonizing.

When self-hate is in place, it is difficult to find solid ground for self-compassion, self-care, or the development of a resonating self-witness (RSW). The brain linkages from the sense of self don't get to connect with the capacity for warmth, as they are hijacked by an old pattern that links self with unbearable pain.

When there is no welcome for an infant in this world, for example, when a mother has postnatal depression, or when a family is struggling with trauma, which means the baby's emotions are not caught and resonated with, and when the only level of intensity or aliveness that is welcome is zero, the body of that infant has a rough time. The sensations of needing not to exist can be very uncomfortable physically (and can lie at the root of anxiety or depression). It is also possible for such a situation to push a person toward a lifetime of dissociation.

A self-hating DMN is trying to do an impossible task: find a place for the person in a system that cannot both acknowledge that person and survive. This begins in the family of origin. Traumatized and disconnected parents, in other words, parents who didn't get to have a place themselves, may have a difficult time even seeing their children, let alone creating space for them. And children who are not seen can grow up with very little sense that their existence is a good thing for the world. Children always want to contribute. If there is no way for a child's presence to contribute to delight, warmth, or love, then the child may believe that he or she should not be in this world. The child then may try to become small enough to fit into negative space. Existence itself becomes a double bind.

Self-Hate and Disorganized Attachment

The habit of using self-hate to try to fit in is a reliable sign that a child has grown up with disorganized attachment. In this style of attachment, the nervous system's response to emotional closeness is unpredictable, even to the point where the child can become tense in the presence of intimacy and can relax with more distance. This can leave people feeling terribly uncomfortable inside their own skin. It can also make people act out dangerously in close relationships, leading to emotional, physical, and sexual violence.

The experience of living with such a fragmented brain can be nauseating. It can come with a feeling of green, infectious sickness in every cell, accompanied by an incessant slide show of painful memories of times when it seemed that harm had been done to other people just by existing. The show can run on for days, usually the same incidents over and over again, often featuring people who are long gone, or dead, with no way to make repairs or receive reassurance.

It is all well and good when there is a clear path of trauma leading to self-loathing, but it can be particularly confusing when there are no memories of abuse to help make sense of self-hate. To fully understand the possible ways that self-hate can arise, we also need to understand disgust and contempt.

The Contributions of Disgust and Contempt to Self-Hate

Disgust is a natural emotion that serves an important purpose. It helps protect people in a world where they can get sick from eating food that has gone bad. It is possible to get a feel for what disgust is by imagining maggot-infested meat (yuck!). When people feel disgust, their body temperature goes up.[1] This is the body's natural response to fighting infection.

Disgust is important to understand when the discussion is about self-hate because the two go hand in hand. People often recoil from their own physical body when they are depressed.[2] And children of depressed mothers are more likely to consider suicide,[3] a sign that self-hate is part of the picture. People can tell that they are experiencing self-disgust if they hear themselves saying they are flabby, skinny, fat, ugly, or undesirable (or, of course, revolting or disgusting).

How is it possible for disgust to be wired to a person's own body, or even with the sense of self? It often has to do with how people were looked at when they were babies. It is possible for babies to be fun. It is possible for their eating to be joyful. It is possible for the mess that they make to be funny and delightful. It is even possible for their poop to be welcome as a sign of health and life. If a mother is depressed, overwhelmed, stressed, or abused, or is suffering from an obsessive condition like obsessive-compulsive disorder, an eating disorder, or addiction, then it is less likely that she will be able to experience her baby as fun, and more likely that she will see the baby's body as a nuisance, as disgusting, or as overwhelming.

Babies need to be looked at with soft eyes. For the first two years of life, the preverbal relationship part of the brain is growing and developing. When the newly forming relational baby brain is delighted in, and experiences being in relationship with other brains that have also been delighted in, it internalizes an experience of resonant responsiveness, soothing, and care. This is the setup for future secure attachment, an easy spring of bonding and oxytocin (the bonding hormone), self-regulation of stress, and the capacity to be essentially human and feel a sense of belonging with the human community. There is a flow of love from generation to generation that can meet a baby when he or she is born. When the mother was held with love and can pass it on, everyone has more of what they need for well-being.

People cannot thrive unless they are looked at with delight. When a mother and father are depressed, have obsessive-compulsive disorder,[4] are highly avoidant, or are distracted by high levels of stress, addiction, domestic violence, or other traumas, then their eyes cannot be soft when they look at their baby. And the baby's body with its ongoing needs to eat, to be loved, to cuddle, to create poop and pee, can be a source of disgust for the mom or dad. This is a kind of trauma for the baby. It is not the parents' fault. They are not evil. They can even clearly love their children. And at the same time the child can experience confusion and loneliness, living with the strange combination of being cared for and treated well and still trying to survive the internalized self-disgust that comes with the appraising, evaluative, and/or disgusted look.

The only way the baby can make sense of this is by believing that she or he is disgusting. Babies don't understand stressed-out, traumatized, or obsessive-compulsive disordered parents. Young children tend to blame themselves. And neurons that fire together wire together. If the sense of self and the body are always linked with disgust, then people can carry forward the belief that they are disgusting almost without knowing it. Because disgust is such a physical emotion, a person will often believe that its message is true. Part of healing work is to understand the effects of disgust and to disentangle the sense of self from early experiences of not having been a source of delight.

Of course, things become even more complicated when the love is not there. Examples of loveless existence include when neglect and parental dissociation make a child unsure whether he or she exists; when abuse makes having a body dangerous and vulnerable; when torture and shame make having a body painful; and when people are being fragmented by facing terror or rage in any form, and the presence of contempt and ridicule in the family.

Contempt is slightly different from disgust. Disgust is very connected with rot and possible infection and the decomposition of organic matter. Contempt removes people from even existing as human—it is a discounting or dismissal of the other. It is so difficult to receive that it impacts the immune system. Noted couples psychologist John Gottman can predict with 94 percent accuracy whether marriages will last after watching a video of an exchange between a couple, based on whether contempt, criticism, defensiveness, and stonewalling appear.[5] Hostility depresses the immune system, bringing with it susceptibility to viruses and infections.[6] This means that it is very difficult for children and partners to receive scorn and still be emotionally and physically healthy.

The dismissal of humans as not being worth the air they breathe is at the root of the worst evil that we can do to one another. We see it in events as common as bullying, racism, and ageism, as brutal as hate crimes, and as unthinkably evil as the Holocaust in World War II and the genocides in Africa, Southeast Asia, and wherever they occur in our world. This ability to dismiss other humans is a marker of disconnection from the body—an extreme of avoidant attachment that allows global levels of murder and destruction. Whether personal or global, disconnection from the body makes us only partly human. It is horrifying that all humans seem to be capable of disconnecting from others on a large scale or small scale.

Another aspect of disgust and contempt is a kind of contagion. To comprehend this, we need to understand that people participate in one another's emotional worlds using the brain's predictive neurons.

BRAIN CONCEPT 11.1: MIRROR NEURONS

When monkeys watch other monkeys, and even when they are watching people, neurons in their brains create an internal movement prediction of what is going to happen next. Researchers call these **mirror neurons**, a particular kind of neuron threaded throughout various areas of the brain, particularly in the motor cortex, interpreting and predicting intention from the movements of others. Mirror neurons become active both when a person performs an action and when a person sees someone else performing that same action.[7,8] The same thing is true for humans. For example, a person watching someone else pick up a glass of water will predict whether that person is going to drink or pass the glass to someone else. Since facial expressions are made up of muscle movements (there are muscles everywhere under the skin of the face, except for the tips of the nose and the chin), the theory is that people are continually supported by the automatic mimicry of mirror neurons to understand the emotions that are happening around them.[9]

The kind of meaning people make from what is seen in the faces around them depends on their age and their emotional state. When a child is little and sees someone looking at them with disgust or contempt (which might be left over from something else the adult is thinking about), the child might believe that the person is angry, disgusted, or contemptuous with them, even if that adult is actually aiming these emotions at someone or something else. Whether the world a child lives in is actually hostile or just blank and unresponsive, that child will often believe that the parent is angry and that the child has done something wrong.

Anger is an emotion that we feel when there is a threat to ourselves or to others we care about. And we definitely care about our children, so a lot of anger can be involved. When people are parenting without much ability to manage their worry by holding themselves and their children with warmth, they are in a constant state of alarm. People can live in a constant state of irritation and overwhelm at either their children or themselves. Parents can still carry within themselves powerlessness, helplessness, overwhelm, pain, the sense of not mattering. They can become angry at their children not because of what their children have done, but because of their current worries and their own past.

Because of mirror neurons, children experience what their parents are experiencing. So if, in addition to any anger, contempt, or disgust parents feel when they look at their children, the parents are also feeling their own self-hatred, the children can take that inside themselves, too, and believe that it's about them. People can turn the entire emotional soup of childhood into self-hatred, self-disgust, and depression. And of course, if this is the case, they are left without an RSW that would be able to stop their self-assault and self-battery. And so they may continually cut themselves to bleeding ribbons simply because that is how they are used to living. Self-hate is a pattern of self-management that is imported from others who are using it to control self and other: people who have more power in the relationship, like parents, teachers, older siblings, and other important figures.

To heal, people need to see their critical self-hating voice not as the truth but as what they have learned to do to try to manage pain and punish the self so that there is hope of learning to be better. As long as people believe their critical self-hating voice, they stay confused. It sounds like it knows what it's talking about, but it has no clue. People desperately need warmth and resonance to live well with themselves, their children, and their world. It can be easiest to understand self-love if we can learn it by internalizing the experience of being loved by others. However, if the self-hate is strong enough, people will stop any new love in its tracks. People can be absolutely unable to let in the understanding that others love them.

When people have no good place in a family or group, they create a narrative that explains what is happening. The narrative can blame others:

"They hate me."

"I live on a planet of robots."

"These people are sick."

Or the narrative can blame the self:

"I'm wrong."

"There's something wrong with me."

"I'm disgusting."

"I should be dead."

"The world would be better off without me."

What Is Your Narrative? Are Any of These Self-Hating Thoughts Familiar?

When reading this list, it is important to remember that these beliefs are just the words that the brain has given to emotions and longings. They are the stories brains use to explain people's lives. Any one of these statements is a condensed version of meaning we made out of something painful or traumatic. These sentences are not the truth.

If you get any body sensations as you read the list, that is a belief that is ripe for transformation. As the proverb goes, *if we can feel it, we can heal it.* Remember, when we can feel things in our body, and especially when we name our emotional experience, our brain is neuroplastic—we are ready for healing and change. Over time, by experiencing the practices offered in this book, the DMN will shift in tone, become less of a continual experience of self-inflicted injury, and start to become a concerned and warm background hum of care, planning, and reviewing to see if repairs are needed. As you read through the following statements, choose the one that seems most familiar or creates the most body sensation for you to use in exploring the guided meditation that follows.

- There's something wrong with me.
- I'm unlovable.

- I'm socially unacceptable.
- I'm a failure as a human being.
- I'm a bad person.
- I'm lazy. I'm irresponsible.
- I'm no good. I'm a loser. I'm a screw-up.
- No one understands me.
- I've let everyone down.
- I can't go on. I'm totally exhausted.
- I'm so weak.
- Nothing feels good anymore.
- I can't stand this anymore.
- I'm no good at anything.
- What's wrong with me? I'm not viable in the world. I'll never belong.
- I'm sick and twisted. I don't deserve love or understanding.
- I'm too broken to be loved. I'm too dirty and unwanted.
- I'm not trustworthy. I can't do relationships.
- I'm in danger.
- I'm such a coward. I have no backbone.
- I hate myself.
- I'm toxic.
- I'm too needy. Nobody wants me. Nobody would ever want me.
- I'm ugly, fat, undesirable.
- I'm so stupid. I'm too dumb. I'll never learn.
- I can't finish anything.
- I don't deserve to live, let alone do something I enjoy.

The following meditation will take you through your own process of hearing the voice of your heart inside your story of pain.

GUIDED MEDITATION 11.1: Transforming One of the Savage DMN's Stories

Before you begin, choose the statement from the list above that packs the greatest emotional punch for you, or use one of your own that you often hear repeated by your DMN and that you find painful to receive from yourself.

Begin with your hands. Move and flex your fingers, rotate your wrists. Can you let your consciousness enter your hands? If you can, follow the sensation of being inside your own skin up your forearms to your elbows, up your biceps to your shoulders. Do your shoulders attach to your torso? Is your torso bringing any breath in and out? Do you have a heart beating in your chest? Can you feel your heart beat? Hold your breath for a count of ten, and then check again to see if you can sense your own beating heart. If you can catch your heartbeat sensation, invite your attention to stay with it. If you can't find your heartbeat in your torso, bring your attention back to an alive sensation in your breathing. As your attention wanders, gently and with warmth invite it back to your breath or your heartbeat. Take your time with this, giving yourself three or more minutes to be in the wandering dance of attention to breath and heartbeat and kind attention to where your attention goes.

Now, say the statement that you have chosen. As you say it aloud, allow yourself to notice how your body responds to it. Maybe you feel a collapse, some tearing in your eyes, a heaviness throughout your body. And if the sensations were an emotion, what might it be?

Maybe there is exhaustion, discouragement, hopeless despair? Is there a longing for self-love?

Is there anger or impatience, and a need for acknowledgment of how long you have been struggling with this? Do you long for change and transformation? Just for a moment, would you like to inhabit someone else and have a rest from yourself?

Is there sadness? Do you long to be able to treat yourself with tenderness and care?

Is there confusion? Do you wish to experience crystalline clarity?

Is it scary to hear the cruelty in your own words? Do you need gentleness?

After you guess a need for yourself that feels true, say the statement again. Maybe you feel a burning in your abdomen, which might be horror and shame. And maybe beneath the emotions there is a need to be supported, to be precious in someone's eyes, or just to be loved. Again, stay with your feelings and needs guesses until this level of tension in your body eases.

Repeat this process until your body no longer reacts to the statement, each time noticing the changes in your body's message about what it is like to say the words that you have been using to explain your pain to yourself.

Now stop and see if there is different truth that your body likes better. How would you change these words to make them true?

WHY PRACTICE THIS MEDITATION?

When working with a toxic belief, it is important to find the most intense physical sensations connected with the beliefs. Once people have found the sensations, they have found the key that opens the door to change. They can now invite their insula (the part of the brain that lets us give words to emotions) to see what kinds of feelings and longings gave rise to this belief. It is like people are wrestling with a knotted tangle of yarn, starting at one end and untying the knots as they go. As they discover the emotional meaning that lies behind the words they have been saying to themselves, they let go of the conviction that their thoughts are true, and they start to see themselves as just telling stories that try to capture what their experience of this life has been. Beliefs about the self shift from "I'm not enough" to "I have always believed that I was not enough because that was easier than seeing how incapable my family was of warmth and acceptance," and then to something like "I am enough, I am big enough and strong enough to live my life, and I am willing to receive support."

There is another aspect to the question of self-hate that brings us back to the research into the way that infants limit their emotional expression to match their mothers' emotional vocabulary: what happens to an infant when there is no welcoming of the baby's emotional experience?

Belonging and the Window of Welcome

For humans, fitting in and belonging are almost the same thing as survival. I write the word *belonging* as if it were nothing, just a regular word, but it is one of the most important words we can use. People are made to live with and be loved by other people in the social world. When children are securely attached, they can reach out for support from their adults in difficult moments, without even showing much increase in their stress response: no rise in heartbeat, no spike of adrenaline or cortisol.[10] As you may recall from Chapter 2, when we look at a hill and we're alone, we see it as steeper than it seems to be if we have someone to accompany us.[11] When we experience minor pain and there's someone with us, the pain network doesn't light up the way it does when we're alone. Even if the person is a stranger, it still helps, and it helps even more if they are an intimate partner.[12]

Do you recall all of our learning so far about fight-or-flight and immobilization? Other authors use the phrase **window of tolerance** to refer to the amount of stress that an animal or human can experience and recover from without moving into fight-or-flight or immobilization response.[13] When we were learning in Chapter 10 about children's heart rate variability in the different attachment styles, we were actually learning about the window of tolerance for each attachment style.

The **window of welcome** is a different concept that specifies the emotional expression and intensity that can actually be met with warmth and understanding and is easily reflected and resonated within a relationship. What is read by others or self as going beyond the bounds into the inappropriate or unacceptable is outside the relationship's window of welcome.

Humans have the capacity, starting at the age of four months, long before they can talk, to carefully track the amount and kind of emotional expression that is acceptable to whoever has the power in the human system—parent-child, older sibling–younger sibling, family, group, class, work team, church, intimate partnership, and so forth. You can test this for yourself. Think about whether it's easier when someone who is dependent on you is sad or when that person is angry. If it's easier when that person is sad, you have a wider window for grief than for rage.

Individuals, families, and communities can have wide or narrow windows of welcome, and they may vary depending on which emotion we're talking about. A certain workplace may have a wide window of welcome for irritation and anger and a very small window for sadness or grief. A family can have an easy time with expressions of fear and almost no room for anger. The stronger their connection with their RSW, the more stability and self-connection people have, no matter what emotion is being expressed.

Interestingly enough, families and communities also have windows of welcome for the simple expression of life energy, expressed through movement, volume, intensity, variety of vocal expression, aliveness of gesture, and liveliness of facial expression. It is about how much inner experience is revealed. For children, and even for most adults, the need to belong is almost as important as the need to breathe. If a very alive and expressive child is born into a family without much welcome for expression, and there are no hidden currents of warmth to sustain the child and teach the child easy self-modulation, that child may learn to self-manage using the anger-shame cycle known as self-hate. The intensity of this can be understood only by acknowledging that, when humans are expelled from their family groups, it is experienced as a death. Children save their own lives by staying small enough to belong.

The more social intelligence and social fluidity people have, the more easily they find their place in human groups. Children who have been met with welcome and resonant understanding for their emotional expression are already being supported at the nervous system level to be in a resilient state of social engagement. They are able to read social cues about what kinds of expression are welcome and modify their behavior to be able to fit in with ease. And they are able to carry their own internalized sense of belonging wherever they go, so that their sense of being acceptable to themselves is so strong that they can support themselves in expressing ideas, intensity, and emotion, no matter what is happening with others. These people then invite others into being able to stretch into new emotional territory.

If you recognize that you dissociate or turn away from yourself when you are angry, frightened, or sad, and you'd like to expand your own welcome for emotion, you can use the skills you have been learning in this book. The same is true if you lose your confidence around others and try to become small in order to fit in. Notice the nuances of how your body responds to moving into a specific relationship with one person or a group of people, and offer your body some wonderings about how it is feeling and what it might be longing for.

RESONANCE SKILL 11.1: EXPANDING THE WINDOW OF WELCOME FOR EMOTION

What we can feel, we can heal. At the same time, if we are flooded with emotion, then we are overwhelmed, and change is less likely to happen. It is important to be gentle and to find a way to make the edges of the emotional experience small enough to be able to feel them without being overwhelmed by them. As we learned in Chapter 2, it might be possible to do this by imagining holding one cell of the body with resonance. It is also possible to work with imagined distance in order to make emotion manageable. Sometimes people can put their RSW on top of a nearby mountain and then shift their attention to being inside the RSW and looking at themselves from afar in order to get the level of emotional intensity low enough to be able to find the edges of sensation or nuance of a feeling.

If people want to expand their welcome for their own emotions, then they need to notice how their automatic DMN responds to these emotions. For example, when people feel sadness, shame, anger, or fear they can activate their SEEKING circuit (an automatic self-care reaction, one of Jaak Panksepp's circuits of emotions described in Chapter 3), which leads them right to their addictive substance or behavior. They can find themselves with a half-eaten cookie in their hand, without even knowing that they were taking action in response to feeling an emotion. It takes gentleness, warm curiosity, and commitment to start asking the self, "Before I went for my addiction, was I sad?" "Angry? Ashamed? Afraid?" If this rings bells for you, you can use the following guided meditation to support yourself with resonance so that you have a little more ease in the world with your own and other peoples' emotions.

Now that we have learned that people can try to make themselves nonexpressive in order to fit into other peoples' windows of welcome for emotions, it might be possible to understand how powerful a tool self-hatred can be. It is used when people are trying hard to fit in but when fitting in is hopeless. If people can bring the force of self-loathing to bear on themselves, they may be able to drive themselves so far into nonexistence that they can stay small forever and preserve some hope that they will get to belong.

GUIDED MEDITATION 11.2: Expanding the Window of Welcome for Emotion

Choose a moment in time when your own emotional expression left you feeling uncomfortable. You can choose a moment of sadness, irritation, outrage, doubt, skepticism, exhilaration, overwhelm, rage, anxiety, fear, or terror.

When you think of that moment, what do you feel in your body? Notice the nuance of contraction or constriction. Where do you feel it? Anything in your face? The face is often the easiest place to begin. Is there any sensation around your nose? This is where you may notice disgust or contempt. Around your mouth? Sometimes we can feel sadness or irritation in the corners of our mouths. At the corners of your eyes? Or between your eyebrows? Is there confusion? A little fear? Exhaustion?

As you connect with these edges of sensation and what emotions might lie beneath them, what is most important for you and your body to acknowledge?

Is the emotion itself unbearable, unresolvable, and uncomfortable? Do you have a hopelessness that naming it will help in any way? Is this an emotion that was unknown or unnamed in the family you grew up in? Does it bend your body into negative space, where you no longer get to exist? Feelings that have never been resonated with can collect in a hollow-feeling space in the chest or the gut. If your experience is wordless, then you can imagine bringing a soft cloud of attunement, a response of "of course," to every nuance that is here.

If your thoughts lead you to remembering other people's emotional expression, do you need acknowledgment that someone in the past has overloaded you with their emotions? Are you longing for absolute freedom from other peoples' emotional experience? And for emotional self-responsibility? Do you want to live in a world where people calm and soothe their own annoyance and frustration, rather than taking it out on others? Do you wish to know that everyone who is grieving will be cared for, and that it is not your burden?

Is there any edge of contempt or annoyance that you would like to name when you are in the presence of your own or others' emotions? Do you sometimes want to live in a world that is absolutely free of all emotions? Or, conversely, are you tired of people hiding what they feel, and do you ache for expression rather than numbness?

What other longings are rising toward consciousness?

Are there any other emotions that you have caught the edges

of, that would like to be named and linked with your deepest dreams? What is here to mourn or acknowledge that keeps your heart closed toward yourself?

Return to thinking about your physical response to your emotional experience. What happens in your body now? What is the next nuance of feeling that needs to be named or held?

If you find that disgust is here, imagine lifting the rug of that emotion to look underneath it for what frightens you or makes you angry. Hold any discoveries with gentleness. If you find self-contempt here, name the way that you have stepped outside human acceptability with this emotion.

Check in with your body again. If there is any change in body sensation at all when you think of the emotion, you are starting to experience neuroplasticity, and the gradual change in the window of welcome that resonance can bring.

WHY PRACTICE THIS MEDITATION?

This meditation touches the central question of this book: how do people learn to support themselves emotionally if their initial experience with their family included little understanding or attunement? This meditation takes your now-advanced skills in connecting with and reading bodies to work with the deepest core of contact with the self to create real change in bodies and brains.

Integrating the Window of Welcome Into an Understanding of Self-Hate

What do people do if they have the double whammy of a small window of welcome for emotion and very little capacity for self-warmth? They have to be able to quiet themselves somehow. If they can't calm themselves with resonance, they will use any means necessary to stay contained enough to fit in socially.

One way of doing this is to change the environment so that it is possible to stay calm. Maybe the house has to be neat and spotlessly clean, or quiet—that might help to stay calm. If the people in the family behave the way they "should," maybe emotions will be manageable.

If people aren't trying to change their external environment, then they can try to manage themselves with the whip of self-blame and the collapse of shame, using both to stay within their very small window of welcome. The drive to be a part of human groups is so strong that people will do anything they can to fit in, and if the group they belong to also has a very small window of welcome for expression, then there will be a "self-blame, collapse, self-blame, collapse" pattern: blame for doing things wrong, collapse into shame, self-blame for collapsing, alarm and a little bit of functionality, and then blame for doing things wrong, self-blame, and collapse again into immobilization. This is not a sustainable cycle.

Let's review the spectrum of self-criticism from Chapter 4 that the critical self has at its disposal:

- Insults, put-downs, name-calling
- Comparisons and measurements
- Dissatisfaction and a longing for perfection
- Inhuman expectations
- Blanket statements: "I always . . . ," "I never . . ."
- False core beliefs: "I am not enough." "There's something wrong with me." "I don't belong." "No one cares about me." "I can't love."

Remember that the critical voice has no capacity for understanding, compassion, mercy, or humanity. It sounds like it knows what it's talking about, but it has no clue about humanity or wholeness. The cycle of self-hate can be seen as a series of ricochets between existing and trying to stay small enough to belong. It is also possible for people to aim their hate and blame outward, but here is the way the cycle works if people are aiming their blame inward:

The Self-Hate Cycle

1. Something arises for us that we want to share.
2. We express in words.
3. If we are not accompanying ourselves, we are entirely dependent on the other's response. We watch the other person to see if our self-expression is received. If it is not received, we experience shame or collapse. This is where the self-hate cycle begins. We were too big, or too much. The greater the sense of social exclusion, the more pain we experience.
4. We blame ourselves for doing it wrong, using comparing, criticism, and measuring. (Fight/flight might bring us out of immobilization.)
5. We receive our own self-criticism with shame, regret, and hopelessness. (More collapse.)
6. We use our frozen immobility as the basis for more contempt, disgust, and self-hatred. (As we shift into self-hatred, we might be able to mobilize ourselves with fight/flight).
7. We experience more shame and exhaustion.
8. And so on, over and over again. . . .

This is self-management by self-hatred. It is like trying to keep a house within a narrow temperature range by turning the furnace on high and then all the way off, over and over again. When a person grows up with this cycle and uses it for self-management, rather than using self-attunement and self-resonance for self-regulation, that person is continually exhausted. A person will stay mystified, confused, and paralyzed as long as he or she believes this voice and buys into this cycle. And this cycle can cause a person to descend into depression and stay down for a long time.

The first step in stopping the self-violence lies in seeing the pattern. People are just trying to take care of themselves, using a paint roller dipped in shame instead of an artist's brush dipped in attunement, because that's what the family handed out. The family probably didn't even know that the gentle, precise brush of resonance existed.

The change happens when a person brings in the RSW to regulate with self-empathy and stop the self-assault and battery. The path to healing self-hatred might look something like this:

Steps to Healing Self-Hatred
- Demystify the concepts of self-hatred, self-disgust, and self-contempt: "Oh, so that's what I'm doing to myself!"
- Identify and understand the inner longings of the judging voice: "There's the unreliable voice of my inner critic. I must be trying to manage something emotional."
- Identify the voice of self-hatred within: "Ouch! That just hurt."
- Choose an approach: "Hmm—which meditation might work best here?"
- Access the RSW: "What would it sound like if I were wondering about myself with warmth?"
- Detoxify and disentangle the sense of self from shame, contempt, and disgust: "Oh, here I am—there's nothing wrong with me. I've just been trying to take care of myself as best I could."
- Implement the approach: do the process, follow the meditation, ask for help.
- Let others in: "Oh, you love me? How wonderful."

BRAIN CONCEPT 11.2: BRAIN EFFECTS OF ABUSE

Trigger warning: Graphic material on violence and sexual violence is included here. Do not read this section if it will upset you.

We have been speaking academically of disorganized attachment and the effects of trauma without naming the kinds of acts that terrify children, fragment brains, and create disorganization. The painful and difficult things that happen to children have brain effects, as well as contributing to emotional and memory fragmentation.

Terror fragments people. It makes brains stop working; it floods the system and explodes memory into shards. At its extreme, it takes people into a frozen state of immobilization. It is important to understand how people receive their world with their guts, how people can receive the intensity of someone else's expression—without even words, volume, or physical violence—and how it can fragment a human brain and body. This understanding is important to comprehending the effect of disorganized attachment: if the parent is terrified or terrifying, it creates disorganization in the child's brain.

Without consistent and warm reflection, people can't stitch their sense of self together. Taking this into account, it is probably no surprise that continual exposure to terrifying or terrified caretakers causes people to fragment. This means disconnected neural networks that run through the amygdala are formed (implicit memories), without much contact with the hippocampus, which holds both chronology and clear autobiography (our explicit memories of self).

Brains are affected by abuse in four main ways:[14]

- Irritability and brain wave irregularities in the limbic system
- Deficient development of the left hemisphere
- Problems with the hemispheres communicating with each other
- Abnormal activity in the cerebellum

Since three of these effects reference the hemispheres, in order to fully understand the brain effects of abuse and neglect it is important to recall what we learned about the left and right hemispheres in Chapter 4. Both hemispheres contribute to our well-being, and both are difficult to live with if a person has been fractured by trauma. The left hemisphere is our engine of doing and unites our energy and our efforts with our everyday language. It helps us accomplish things and carry out our intentions. When we have been traumatized, the left hemisphere's capacity to do things is compromised. And, if we've never been resonated with, the right hemisphere hasn't integrated a helpful structure for self-care and self-warmth. When we have been met with warmth and understanding, we reap the benefit of the integrated, resilient fibers of the emotionally healthy right hemisphere.

Here is a partial list of the parenting behaviors that create disorganized attachment and leave traces in children's brains, with information about how these traces affect people. (If these details are not of use to you right now, just skip down to the end of this section.)

Physical abuse

Physical abuse includes, but is not limited to, hitting, spanking, beating, whipping, slapping, punching, pinching, poking, hair pulling, shaking, kicking, burning, pushing down stairs, running over with vehicles, being abandoned away from home (being left somewhere, on the street, or with neighbors), forced physical exercise, and exposure to cold or to cold or hot water. The brain effects of physical abuse include a 38 percent greater rate of having seizures in the temporal and limbic areas of the brain (temporal lobe epilepsy).[15]

Sexual abuse

Trigger warning: graphic details. Sexual abuse, including the horrors of rape, molestation, or oral, vaginal, or anal touching or penetration during childhood, as well as other forced or coerced visual, verbal, or touch experiences, also leaves a mark on people's brains, creating a smaller left hippocampus (where factual memory lives), causing problems with verbal memory and dissociative symptoms that continue into adulthood. It also causes abnormal blood flow in the cerebellum, the small structure at the base of the brain (see Figure 1.2) that helps regulate attention and emotion. The seizures mentioned above happen at a 49 percent greater rate for sexual abuse survivors than in people who are not abused. And if both physical and sexual abuse is experienced, the person is 113 percent more likely to experience seizures. In girls, the corpus callosum, the bridge between left and right hemispheres, is particularly vulnerable and is smaller in girls who have survived abuse.[16]

Emotional and verbal abuse and witnessing domestic violence

Verbal abuse includes name-calling, contemptuous comparison, ridicule, humiliation, scapegoating, discounting (being called too sensitive or too childish, or told we have no sense of humor), threatening, demanding, denying, yelling, and screaming. When people have suffered emotional abuse, including parental and peer verbal abuse (bullying), or have witnessed domestic violence, they are more likely to have abnormal brain waves in the left hemisphere.[17] These problems and compromised development in the left hemisphere also occur with the other types of abuse but are even more marked with psychological abuses.

Neglect

Neglect might initially seem less harmful than abuse, but as mentioned in Chapter 2, severely neglected brains can weigh significantly less than normal brains. Brains are nourished and fed by relationship, and when they don't get it, they starve. Neglect harms both girls and boys; boys show much more damage from neglect than from physical or sexual abuse, especially to their corpus callosum. Experiences of neglect make people more likely to live in fear and to overreact to danger and can lead to altered metabolism and suppressed immune and inflammatory responses, neuronal irritability, and enhanced susceptibility to seizures.[18]

Humiliation and privacy abuse

Humiliation and public ridicule are old types of abuse that have a new forum: the Internet. Before the Internet, parents would do this by telling painful stories about their children or putting signs on them and forcing them into public. Now parents are posting online videos of their children having a difficult time emotionally. This is abuse. Children have temper tantrums and explosive experiences because of brain imbalances, trauma, abuse, and problems in the family. When a parent first takes such videos and second posts them online, the experience is one of unrecoverable shame for the child. The same is true for peer humiliation. When personal material is posted online without the consent of the person concerned, it is violation of trust and even of existence.

If you have experienced this form of trauma, it is very important to bring your RSW to support you, especially in the first moments when you realized what was happening. Those are moments of shock and horror that must be resonated with and acknowledged, and the losses that come with these experiences must be named and mourned.

So, is it hopeless for people who have survived abuse? Not at all. The brain is enormously complex and capable of growth and change. People may not be able to change the structural marks left by abuse, but they can grow new and supportive fibers that help to compensate for the imprint left by pain. People need to take themselves seriously, though. It is only as they begin to be able to fathom the enormity of the fear that they took into their bodies, and how it stopped their nervous systems, that the little ones within start to relax, and people can reclaim the life energy that is frozen inside their disconnected brain territory.

Quentin's Story

Trigger warning: If you would prefer not to read about children surviving years of sexual abuse, please skip this story.

One day at the men's prison, one of the men shared that he had made the decision to let his abuser live. He had been raped for years, and when he got old enough to stop it, he realized that he had a choice. He could actually kill the man who had hurt him, or he could tell the police and take his chances with having a sense of justice from the legal system. He chose to tell the police. Each member of the class made a guess for him about the complexity of what he had felt, and what he might have been wanting: that he might have been full of rage and longing for acknowledgment and some sense that retribution and balance were possible; that he might have been exhausted and needing peace; and that he might have felt determined and acted from integrity.

The next week the man was not in class. I worried that he had dropped out because of the intensity of the subject matter. But the next week he came back again. "They took me out of prison last week for emergency surgery, and then stored me in the city jail," he said. "When they put me in my jail cell after the operation, it turned out that my abuser was in the next cell over. I was stuck next to him for three days. If we hadn't had the conversation here two weeks ago, I think I would have killed myself. I only survived by remembering everyone's understanding."

This story reminds us that we don't change our history, but that when we are accompanied we change our own ability to survive it and to keep our integrity, and to continue to grow and heal. People are not victims with no hope for change. Yes, many of our patterns are laid down very early, but we can build our capacity to respond to what is happening in our world so that we can live differently. First we learn (with the help of others, or a book, or some other resource) to respond to ourselves differently, and then we naturally learn to respond to others and our world differently.

Solving the Mystery of Shame

People are finely honed to be social and to belong. As we have learned, it is almost physically impossible for humans to go outside the range of expression of emotion and intensity that is acceptable in a pair, in a family, or in a group. The price that is paid for being more emotional or more intense than what is welcome is the set of body sensations that we call shame. These can include a weakening in the upper back and the back of the neck, a flushing of the face and chest, difficulty in looking up or meeting people's eyes, nausea, and nonspecific pain sensations. The self-consciousness that comes with shame raises the body's cortisol levels more than any other emotion. In addition, self-conscious emotions also increase inflammation, compromising the immune system.[19] This is how important belonging is to humans. Shame has a psychobiological response in the body that is similar to the effects of abuse described above. All these conditions have long-term impacts on both mental and physical health and well-being.

The most visible and explicit example of the curtailing of expression in social situations is using contempt to induce shame. Since inducing shame is so effective at making people quiet, it is commonly used by parents and teachers to manage children's behavior. And then children grow up and use it to manage their own emotional experience, saying to themselves, "How could you be so stupid?," "What an idiot!," or "When will you ever learn?"

Sometimes shame can be confusing. People can feel it suddenly in social situations without being able to track how it began. In these moments it is helpful to know that when people extend their life energy, their contribution, or their vulnerability to others and it is not acknowledged, there can be a neurobiological collapse. Imagine that when a person is reaching out they are putting out one half of an extension bridge. For example, this person starts to tell a joke at a cocktail party. Halfway through the joke, the other people in the small group turn away and start speaking excitedly to someone else. The person who was telling the joke would have to deal with his or her own neurobiology crashing as a result. If no one meets the bridge a person is putting out with another half of a bridge, the neurophysiological load is too heavy to sustain alone, especially if the extender is vulnerable or has less power, less support, or fewer resources. When someone else reaches out with communication, verbal or nonverbal, that responds in some way to what we are offering, the bridge is met and supported.

Shame comes in a number of different neurobiological flavors. Sometimes it elicits a fight-or-flight response, with a flow of alarm and cortisol. Sometimes it seeps through a person like a numb nausea, bringing helplessness and resignation in its wake (a sign that the body's flow of energy and information may be moving toward dissociation). In Panksepp's circuits of emotion, shame is one of the flavors of PANIC/GRIEF and comes with a decrease in levels of endogenous opioids and oxytocin, so it is no wonder that it is such an unpleasant experience, so difficult to recover from. And no wonder people work so hard to belong.

RESONANCE SKILL 11.2: TRANSFORMING SHAME INTO SELF-KINDNESS

Once a shame reaction has begun, there is an inherent challenge to bringing resonance to the self, because shame is a miniature trauma, a moment when we are inherently unaccompanied. (The accompanied self cannot be shamed.) Recall from Chapter 6 how, when we were working with time traveling to heal trauma, we froze the environment to make it safe. A shamed internal environment is not safe—that is part of the reason that resonance is hard in this situation. It is hard to freeze the contemptuous self and keep the shamed self awake for resonance, so instead it may be necessary to start by offering resonance to the judging self.

The first step is to find out if a part of you has turned away from yourself in the shame experience. One way to do this is to say to yourself, "If I had contempt or disgust for myself right now, it would be because I so value _____ (honesty, commitment, loyalty, integrity, social grace, understanding, care, etc.—choose whatever words work for you)." Is there any easing in your body with that self-inquiry?

Now see what kind of resonance lands for the self that feels shame. This is one moment when reassurance can be truly supportive. "Do I need to know that I belong, no matter what? That no one can take my belonging away? That I am precious? That my voice is important and my contributions are essential? Do I need to know that I am okay? Am I aching for a clear sense that I matter to my community? To know that I am wanted?"

It is important to explore, be creative, and take note of what really supports you in your well-being, so that you have structures and understandings to support you when shame takes you offline.

A Word About Thinking About Suicide

When people live with self-hate and disorganized attachment, they can have a sense of being so exhausted that death might be the only possible rest. They can feel a never-ending weariness in their bones. This may be the closest people come to thinking about suicide: a repeated image of something like driving a car off a cliff and soaring into what might seem to be absolute peace. But there are many who come much closer, making actual attempts, and some who, sadly for those of us left behind, succeed.

Exhaustion is the result of a toxic DMN. Disgust, self-revulsion, and self-dislike are fatiguing to live with even for moments at a time, let alone day in and day out. Hopelessness and meaninglessness are close companions. All of these feelings take people away from their own life energy, leaving them stuck in an ever-decreasing pool of resources.

Again, the links between trauma and difficult lives are profound. People who have experienced four or more different kinds of adverse childhood experiences are much more likely to be depressed than those who haven't experienced childhood trauma. And if they have a score of 7 yeses to the ACES trauma questions described in Chapter 6, then they have a 30 percent likelihood of attempting suicide. Between two-thirds and four-fifths of all attempted suicides can be traced to adverse childhood experiences.[20] So doing the healing work that brings us back to warmth (or gives birth to it when it has never been there) for self and others can lead us away from thinking about and attempting suicide.

The mystery of suicide includes this difficult relationship with self, but it also includes the effects of traumatic brain injury, side effects of medications, economic and employment difficulties, and "suicide contagion." For adolescents, exposure to suicidal behavior in a friend or family member is as risky as becoming severely depressed.[21]

The feelings of devastation, grief, and bewilderment for those who are left behind when the attempts are successful are mind-numbing, incomprehensible, and never ending. There is shock enough at just an attempt. When the effort ends in death, it almost seems like the earth has opened up and swallowed the missing person whole.

Empathy can't change anything that has already happened, but we can begin to acknowledge the enormity of the experience of loss for survivors, and we can learn to support everyone involved so that it is easier to live, no matter who they are.

Self-Hatred Is Part of a Larger Picture of the Transmission of Disorganized Attachment

Disorganization (the effect of abuse) passes from generation to generation, even if abuse is not present. You might be thinking, "Okay, I understand how a terrifying, abusive, or neglectful caretaker would fragment me, but why is she talking about terrified caretakers?" Caretakers create the ground of our being. Children rely upon them to be present and responsive. When children look into their eyes and see that they are terrified, the children's ground of being disappears, and this experience stops their nervous system in its tracks just as fully as being really scared by a mother or father does. Additionally, it is unbearable for anyone to live in an ongoing state of terror, so terrified caretakers tend to dissociate, which means that they are unable to understand or respond to their children's emotional communication. Their neglected children walk through the world unknown and thus unable to know themselves. This is the land of the second-generation effects of child abuse and neglect. It explains why people may experience fragmentation and disorganization even if their parents were not themselves abusive or overtly neglectful.

If our children have already grown, learning about these effects can come with big doses of pain, regret, and mourning about not having been able to stop the transgenerational transmission of terror and disorganization for our children when they were young, even if our houses were very safe. If this is true for us, we get to hold ourselves with immense tenderness and acknowledgment and to remind ourselves that repairs are possible as long as we are alive.

Carrie's Story

Reading these words I feel a stabbing pain in my heart. I was a second-generation abuse child. My parents were physically gentle with me, even when they were unable to respond to me or understand me. My mother was most often dissociated and non-responsive to me, with moments of being terrifying, though not physically abusive. So I left childhood very confused about my lack of resilience, my depression, and my suicide ideations. They seemed to come from nowhere. I remember how unable I was to understand my son's emotional world when he was small. One day a friend asking me, "Can't you see that he's scared?" In that moment, I knew she was right, but that I couldn't see it. I would play with him in ways that were really terrifying. I would chase him and not be able to tell that his shrieks were real fear rather than joy. I feel grief, regret, and shame, and I long to have had this information fifteen years ago, so that I could have held my child with more care and responsiveness. There are small tears behind my eyes, and I hope that in writing this I will open the door for other parents to see themselves with compassion and tenderness in the bewildering experience of not being able to be there for their children the way they would like to be.

As we begin to understand these ideas, we are clearing brain space for the importance of our RSW and teaching ourselves to always go back to the body, to warmth, and to connection to make it through, instead of to self-criticism. And as we start to have compassion and tenderness for the child that we were who survived all this as best we could, then we are beginning to heal.

CHAPTER TWELVE

Gently Healing Depression

"My life is meaningless."
(actually, "I can find richness and create meaning.")

Bringing Self-Warmth to Overwhelm and Depression

People can live with depression for years. It can be particularly hard to get out of bed in the mornings and to do minimal self-care, such as brushing teeth, showering, and eating. People will try different approaches to getting moving: self-scolding, cajoling, prayer, or reminding themselves of everything that has to be done. Often the fear of falling farther behind is what will motivate people to swing their legs over the edge of the bed and stand up.

A change can happen as the resonating self-witness (RSW) becomes real and more accessible on a minute-by-minute basis. When a person lies down to sleep at night, it is possible to imagine covering the self with a blanket made of acknowledgment of longings. People can let truth warm their chest; reassurance and comfort can nestle into the belly, and a little support and tenderness can cradle the head.

The mornings can become different, too. What happens when people meet themselves with warmth when waking? When people don't want to get out of bed, instead of messages of self-contempt they might ask themselves, "Are you already tired and overwhelmed? Do you long for space to breathe? Would you like to be connected to your own capacity for delight? Do you wonder where it has gone? Are you wanting to have a sense of being enough and of being welcome just as you are? Would you like your day to be just right for you and to have the experience of lightness and being carried, rather than that you are carrying everyone and everything else?"

When this is their first experience of the day, people can be lifted out of bed effortlessly. It becomes more possible to see the world with a glint of humor. Play can begin to awaken, which in turn creates more resiliency to depression.[1]

And those changes are more likely to happen if the depression is a light, low-level grayness. It is harder, but still possible, to change bigger depressions. Here are some of the patterns people live through when depression takes hold of them.

What Is It Like to Be Depressed?

Depression can come on a person suddenly. It can be intense and life altering, or it can be low-grade and last for decades, almost under the level of conscious awareness. People can become depressed when they get sick, when they stop an addiction, or when they are under long-term stress. People can also get depressed when they experience a trauma, especially after they lose someone they love to a breakup or death. Depression occurs for some people when the weather is continually dark or rainy, or during the hormonal fluctuations of menstrual cycles or menopause.

It is possible for people to have lived with depression forever, especially if their mother had pre- and/or postpartum depression. People might live in a depressed state because they believe they are bad, disgusting, or wrong, as a result of trying to make sense of coming into a family where they are not welcome, or even where they were welcome but their parents never had a sense of belonging to this world. Nearly half of all people with depression also have anxiety. Nearly half of all people with anxiety also have depression. Depression can alternate with mania, or intense energy, as when people are bipolar. In this condition, the mania can become so all-consuming that they lose touch with reality.

Sometimes it seems as if depression is the brain's own inertia, as if the brain has given up on ever getting any needs met. It's like everything has gone into a painful, draining stillness that has suffering as its core, without enough energy available anywhere to do anything but keep breathing, and that only because it is involuntary.

This life within a dark cloud is different from sadness and grief. It's more like gravity has gotten much heavier than it used to be, and there isn't enough energy to lift the body to eat, sleep, do any self-care, work, or carry on relationships. The word *pleasure* no longer makes sense. It is like the brain has been robbed of all its resources and all its sources of energy. For this reason, depression can be hard to get out of without support. People struggling with depression need help, and it can be hard to have enough hope even to reach out to try to get it.

Signs and Symptoms of Depression

- Feelings of sadness or unhappiness
- Irritability or frustration, even over small matters
- Chronic dissatisfaction with other people's or our own performance or contributions
- Articulate verbal shredding of performance and contributions
- Loss of interest or pleasure in normal activities
- Reduced sex drive
- Insomnia or excessive sleeping
- Changes in appetite—either decreased appetite and weight loss or increased food cravings and weight gain
- Agitation or restlessness, for example, pacing, hand-wringing, or an inability to sit still
- Irritability or angry outbursts
- Slowed thinking, speaking, or body movements
- Indecisiveness, distractibility, and decreased concentration
- Fatigue, tiredness, and loss of energy—even small tasks may seem to require a lot of effort

- Feelings of worthlessness or guilt, fixating on past failures, or blaming yourself when things aren't going right
- Trouble thinking, concentrating, making decisions, and remembering things
- Frequent thoughts of death, dying, or suicide
- Crying spells for no apparent reason
- Unexplained physical problems, such as back pain or headaches

Let's think about the things that can start a depression in motion. It's good to know that depressions have starting points, so that we can also anticipate the movement out of depression and get to the ending points. Sometimes awareness of these triggers helps people let go of judgments when they start to slide. This knowledge can also help people not to blame themselves so intensely for not being able to do ordinary self-care, such as taking a shower.

Possible Causes of Depression
- Long-term stress
- Attachment trauma
- Loss of a significant other (breakup or death)
- Faulty mood regulation by the brain
- Recovery from addiction
- Mother's pre- and/or postnatal depression
- Genetic vulnerability
- Hormonal fluctuations
- Stressful life events, including poverty and abuse
- Professional, career, or job-related loss
- Issues of finances, security, or stability
- Seasonal light changes
- Medical problems
- Medications
- A savage default mode network (DMN)

Depression and Trauma

Difficult early-life experiences make it more likely that people will suffer from depression. The more different kinds of trauma people experience, the more likely they are to experience depression.[2] Let me say this a different way: the harder things were for you when you were little, the more kinds of abuse you had to endure, and the more bad things that happened for your family, the more likely you are to find life meaningless and to struggle with hopelessness and lack of energy. You may read this and think, So what? My life is hard because my parents were mean to me and had a hard time, because their parents were mean to them and had a hard time, so where's the hope and promise of change? The more people learn to think about themselves with gentleness and warmth, and the more meaning they make about their lives, the more choice they have in how they treat themselves and others.

The healing work is important. Depression has an effect on you, your friends and neighbors, and your children and grandchildren. One study of people with major depression found that nearly all of the participants had been raised by parents using "affectionless control" as their parenting style (meaning the parents would tell their kids what to do and discipline them without warmth, affection, or any expression of love). And in this study, all the people had increased inflammation in their immune systems. The more they had been physically neglected and maltreated in childhood, the more their immune systems were affected.[3]

What is it like to take in all this information about depression? Is it depressing, when you are longing for lightness and support? What do you notice in your body? Is there relief at the confirmation, validation, and shared reality? Are you curious and wanting more information? Do you feel sick to your stomach with the pain of self-recognition, and do you need acknowledgment of overwhelm? Do you need a hefty dose of hope seasoned with a little optimism and faith?

RESONANCE SKILL 12.1: GENTLENESS AND ACKNOWLEDGMENT

When working with depression, the two most important skills are (a) knowing how to embrace an exquisite gentleness, and (b) being able to acknowledge what is true for the depressed self without making that self wrong and without believing that the depressed voice is the true voice. Both are paradoxical positions in the relationship with the self. Both require a "being with" that is not asking for any change while simultaneously remembering the undepressed self and wanting the return of life energy and ease.

The most helpful stance is to want the best for ourselves while not pushing in any way. This kind of gentleness with the self is a gentleness of presence and accompaniment that lets softness and comfort enter the harsh and energyless zone of depression.

The acknowledgment that is needed here is whatever is true for the depressed self: "Do you need acknowledgment of the grinding lifelessness of this state?" "Do you need some shared reality that there is no hope for this world?" It is radical to speak in this way, and you may protest reflecting such stark, harsh statements. But if these questions are asked from the point of view of exploring what is real for the depressed self, then the result can be very interesting, so do not judge before you try it. You can try it right now: what is the most depressed thing that your being would like acknowledged? Ask your depressed self if it needs acknowledgment for this thing. What happens in your body? Sometimes a bubble of giggles arises with the unaccustomed acknowledgment, sometimes a deep breath of relief, sometimes a clearing of the head. It seems that, although we can fight depression by trying not to talk about it, it can also be a huge relief to start naming what the brain perceives.

With all of the different ways that depression shows up, a person might wonder if there is some unifying pattern of brain activation that lies at the root of this state. Let's look at what the research shows.

BRAIN CONCEPT 12.1:
AREAS INVOLVED IN DEPRESSION

When we look at functional magnetic resonance images of depressed brains, we see barely any brain activity, just the small embers of life glowing in the limbic system deep in an otherwise dark brain. This helps us to understand why depression is notoriously difficult to come out of. It turns off and tears down the parts of the brain and the resources that would move us toward recovery.

In depression, the amygdala registers distress and overwhelm. The more active the amygdala, the more cortisol flows in the brain and body. The less the amygdala is supported by the prefrontal cortex (PFC), and the smaller the voice of the RSW, the more intense the depression.[4] The more cortisol flows, the less active the hippocampus.[5] The hippocampus works with and coordinates all the areas that are responsible for memory and learning. This may be why small children who are depressed or overwhelmed with trauma have a hard time at school and grow up believing there is something wrong with them.

As people heal from depression, they are awakening their RSW and bringing their brain back into balance. The PFC in both hemispheres is less active in depressed people.[6] In particular, the left PFC, the part of the brain that people depend on for executive function, to make decisions and get things done, shows very little activity.[7] In depression, the inferior frontal gyrus (see Figure 1.5), a part of the PFC involved in connection problems that link negative events with the sense of self, resulting in a savage DMN, is more active.[8] When this happens, a person can be overwhelmed by shame, sadness, depression, pessimism, and despair and can be caught in a never-ending cycle of negative emotions, pessimistic thoughts, and unconstructive thinking styles. As people get stuck in this negative looping, they can become more alarmed and vigilant, it can be harder to stop the cycle of thoughts, and they can even develop sleep disturbances.[9]

Other effects of being at the mercy of unregulated emotions in depression (which means that the PFC is not active, so no RSW is available) include

- Rumination: a tendency toward painful self-reflection where people withdraw from the world and focus their attention inward.[10]
- Hypervigilance: when the amygdala is running a low-level, constant anticipation of danger, causing more stress. The body pumps out cortisol, keeping people continually on alert, which deteriorates immune system functioning, increasing risk of developing other illnesses (why it is common for other diseases to occur along with depression).[11]
- Anhedonia: the brain's entire reward system goes offline and people move into the complete loss of pleasure that is a part of depression.[12]

Two Main Pathways of Depression

You will recall that throughout the book, starting in Chapter 3, we have been discussing neuroscientist Jaak Panksepp's seven circuits of emotion. We use the SEEKING circuit to get and do what we need. We use the PANIC/GRIEF circuit when we are abandoned. The FEAR circuit gets us away from danger or immobilizes us so we are safe. The RAGE circuit helps us protect ourselves and others. The LUST circuit helps us have sex. We use the CARE circuit to support and nourish ourselves and others. We activate the PLAY circuit when we are safe and happy.

Just as there are two types of anxiety, as discussed in Chapter 5, Panksepp's research shows two main pathways of depression: the savage DMN and lifelong loneliness.

The savage DMN in depression

Moving people away from depression involves transforming the savage DMN. This has been the focus of this whole book: the exploration of what happens when we bring in the self-warmth of an RSW, particularly the care that our PFC can provide when we aim it in the right direction. The untransformed cruel DMN puts people under chronic, long-term stress that leads to depression. (Other life events can create the chronic stress that leads to depression, too—financial worries, job stress, or family or health worries can wear away at us.) Panksepp traces the depressive effects of long-term stress on these circuits of emotion in this way:[13]

- The FEAR circuit gets neurotransmitters going in response to stress.
- As the stress continues, these chemicals that make the brain work run low.
- This stops neurons from growing and increases inflammation in the brain.
- The SEEKING circuit slows and has no goal or purpose. (PLAY and CARE are also slow.)
- Depression follows.

Working with this type of depression, it is helpful to focus on ways to ease and quiet the savage DMN.

Lifelong loneliness in depression

In addition to the difficult-to-survive relationship between the brain and long-term stress, another kind of depression arises from lifelong loneliness. If a mother, the very first person who is supposed to welcome children to this world, is nonresponsive, particularly if she suffered from the profound lack of responsiveness that comes with pre- and postpartum depression, her children can live with the PANIC/GRIEF circuit perennially activated. Lifelong depression can arise from profound loss or total breaks in connection, such as postnatal depression, adoption, early death or departure of a mother or father, or loss of a twin.

People suffering from lifelong depression need attachment repair work even more than they need to change their savage DMN (and the savagery will change along with the attachment repair). People need to obtain and maintain close and nurturing interpersonal relations, and they receive benefit from being emotionally supported. Panksepp tracks the development of this type of depression to difficult attachment patterns:[14]

1. Separation leads to activation of the PANIC/GRIEF circuit, leading to feelings of grief and abandonment.
2. When grief and panic are aroused, there is a depletion of comfort chemicals such as endogenous opioids, as well as decreases in oxytocin and prolactin, and increases in the flow of cortisol.
3. The lonelier a person is, the greater the experience of pain, depression, and fatigue.
4. Again, the SEEKING circuit is diminished and has no goal or purpose. (PLAY and CARE circuits also slow.)
5. Depression follows.

In service of these two different roots of depression, this chapter offers two different meditations to support healing. Both of these meditations are meant to be integrated with a supportive daily practice of self-warmth in the service of long-term change, rather than being one-time experiences. Change or modify them in any way that supports you

GUIDED MEDITATION 12.1: Working With Depression Connected With a Savage DMN

Start with your body, and be very gentle. Instead of following your breath this time, invite a sense of a golden protective aura to form around you, to form around your heart. Let this aura become tiny glowing rays of care that are capable of protecting you from yourself.

Take a moment to see what this might be like, this sense that there is a part of you that is worth being protected and cared for, even against yourself.

Now, bring support in to hold that angry, bitter voice of self-hate. Ask this part if it is at its wit's end, completely exhausted and bewildered, and hopeless about how to support you. Ask this part if it longs for your invulnerability, for you to be bulletproof and beyond reproof in this life. Ask this part if it is angry at you, so angry at your weakness and your pain, and if it longs for the strength of steel. And ask this part if its standards are so high that they are inhuman. How is this part responding to your care and understanding? If there are more feelings and needs guesses for this part of you, follow your body to see what emotions and longings are there to be named.

Now come back to your heart, and see whether your heart is willing to receive the sweetness that you are offering it. Does your heart feel healthy and whole, or is it giving you imagery of being ill, burdened, another color besides pink, or made from a material other than heart tissue? Whatever you find, ask yourself, if this communication were letting you know about an emotion, what would it be? And what is the longing or need that lies behind that emotion?

Is your heart exhausted and needing replenishment and support? Is it almost like it has been creating the blood that has been nourishing you all by itself, without anything coming in from outside, and it's worn out? Is your heart needing and longing to be loved, just for itself, even if it were just in a state of rest? Does it need a cradle of clouds, or a nest made of spun oxygen and dreams?

Is your heart broken and split from grief? Does it need acknowledgment of the losses it has endured? Of how little it enjoys continuing to live when those it has loved are gone? Check to see if it is carrying other broken hearts or other pain besides its own.

Let the rays of protection resonate and hold your heart with care and acknowledgment, not needing any truth other than your heart's truth.

Now let your attention return to your full body with affection and care, not expecting anything to change, just holding your whole being with acknowledgment, and, if possible, a little bit of black humor about the way we humans can make our own lives unlivable.

GUIDED MEDITATION 12.2: Gently Holding Depression Connected With Lifelong Loneliness

Bring your attention to your physical body in the world. As you breathe in, notice where you can feel your breath moving: movement of your muscles, movement of the air. Invite yourself to bring warm regard to your attention, gently supporting it to stay with or return to your breath sensations. What is the texture of your breath? If your breath were a color, what would it be? Would there be different colors for inbreaths and outbreaths? Let yourself sit for a few moments, feeling into the inner life of your breath.

Now, let yourself imagine, if you are willing, that as you breathe in, you are bringing in an emotion that supports you, and that as you breathe out, you are breathing out an emotion that represents your pain: anger, depression, fear, or grief.

As you work with this, notice if you are profoundly alone in your experience. What if you might not be so alone? What if you really belong here? Let your breathing be an acknowledgment of your emotional self in the larger world. As you breathe in, let the world nourish you with resonance. Bring your resonating self-witness in to support you.

Let this compassionate inner voice ask you, "Are you exhausted and do you long for a safe place to rest?"

"Are you angrier than you can bear, and have you given up? Do you need hope, balance, and self-responsibility?"

"Are you so lonely that your bones creak? Do you wish to experience even a few seconds of both a feeling of being deeply embedded in a warm, loving community and simultaneously a feeling of soaring freedom and individuality?"

"Would you like to be sure that your self-expression would bring you closer to others rather than pushing them away? Would you like to know that it is possible to both be yourself and be connected to others?"

Let your outbreaths carry the way you feel into the world,

breathing your emotion out. With your inbreaths, let the world respond to you. Let it share and console your grief. Let it quietly savor any stirrings that might arise.

Let's move farther into your physical being. Find the loneliness that lives at the level of the very small beings that comprise you: your cells. If there were longings or dreams that were traveling into your cells, and a call to the universe traveling out from your cells, what would that exchange be? Are your cells longing to relax into being truly known? Or are those words so foreign that they are almost incomprehensible? Would it be nice if they made sense?

Let your resonating self-witness speak with the lonely cells. If you don't have a sense of your self-witness, bring in someone else as a resonating witness, someone you trust. If there are no people you trust, are there any animals? Is there a tree or a place in nature? How do your cells respond to this being or this essence? Do your cells need acknowledgment that they have been alone and bewildered for as long as they can remember?

And do you as a whole person need there to be someone bigger than yourself, someone warm and dependable that you could lean on when you want and wander away from when you want, and who would still be there in the same place for you to come back to? Is there a longing to know what support and intimacy might feel like? And how about being loved no matter what? Would it be sweet to have experiences of love that truly had nothing to do with what you did or didn't do? Would you enjoy being able to know what "unconditional love" meant? Would you like to know that you belong utterly, that you are beloved, and that you are understood?

As we work with these concepts and talk about them, are there a mourning and a grief that need to be acknowledged? Have you been alone more than any little social mammal should ever have been alone? Each and every cell in your body has a tiny bit of the original mother in it, in the mitochondrial DNA. If we think about cells in this way, each cell in your body is being supported and loved by the long line of mothers that stand behind us.

Now come back to your breathing, and see what emotions might be being breathed in and out. What is your sense of your body as a whole? Say goodbye for now to this work of acknowledgment, and let yourself return to your regular life.

WHY THESE MEDITATIONS ARE HELPFUL

When working with depression it is important for gentleness to be the first priority. People have spent lifetimes trying to affect the depressed self by using anger, bitterness, resentment, irritation, and criticism. The combination of warmth and solid presence is a radically different approach for us to integrate and is an invitation to come all the way back to safety and social engagement instead of forever vacillating between the anger and shame of self-hate. It is also important for warm presence to be consistent. Thirty seconds of warm breathing meditations twice a day might be a doable request and is much more reassuring than fifteen minutes once a week.

A couple of brain chemicals are important to reference in thinking about the usefulness of these meditations. Whenever people experience emotional warmth, it is likely that they are balancing the flow of oxytocin. Oxytocin is the substance that the brain creates when there is a sense of belonging. This is immensely calming for human systems (once closeness feels safe—if warmth has never felt safe, then people tend to try to avoid it). It is important to understand that expression and individuality are essential if intimacy is to be complete. If people have to give up parts of themselves in order to belong, they can end up living within a profound depression and a bone-crushing loneliness. A person has to be fully known, as well as have experiences of deep warmth, to move fully out of depression. If people don't have a warm community in their present-day life, it is possible to begin to grow and nurture one, maybe even by imagining dipping into the circle of other people who have read this book and are on this same journey of transformation.

Another brain chemical that is useful to have in balance is dopamine. The experience of depression includes helplessness, hopelessness, paralysis, and bewilderment about what action to take, all of which indicate that dopamine may not be flowing. So as people take action, they invite movement in the brain. Experiencing a guided meditation is doing something. Asking the brain to turn toward the self with warmth is taking action. Giving the left hemisphere something it can do to offer support can be a helpful movement from within the sometimes-frozen experience of depression.

It may be supportive to know that almost any approach to healing depression that has been researched appears to work for about 50 percent of the people who try it—exercise, antidepressants, acupuncture, and so on. There are many other places to find these resources, so let's focus on getting support from resonance-based approaches.

Using Resonance to Support Healing From Depression

Things change gradually, rather than all at once, for people struggling with depression who are developing a relationship with their RSW. Here are some possible starting points that integrate the learning from this book:

- Acknowledge the savage DMN.
- Capitalize on the space between bouts of depression to nourish the relationship with the RSW.
- Start a resonance-based mindfulness practice with any of the meditations in this book.
- In a depressive episode, begin small—begin with counting three breaths with warmth.
- Remember to use gentle warmth to bring the attention back to the breath (not cold or disgusted impatience).
- Disarm the savage DMN by translating and transforming automatic thoughts, naming emotions, wondering about longings, and using new skills.
- Work with the exercises shown in this book to heal outdated attachment patterns, reverse the effects of affectionless con-

trol and early trauma in childhood, and heal trauma that may underlie inflammation, which could contribute to depression.

• Find ways to start experiencing the PLAY circuit.

Carl's Story

I started working with this material after I lost my wife to cancer and no longer had a sense of meaning in my life. When I wondered about what was happening in my body, I could feel my feet and my hands, but the inside of my torso was a mystery to me.

The idea that I could have a resonating self-witness was absolutely foreign. After getting used to the idea, I became willing to use the book as a basis for an RSW who would make empathy guesses for me. I asked myself, "Do you need to acknowledge the shock and the enormity of the loss when your wife was first diagnosed, then when she was debilitated by the medical treatments, and finally when she died?"

I took each of these events in turn, making sure that my body didn't have to stay frozen in time with any one of the shocks. I asked myself, "Did your heart stop beating when you heard the word *cancer*, and has it never really started again?"

"When you saw how the treatment affected her, did you suffer with her? Were you filled with an enormous, unreasoning rage, and did you have a need to express tenderness and care?"

"When your wife died, was it as if a part of you died with her?"

As I made the guesses to hold the hugeness of these events, sensation gradually returned to my body. As my body came back to life, the depression began to recede, and I made more guesses for myself. I moved very slowly and gently, following whatever voice my body had, following my thoughts with empathy when my body had no voice.

As I fully acknowledged myself, I became more willing to live again, both grieving the physical absence of my wife and holding the sense that her love remained with me. I reclaimed the idea of meaning for myself. With the commitment I had made to living in this new way, I was growing and strengthening my fibers of attachment and making my brain more easily regulated and balanced. With the growing sense of meaning that I was discovering, my own RSW became fully present, and I began to be able to hold myself with compassion and gentleness in my everyday life.

CHAPTER THIRTEEN

Leaving Behind Addictions and Compulsions: The Contributions of Self-Understanding and Resonance

"I can't stop," or "I will never have choice."
(actually, "As I become gentler with myself and my
nervous system relaxes, I have more choice.")

The difficulty of human struggles with addiction reveal that early-life experiences can have enduring influences on nervous systems. The interaction of mother and child leaves its mark on a person's capacity to effortlessly respond to life itself, transforming the structure of the brain and the balance of the nerve pathways that regulate the heart.[1] The less support received in those early relationships, the more effort it takes to sustain the self in connection to others and the outer and inner world. And the more people have to cannibalize their own inner strength to survive, the more attractive external supports (sugar, alcohol, opiates, speed, nicotine, etc.) become.

Then people ask themselves to stop doing an activity or taking in a substance, and panic hits. People are truly asking themselves to become naked and alone. And they rarely understand the seriousness of this request.

Once a person learns about the brain's response to going it alone, it makes sense that whatever comforts them or makes them feel good or even a little high (like the way sugar, fat, and salt release endogenous opioids and oxytocin into the brain and body) might become a craving. The chances are very good that whatever can give people what they are missing so badly will become something they don't want to live without. This is the essence of addiction.

It is far easier to change the way brains are working by taking some brain-changing substance (indulging in an addiction) than it is to bring the resonant self-witness (RSW) in as support. Luckily, the more of a habit relying on our own warmth becomes, the less effort it takes to embody warmth for the self, so each time we choose this approach, it becomes more available.

The very best addiction programs help address the roots of loneliness and disconnection. This happens in powerful twelve-step groups with warm community and deep connection with higher power, whether they are for the addicts themselves or for the families of addicts. This has happened in Portugal, where the country decided over a decade ago to decriminalize addiction and instead pour the monetary resources into drug treatment, warm community, secure housing, and subsidized employment. Drug addiction is down 50 percent now in Portugal.[2]

Healing the roots of loneliness and disconnection can also happen in mindfulness-based relapse prevention programs that introduce people to the concept of self-regulation and help bring the fibers of attachment and self-connection to life. Outpatient and inpatient treatment programs where people weave together a sense of being warmly held by one another are also profoundly helpful. And this type of healing can occur when people awaken their RSW and begin to respond to themselves with more warmth and reassurance. For some, this will be the first time they have felt a true sense of being able to come home in body and mind.

BRAIN CONCEPT 13.1: TRAUMA AND THE NEUROBIOLOGY OF ADDICTION

There are a lot of different definitions for the word *addiction*. One of the simplest is "continued use despite harm." Addictions can be substances like alcohol, cigarettes, food, or drugs. Addictions can also be behaviors like compulsive buying, sexual activity, gambling, or working. Whether they are substances or behaviors, addictions are the brain's best effort to solve a problem. On a brain level, something is out of balance: people don't have the energy they need to function or socialize; they are experiencing physical pain or the pain of exclusion; they long to moderate their inner coldness with themselves so that they can feel warmth; emotions arise that they have no way to deal with; or they want to obliterate the voice of a savage default mode network (DMN). Any of these can lead to the craving for a substance or behavior. People are always trying to come back into a state of well-being and calm. Something emotional may be happening—often something that they don't even know about that their brain is trying to manage or resolve. The addiction is a strategy that the brain is sure about—it has worked before, when there hasn't been access to the RSW's warmth and understanding for self-soothing and to create well-being.

A person can carry an ongoing stimulus for pain within them every minute, such that they need their addiction every minute of the day. For example, if disgust or self-hate is intertwined with the sense of self, then every time a person thinks of anything that has to do with the self, there will be pain and the desire for the relief that the addictive substance or behavior originally gave them. Unhappily, the brain gets used to the addiction and starts to believe that its presence is the new normal, so it adjusts the flow of brain chemicals to keep everything balanced in the context of the feel-good experience of the addiction. In the flood of the addictive feel-good experience, the new balance reduces the flow of neurotransmitters and decreases the number of receptors for feel-good chemicals, creating a state even worse than before the addiction began. But with the reduced receptors, the compulsive behavior or substance no longer stops the pain, and then the person is in the grip of a compelling memory and habit, but the craving never stops. People live in a never-ending cycle of wanting their pain to stop, trying to get it to stop, and harming themselves and others in the process, causing even more pain. The use of external strategies to change the inside of the brain is ultimately self-defeating, as they harm our health and are a poor substitute for real self-care. The change needs to happen in the way we use our brains, not in the way we try to self-medicate our brains.

The more pain a person is in, and the more burden the brain carries from the fragmenting effects of trauma, the more compelling addictions can be. The ACE study (described in Chapter 6) shows us that each emotionally traumatic childhood experience doubles or triples our likelihood of using alcohol at an early age. If people experience both physical and sexual abuse, they are at least twice as likely to use drugs as those who only experienced one kind of abuse. And boys who experience four or more types of trauma are twelve times as likely to use intravenous drugs as boys who have not experienced trauma. If the boys experienced six different kinds of trauma, they are forty-six times more likely to use intravenous drugs.[3]

Of all the veterans that served in Vietnam, close to half tried heroin, but only 5 percent continued to use it addictively when they returned home.[4] Heroin's rate of addiction after one use is typically reported at around 23 percent, but these numbers contradict that statistic. Alcohol's reported rate of addiction is 23 percent, cocaine is 21 percent, and marijuana is 9 percent. The most addictive substance after one exposure is nicotine: of people who have used nicotine just once, 68 percent went on to long-term, habitual use.[5] But overall, you can tell by these numbers that the drugs themselves are not as addictive as we commonly believe. What is addictive is the desire to kill the pain or balance the brain. This may be surprising, since mostly people talk about substances being addictive and needing to avoid exposure to them (or "just say no" to them) rather than talking about pain causing addiction, and needing to heal and regrow the fibers of attachment in the brain.

One of the reasons for this focus on substances rather than pain and imbalance is that much of the addiction research has been done using rats living in laboratory conditions, which are extremely stressful (although this is usually unacknowledged): the rats are powerless, overcrowded, and stressed.

Canadian addiction researcher Bruce Alexander tested to see if the rats' addictive behavior would change if their living conditions changed.[6] He built an airy, spacious, and sociable environment for the rats in his care. He called it Rat Park, and put both male and female rats into it.

Alexander put two dispensers up for the rats in Rat Park. One contained morphine and the other did not. The rats did not want the morphine, not even when sugar was added to it (which they usually loved). So the scientists made some of the rats "addicted" by forcing them to drink morphine for weeks, so that they went into withdrawal if they didn't use it. The rats still avoided it when they had the choice.

In Rat Park, the more nurturing environment, the rats stayed away from the drug if they had the choice, even when they were physically dependent on it. In contrast, regular caged rats drank up to twenty times more morphine. No wonder so many soldiers stopped using opiates once they were outside of the environment of war and in the more nurturing environment of home.

Overall we do not hear much in the general press about the connection between pain and addiction. People who teach about addiction are reluctant to raise the subject of trauma as a root of addictive behavior because they don't feel prepared to discuss emotional material. I recently attended a school-district-sponsored class about addictions and teens, where the root cause of trauma was not mentioned once. I asked the educator whether she was aware of the ACE study and the connection between adverse childhood experiences and addictions. "This is not a therapy group," she replied. "There's no support for emotional processing here."

Another reason people don't talk about pain being at the root of addiction is because it takes embodied self-awareness, in itself an antidote to addiction, to be able to understand this. If people don't have an RSW in place, they ricochet right out of the connection between trauma and addiction. It is not possible for an unembodied brain to comprehend how interwoven addictions and compulsions are with trauma.

As people begin to work with addictions, they will often hear themselves saying, "There was nothing happening—I just wanted my addiction out of the clear blue sky. The craving came suddenly, and without reason." When things are really slowed down, though, the trail of clues that can lead us back to an understanding of the root problem or pain may become clear.

Let's take a look at the brain complexity of the so-called simple "just say no" approach to addiction.

Addiction and "Self-Control"

A helpful image in understanding the complexity of managing an addiction or compulsion is the metaphor of the elephant and its rider. An elephant's strength is far greater than its rider's. The deep brain structures, with their currents of habit, are likewise much stronger than an unregulated connection between the prefrontal cortex and the amygdala. What is necessary in both cases is communication between rider and elephant, between the RSW and the deep currents of brain habit. This can be done coercively—the dominant approach to addiction management in North American culture—or it can be done with acknowledgment of relationship and long-term habits of self-warmth, so that in the best of all possible worlds the elephant (body and deep habitual impulses) will have some willingness to be cared for and guided by the rider (the RSW).

One of the facets of addiction recovery is called "self-control," which has three main components: deferred gratification, response inhibition, and maintaining a goal in the face of distraction. The learning we have been doing in this book supports each of these three facets of the movement toward sobriety and choice.

- *Deferred gratification:* We need to remember that there is a longer-term goal than simple immediate satisfaction. In the best of both worlds, all parts of the brain are recruited to contribute to our move away from our addiction, including by helping us choose a different strategy and acting on this choice, and also by keeping our long-term well-being in mind.

- *Response inhibition:* How long does it take us to stop a behavior or impulse that we have already started? Stopping the automatic addictive reaction to a craving is a very complex act, requiring a lot of emotional resourcefulness. If we can get support from our RSW or from others, often we are more successful than if we try to muscle through on our own.
- *Maintaining a goal in the face of distraction:* In the midst of life and everything that it throws at us, are we able to stay focused on our goal of having a better life and making more life-serving choices? Again, staying connected to the RSW and any intentional community that supports us helps us to remember our long-term goals.

Recommendations for Support in Changing Addictive Behaviors

As people develop a warm yet firm responsiveness, they move closer to the life they were born to live. It is important to work on two levels: (a) to begin to clear the implicit minefield that knocks people off balance and sends them scurrying for the comfort of addiction (calming the elephant), and (b) to create the external and internal environment of conviction and support that comes with full commitment to an approach—if it is a twelve-step approach, then doing the step work; if we've chosen mindfulness, yoga, or exercise, then doing the daily practice (empowering the rider). The guided meditation that follows uses an empathy process to do a posthearsal (see Chapter 7) around a craving, clearing out emotional minefields that lead to relapse.

It is also important to understand that if people are using their addictions to manage absolutely everything, then they also need to structure their environment and their lives to minimize access to their substance or activity of choice. Every time people have to say no to their addiction (fight off a craving), they deplete their energy reserves for willpower and decision making. Therefore, the less often people are reminded by a cue of the addiction and have to say no, the more resources they have left to support themselves in their new behaviors. My recommendation is to clear the cookies out of the cupboard and put them down the garbage disposal, mix the marijuana stash into your compost, double bag the stash of pills and put them deep inside the coffee grounds in your garbage on garbage day, or unplug your computer or the television and put a cover over it when you aren't working or haven't planned to use it.

Healing from addictions includes working with the internal world: beliefs, memories, and emotions. It is also easier if our external world supports us—remember the rats in Rat Park. It doesn't matter if people can't change their external environment right now; they can just hold that change as an intention and as part of their self-acknowledgment. Even finding a twelve-step meeting that feels warm and supportive can be a positive change in our external environment. The most important thing is that we feel welcome in our world.

Healing from addictions is not simple. It's doable, but it asks a lot of people. It asks them to become truly alive. Addictions allow people to hide from and survive vast landscapes of pain. More than anything else, people need self-compassion, persistence, an understanding of the after-effects of trauma, and sources of resonant empathy outside of the self to allow them to heal and put in place brain pathways for self-connection.

Here is a guided meditation to help on this journey. Please note that research finds that distraction from cravings (diverting energy to exercise or other self-care strategies) is more supportive of moving away from cravings than is traditional mindfulness. This meditation should be used when you are feeling strong as a way to work with implicit mine-fields and to transform the inner landscape, rather than as a daily or minute-by-minute fallback to deal with cravings.

GUIDED MEDITATION 13.1: Holding a Craving With Gentleness and Open Curiosity

First of all, notice that you are experiencing a craving. In this moment of craving, invite a new response. While remaining aware of the craving, start to breathe, and bring your resonating self-witness into relationship with both your attention and your craving. See what the sensations of this craving are.

At first when you step into this invitation, you may think that your craving is just in your head, and that it is unbearable and irresistible. How does this craving speak in your body? As you breathe, how does this extreme wanting make itself known? Sometimes it is a heart-centered sensation. Sometimes it is in the face near the jaw. Sometimes it is in the gut.

As your body experiences this craving, ask it if it is trying to take care of you. Does it want to take care of your anxiety? Does it want to "gird" you against times of scarcity and lack? Is it trying to divert your attention from the pervasive sense of panic and emptiness?

Wherever you find sensations, ask yourself, if this sensation were an emotion, what would it be? Loneliness? Fright? Irritation? Hopelessness? And what would the needs that underlie these emotions be? Are you exhausted and longing for warm support to float you effortlessly through your life? Would it be lovely to have a magic cloud personally dedicated to your every comfort and success? Do you feel helpless in the face of the complexity of your days, and do you wish for simplicity and ease? Would you like to know the exact next best step for you and the people you love? And the best step after that? Do you long for an assurance of safety? And even saying that, do you need acknowledgment for how delicately balanced everything is, how fragile your life and the lives of the people you care about are? Would it be sweet, even for one instant, to have someone else actually understand everything that you are holding and balancing, and the care you take with it all?

Come back to your body, and see what is happening now with your sensations, your emotions, and your needs. Follow this emotional trail where it leads you, noticing that you can use any of the processes that you have learned so far: if you find that you are telling yourself a harmful belief about the self, follow it. If you find a painful memory, allow your resonating self-witness to move back into the memory with gentleness and care, again following body sensations with feelings and needs guesses.

As your body relaxes, take this opportunity to implement whatever self-care approaches work best for you in relationship with your addiction, whether that is calling someone in your support network, starting your mindfulness meditation, moving out for exercise, or something else.

WHY PRACTICE THIS GUIDED MEDITATION?

All of the work that we do, connecting with our bodies and clearing out the old stuff that trips us up and makes us mad, afraid, or sad, makes room for more choice, more ease, and more willingness to receive support from others. When we have more space to exist in balance with ourselves, it helps us make room to join the groups and learn the material that can change the existential aloneness of addiction into the capacity to be part of a warm community and rejoin the human race. Reconnecting to our RSW during this process, whether we relapse or not, puts us firmly on the path of healing (as we shall see in the next section).

Just as when we were looking at recovery for depression (see Chapter 12), it is most helpful to be creative and bring more than one approach to bear in our healing. For example, recovery rates for addiction are better with combinations of formal inpatient or outpatient treatment programs, counseling, and whatever twelve-step program is applicable, rather than any one approach on its own.

Working With Relapse

The statistics for the number of times people try to stop an addiction before they have periods of stable recovery reveal that the most important thing is to keep trying. Cigarette smokers "quit" many times before they actually stop for any period of time, and people who are alcohol dependent stop drinking a number of times before they make significant changes. What people most need as they struggle with the very human tendency to self-soothe with substances or activities are hope, self-trust, faith, and resilience.

The longer a person can stay in recovery, the greater the rate of long-term abstinence. For example, only about a third of people who are abstinent for less than a year will remain sober. For those who achieve sobriety for a year, less than half will relapse. Among those who make it to five years of sobriety, the chance of relapse is less than 15 percent.[7]

The more abusive we are to ourselves when we have a relapse, the longer our relapse will last, since addictions fit nicely into the anger-shame cycle of self-hate. If I am trying to create change in the way I eat, for example, and I have a piece of chocolate when I asked myself not to eat candy, and that makes me angry with myself and ashamed, then my system goes further out of balance, and I need more sugar to try to cope—I feel more shame, eat more chocolate, and so on, in a continuing cycle. If we are gentle with ourselves, then we don't add fuel to the fire of the relapse, and with the help of our RSW, we are able to move back into integrity with our original intentions for recovery.

The self-resonant approach in case of relapse might sound more like this:

Sarah, are you feeling angry at yourself? Do you long for committed self-care? Are you discouraged and exhausted when you think of how many times you've said you were stopping? Do you remember saying you wanted to change your life, and are you bewildered by the way that your intention loses meaning as you hit rough patches? Do you want sustained focus and to be able to rely on yourself? Are you

ashamed and worried, and do you want integrity? Do you need sup-
port, warmth, and gentleness? Do you long to know that you have
worth and can make contributions even as you struggle with your
humanness? Do you long for all people to know that they are a part of
the dance of true relationship, even as they are also using substances
or activities to survive?

What If the Pain Is Not Ours?

And sometimes what people are surviving goes far beyond the personal. People can be struggling with the socioeconomic effects of poverty, educational levels, war, and displacement, as well as the aftereffects of trauma. People can also be living with the multigenerational effects of all of these influences, which means that they are holding the pain of past generations in their own bodies, as the field of epigenetics shows.

Epigenetics researcher Moshe Szyf's prediction is that soon we will be able to read the history of trauma in our families by looking at our epigenetic structure. He bases this conclusion on his work with survivors of the 1998 ice storm in Quebec, who all showed similar epigenetic patterns of trauma.[8] This research indicates that, with both depression and addictions, people may be carrying emotional pain inherited from past generations. After hearing Szyf speak, I started to look at others in wonder, asking myself, are we all carrying the patterns of emotional pain from our parents and grandparents in addition to what we ourselves have experienced during this lifetime?

This curiosity has deepened my consideration of how to create supportive change with resonance, even when the question at hand is grief, depression, or addiction. In my practice I have used the basic processes developed by Susan Skye and added others that let me work with the body. These processes let us read the body's cues and follow them to where they point.

As I have tracked my body and my clients' bodies along the path of healing, I have found that many people do indeed carry accessible emotional loads that are not theirs, loads that really belong to past generations. My clients' bodies relaxed in new ways as I tested with them the resonance skill shown at the end of this chapter, which lightens the implicit load. In curiosity about my own experience, I also got two friends to sit with me as I dove into the sensation of the bottomless pit of my hunger.

Sarah's Story: My Father's Hunger

I have spent my life with a hollow leg for sugar and sweet things. When I tried to respond to myself with empathy about the longing, the hollow leg eased but never really disappeared. Over my fifty years I have never felt sick or full from eating sweets. When other people would say, "Too rich for me," my eyebrows would come together in incomprehension, wondering what it would be like to experience satiation.

So I decided to try the question on my insatiable hunger that I had been asking my clients: "If this weren't yours, whose would it be?" We're experimenting with our intuition in this approach. We're doing our best to tune in to the truth of our bodies. Sometimes we carry messages that are hard to digest. The question is not so much about literal truth as about the marks that family stories and beliefs have left on us physically.

I asked myself, "If this is not my hunger, whose is it?" I tried out my mother's body superimposed on my own, and it didn't feel like her hunger. When I asked if it were my father's body, the hunger sensation seemed truer. I started to hear his voice. My heart felt heavy, and my stomach felt empty. The thirteen-year-old boy my father had been began to speak from within me. I felt his exhaustion and despair when his father had posttraumatic stress disorder from World War I, and when his mother was put in a mental institution for a nervous breakdown during the Great Depression. When this happened, he and his brothers and sisters were split up to live with different relatives, who were violent and frightening. I could feel from the pain and anxiety in my stomach that I was carrying my father's worry for his mother, his concern for his younger siblings, and his anger and hopelessness when he thought about his father's helplessness. I guessed aloud about his longing to contribute, and about his ache for safety and support. I asked whether he was homesick and had a need for familiarity, and most of all, about his longing for his mother's well-being. My perception of my father's hunger, and his presence within me, faded as the resonant guesses landed.

I stayed with my body, and the sensations I was experiencing shifted. I felt my physical experiences change into my grandmother's quiet terror of breaking down emotionally, with a sensation almost like a black hole opening in my abdomen. I asked if she had a hunger for stability and solidity, and a determination to be well. Now my stomach crawled with a tentative anxiousness about being able to hold on to balance. I asked my grandmother within me if she were longing to be held with care herself. Was she needing tenderness, stability, renewal of her energy flow, and to know where solid ground was?

As my body relaxed and my sense of my relatives' presence within me eased, I thought about my grandmother's cookbook. There are fifty-six different cake recipes in her handwriting: snow cake, fig éclair, banana cake, filbert torte, orange cloud cake. . . . My best guess is that she made a cake every day of my father's childhood, except during the time of her mental illness. As I thought of those cakes, I began to understand the meaning of sweets in my father's body, and what I had learned from him without even knowing it.

Several days after doing the work, and after several weeks of the abstinence from sugar that usually is my best support for dealing with the bottomless hunger, I found myself at a party with my favorite German chocolate cake. I tried out a small slice to see what would happen with the never-ending black hole and found that the slice was just right for me and that I didn't need more. Since then I have become more acquainted with the strange experience of satiation.

As I asked the question, "If this hunger were't mine, whose would it be?", I found that I carried my father's and my grandmother's stories in my body. As I made guesses for the sensations I was feeling, my body eased in a way hat it had not relaxed when I was thinking of myself as subject only to the story of my own life. Whatever we can feel and bring understanding to will shift within us, whether we were the ones who originally experienced the story or not.

So this is the invitation: to ask the simple question, "If this (hunger, addiction, pain, depression, terror, or dissociation) were not mine, who would it belong to?" And to follow the aliveness of sensation in your body to see where it leads. The following resonance skill is an example of how to explore this for yourself.

RESONANCE SKILL 13.1: LIGHTENING THE IMPLICIT LOAD

1. Notice how the depression/anxiety/craving or other emotional pain feels in your body.
2. Ask yourself, "If this pain were not mine, whose would it be?" Check to see whether you have a sense that the depression/anxiety/craving occurs anywhere else in your family (mother, father, uncles, aunts, grandparents, etc.).
3. Allow yourself to feel your effected relative within you. Give yourself over to the imagination or to the felt bodily sense. (Allow yourself to go out on the limb—it's kind of a daring and whacky thing to do, but you never know what the body's wisdom is unless you open yourself to the possibility to hear it.) Are the sensations of depression/anxiety/craving similar?
4. Once you have a sense of who you might be working with, bring your RSW forward to make feelings and needs guesses based on what is happening in your body.
5. Check in with your own sense of depression/anxiety/craving.

6. Repeat steps 1–5, looking for layers of others' experiences—and your own personal pain may be layered into the complex family experience as well. As long as you are following your body, you are in the right place.

This work does not mean that we are becoming our parent's mother or father. We are not taking care of them in the outer world. We are working with the emotional patterns that are living within our own bodies.

If you are angry with any of these people, or if trauma or abuse has been experienced in your family, you may not feel much empathy for them, and this process may not be the right approach. If your body recoils in horror at the thought of doing this work, listen to it. When the time is right, if it ever is, you will not be horrified by the idea of offering resonance for your family as they live on in you.

Even though we are vulnerable to the effects of past generations' traumas, we can make meaning from our place in the family story and our family's history. Any sensation we can feel will shift in some way with attuned understanding. Our work is to become our best selves, the people we were born to be. Sometimes the path to our best self includes understanding and empathy for the lives that our past generations lived. Sometimes we are stopped from moving forward by old griefs and worries that we carry on behalf of a grandparent or ancestor, by outrage, injustice, unacknowledged pain, or heartbreak. As we hold these experiences with compassion, we are released to move more fully into our own lives.

Joy, Community, and Our Outside Voice: Bringing Our Resonating Witness to Others

Welcome to the End of This Book!

Here we are at our last chapter. The work we have done has in some small way engaged our nervous systems and, with any luck, has brought us to view ourselves more gently and more compassionately than we have experienced before.

People need empathy for feelings of delight, anticipation, excitement, happiness, glee, joy, passion, love, and celebration just as much as they need to receive resonance for emotions that are more difficult to experience. When these positive expressions are not shared, sensation can get caught in the chest like frozen champagne bubbles, creating discomfort and even shame. Shame is at its most intense when an emotional bridge of excitement, delight, or celebration is not caught or, even worse, is met with ridicule or scorn.

As we move toward the possibility that we are safe, that we make sense, and that we belong on this earth and to humanity, our nervous systems and our bodies relax. Our heart can be in a dance of relationship with everything that is happening around us. Our facial muscles can be alive and responsive to the faces that we meet. We can look at others and see past their trauma and their reserve to the way that their hearts would be expressing if they, too, felt safe. We can know ourselves and others more deeply.

BRAIN CONCEPT 14.1: THE VENTRAL VAGAL COMPLEX (SOCIAL ENGAGEMENT AND SELF-CONNECTION)

You may recall from Chapter 7 the description of the vagus nerve, the large bundles of nerves that connect the inside of the torso with the brain. You may also recall what happens with the vagus when we feel safe: energy and information traveling between the body and the brain shift into the myelinated (fast) fibers in this large nerve. Researcher Stephen Porges calls this the transition to ventral vagal or social engagement (as opposed to fight-or-flight and immobilization responses). Everything starts to move faster, and our brain can keep up with all the complex emotions we and others are experiencing as we inhabit our social world.

We automatically move into this way of being when we feel safe and welcome. Our breathing is deep and full, we laugh and smile easily, eye contact is easy, our ear is tuned to the sound range of the human voice, social grace comes without thought, we lose our self-consciousness, and we truly relax into flow. No matter how far away this state seems in this moment, it still lives within each of us. If we've never really experienced it, we've never really felt safe, and we still get to look forward to knowing ourselves more fully as we relax.

Here is a list of all the ways our bodies relax and function well when we are in social engagement (when we have a sense that we matter and belong):[1]

- The fine muscles of the face come alive to express emotion and help us understand others.[2]
- The eyes focus on the human face.[3]
- The muscles of the middle ear tighten to focus on the sound range of the human voice.[4]
- The larynx relaxes to support lively vocal expression.[5]
- The heart has high heart rate variability.[6]
- The bronchii of the lungs expand to take in more oxygen.[7]

- The viscera get the "go" signal with full blood supply to support better functioning.[8]

This book is about removing the barriers that stop us from reaching our own individual, natural state of grace. It has taken us on a path that acknowledges what is true, validates all the emotions as having very good reasons for existing, and moves us toward resonance and self-compassion.

Reader's Story: How It's Different Now

More and more these days, when my default network reverts to the memories of pain and shame, I am able to move to sit beside myself with care and gentle curiosity, helping my amygdala to calm with resonance, and transforming the painful memories into simple autobiography. When the emotions are too big for me to hold on my own, I know how to reach out.

To do this, I need to believe that my own experience matters. All the old core beliefs about doing it on my own come roaring up in these moments. The ones about not being worth the trouble for others are particularly powerful. To counteract this tendency in myself, I make dates with my friends to take turns being heard without receiving advice or comments, just resonance, so that those outdated beliefs don't keep me isolated.

This journey has led me to intense delight, sometimes quiet, sometimes noisy. I often feel satisfied and happy about contribution, self-understanding, and compassion. There are moments when I have a dawning understanding that joy might be possible, and might even become common. There are many moments when I still struggle with shame, when I interpret the world through the lens that I have done something wrong. And then I know that I can reach out for support and come back out into exploration and approach life fully.

When we look at our brains and see that we affect one another, we are changed. Words are inadequate to describe the social interconnection that is essential for human well-being. It's almost like we have to say the word *relationship* and then stop, breathe, and let ourselves feel what happens in our body when we say it, with full imagination of richness and possibility.

As we practice these ideas, our brains create a model that other brains can follow for comfort and healing. When we look at the work of James Coan and see that our physical pain and sense of effort in life is lessened by the presence of another,[9] we are changed. We are being invited into something lively and indefinable. It is an invitation to spend time on relationship, to value the contributions we make to one another, and to prioritize warm community. It is also a tremendous and beautiful invitation to self-resonance.

There is more to reach for, more territory to heal into, but this is a solid place to stand on. With this approach, we find reliable and constant ground for ourselves, and we become more able to reach out to others, both to receive and to give support.

GUIDED MEDITATION 14.1: Meditation to Support Joy

It is very hard to fully occupy social engagement if no one else is relaxed. And it is hard to celebrate our accomplishments and achievements on our own. This meditation supports accompaniment for moments of celebration when we might otherwise be alone. Before you begin, choose something that you have done or experienced lately that you are proud of, some small satisfaction, moment of pleasure, or breath of awe that you have not been able to share.

> Begin by breathing. As you feel your breath moving in your body, notice how far down in your lungs the air reaches. Spend a few moments riding your breath in, as far down as it easily goes, and out of your lungs and nose, letting your attention follow your breath. Your attention may wander, as attention does. Gently, and with warmth, bring your attention back to the sensation of the movement of your breath.
>
> Now bring your gentle attention to your satisfying moment.

What are the body sensations of this celebration? Are there crinkles around your eyes? Do you get a slightly deeper breath? Do your ribs expand? Or is there a little pain or contraction in your chest? When celebration has not been held with others, it can lodge in our bodies like a small cramp and prevent relaxation and expansion.

Bring your attention to your heart. Is your heart proud of you? Is it gently (or brilliantly) happy that you have had this success? Is it a pleasure to remember your contribution? As you acknowledge your heart's experience, you may have a physical sensation of a glow of happiness, radiating in all directions from your chest.

And now see what is happening with your stomach. Are your abdominal muscles tight, trying to support you as you celebrate this accomplishment on your own? Are they not sure you are safe to really spend a few moments of enjoyment? If so, offer them a little acknowledgment that it might feel odd to celebrate things on your own. See if they would like to take a little hidden satisfaction, maybe a sensation like champagne bubbles moving from abdomen to chest. As you acknowledge these muscles and their careful holding of you, do they relax at all?

And if you want to, you can explore something more intense— maybe a wild jolt of joy that is sharp and sudden, like lightning in your torso, neck, or head—or perhaps a grin that escapes and lights up your whole face. Do your mouth and throat want to burst out with a shout of fun excitement? Are your feet wiggling? Do your cells want to jump up and down in a happy dance? Are you a little amazed by what you've done? Are you surprised to find yourself at the finish line? Is there a mix of settling into relief and lifting into expressions of delight?

Now, let yourself return to your breathing. Is it any different now that you have made this journey of positive acknowledgment? Let your attention ride your breath down into your lungs. How far down do you go? What happens at the lower end of your breath? And follow it out again, bringing your attention back to the external world.

RESONANCE SKILL 14.1: TAKING YOUR RESONANCE INTO THE WORLD

Another way to learn about resonance is to practice attuning to and wondering verbally with others about whether you are understanding them. It helps to become familiar with the lists of "pleasant" and "unpleasant" feelings (Chapter 3) and the list of universal human needs and values (Chapter 4). The traditional Nonviolent Communication formulation is, "Are you feeling _____ because you are needing _____?" This can feel awkward and a little clunky, and sometimes touching on feelings at all can seem intrusive. Here are four main steps to streamline it and use it with other people:

1. Approach the other person with respect. We don't know what's happening for them, and their experience is sacred, so we are asking them, not telling them. It's a guess, not a report.
2. Unless you have an intimate relationship and a lot of trust with the other person, or a formal agreement to use feelings words, try guessing the person's feelings silently but not naming them.
3. Guess what need might be most important: "Do you need to be heard?"
4. And then listen to what the person says.

I invite you to experiment with just wondering about needs, and maybe with putting them into global terms, like these examples:

- To the cashier who has just dealt with a difficult customer in front of you in line: "Would you like a little respect?"
- To your child when her teacher has given her a demerit: "I wonder if you like it better when your intentions are seen?
- To your brother after he's had a difficult conversation with your father: "Do you enjoy calm tones of voice and maybe even some gentleness?"

273

- To your friend when she's found out her partner was lying to her: "Do you need honesty and reliability?"

If you get your courage up to use language in this unfamiliar way, notice what happens after you ask your question. Does this person say yes and nod emphatically? Does this person say, "No, it's more like this . . . "? Does this person (possibly a teenager) say, "Well, duh!"? Each of these responses signals true communication, because in each case this person is letting you know that your sincere effort to connect has been received. It doesn't matter if we are right or wrong, although we are doing our best to reflect what we understand is happening. It matters only that we are genuinely, warmly interested in what the other person's experience really is.

It can be hard to make guesses with someone who responds "Well, duh!," even though that is a resounding yes, due to the shame you may feel arise within you. Just notice if that shuts you down and don't force yourself to try in that particular relationship, unless you can really hear the yes, and you feel more connected with that person. Hold yourself with gentleness. Explore this new way of communicating when it feels rich and rewarding.

Think back to how you felt before you began reading this book. Do you feel any different? Here is a big-picture look at the landscape we've traveled.

What Did We Find in This Territory of Healing?

Let's think about the journey we have taken. First of all, we invited our brain to start seeing itself by listening for the way we speak to ourselves when we aren't doing anything in particular, listening to our default mode network (DMN). We started to recognize the kinds of words our savage DMN uses to try to manage us.

That recognition opened the door to understanding the relationship between the part of the brain that we are calling our emotional alarm system (the amygdala) and the part we are calling our resonating self-witness (RSW), which includes our prefrontal cortex (PFC), and how the alarm system can turn everything else off in service of survival. We started to understand that when we feel a lot of stress, the parts of our brain dedicated to conscious learning and memory get shut down. We can even grow up believing we are stupid when in actual fact we have all the brain cells we need, but we haven't been able to use them because we have been trying to survive stress and trauma. As our PFC becomes stronger and better able to internalize the warmth we have experienced in our lives, it becomes possible to respond to ourselves in an entirely new way, with resonance. Then we start to release some of the emotional burdens of the past.

Our amygdala is not just our emotional alarm system—in order to keep us safe, it indexes emotional memory without any reference to time. This is the way traumatic memories are stored. When a memory is held in this way by the amygdala, and it surfaces so that we can feel it, it becomes available for resonant response and resolution.

The other type of memory is explicit memory, managed by the hippocampus and stored throughout the brain, time-stamped and ordered, with the past clearly the past. Once we understand this, we see that trauma is present in any memory that continues to nag us, little things like grudges and irritations, or big things like posttraumatic stress. The good news about this is everything that we can feel (step into gently, so that our body is alive with sensation but is not flooded) is available for resonance and healing.

Resonance happens effortlessly when other people really get us. It's like their emotional world vibrates at the same frequency as ours. To bring yourself into attunement with another human, you must bring your body into the picture. You can't attune by offering advice, or by telling someone how to think about something, or by changing the subject. You can come into a resonant state by offering body sensations, or by wondering what people are longing for, or what fuels them, or what they are reaching for. You can come closer to attunement by asking whether a visual image or a metaphor that is coming to mind as other people speak has any meaning for them. There is a kind of precision that both people arrive at when the conversation moves in this direction, an emotional precision about what's really happening that helps create relaxation and meaning making.

As we begin to listen more carefully to our bodies, an acceptance of the importance of our early relationship with our mother's neurobiology can start to emerge. We begin to ask, what was it like in the womb that nurtured us? Was our mother anxious, or maybe depressed? Was she well supported during her pregnancy? What was it like in *her* mother's womb? How many generations of similar emotional tone have come down to our prenatal selves? Bringing together the dawning sense of our RSW with this knowledge, we begin to connect with our earliest body memories and sensations, and we start to notice that we can hold and soothe anything that we can feel.

The relationship that our mother has with her brain gets passed along to us. We tend to use our brain the same way she did, particularly to self-manage or self-regulate. These tendencies are called attachment patterns. We learned about avoidant attachment, an ongoing state of doing it on our own; ambivalent attachment, where we move right from enjoyment of life into a stress reaction, with no middle ground; the paradoxical fear of intimacy that is disorganized attachment; and finally everything coming together in the best of all possible worlds: secure or earned secure attachment. The behavior that distinguishes securely attached parents from all other parents is their sensitivity and responsiveness to what is happening for the child.[10]

All people who are important to us give us the pattern of the way they use their brain. Mothers, fathers, grandparents, siblings, teachers, and friends all give us the gift of themselves. We learn from one another, and we are patterned by one another. We have different styles of attachment with each person, depending on how safe we feel and whether that person is capable of delighting in us.

Being delighted in as a soul, the unique unfolding of what we brought to this life mingled with the contributions of everyone who has ever been important to us, is a key part of the awakening of the felt sense of self in the first two years of our lives. If we don't receive the attunement and resonance that we need when we are infants and small toddlers, we continue to do the work of nourishing earned secure attachment as we get older, taking in warmth and love where we find it. If it's hard to trust enough to take in warmth and love so that we can heal, we can still learn to hold ourselves with acknowledgment and acceptance right where we are.

As we get older and move out into the world away from our parents, we make new relationships with other people. We have styles of attachment relationships with other people different from the ones we had with our parents. And if we come from an insecure attachment connection in our family of origin, but we meet people who are sources of secure attachment for us, we heal and move toward earned secure attachment ourselves. Other people start to exist for us, we notice when we've dropped the relational connection, and we have the capacity to return to it if we choose.

The body plays an essential role in every part of our journey toward integration. It is always a step ahead of us in emotional understanding. The body's pathways for communication with the brain involve the embodied self-awareness network and the vagus nerve complex. As you may remember from previous chapters, the vagus is the nerve bundle in front of our spinal column and behind our heart that runs from the body to the skull-brain (most of the fibers run up, and only 10–20 percent run back down). It's a highway of information that lets us know how we're doing in the world. We so often believe that we are making decisions based on rational ideas about what we should and shouldn't do. However, once we start to come into relationship with the incredible amount of information that's coming in through our bodies, we realize that, when bodies are supported by well-regulated brains, they are our main resource for knowing what we are longing for and taking action to realize our dreams.

You may recall that the vagus nerve complex is the part of the body in charge of movement in response to a sense of safety in the world—fight, or anger; flight, or fear; and immobilization, or dissociation—depending on perceived effectiveness and/or hopelessness. In accordance with the emotional tone of our family of origin, we can arrive at adulthood living largely in a state of fight, flight, or immobilization. Again, for most of us, as long as we can start to feel our body, name sensations and emotions, and find the longings that are at the root of our experience, our states will begin to change, and our bodies will become easier to live in.

It is important to know that we all have our own way of experiencing the world and that we each need to be open to what kinds of resonance are most helpful for us. For those of us with dissociated parts, we can learn to be exquisitely gentle and accepting. We each find what works for us.

As we become clearer about the neurobiological load that we carry along with our emotional burdens, we begin to have a sense about the impact of shame, how it can become entangled with our sense of self, the importance of being received with delight, and how rarely this essential experience may have happened for us. The same circuits that carry physical pain also light up when we are excluded or have a sense that we don't belong.[11] Because of the limitations of a child's brain, we end up believing that we are bad, instead of seeing the limitations of the people caring for us.

We are truly emotion-centered beings. We can't even make good decisions about how to use our money, something we would think would be grounded in logic, if we don't have access to our emotions.[12] Without a strong and resonating PFC, our emotions run us, instead of simply giving us their input. Because we are infinitely inventive beings, we use them against ourselves to self-manage. If we're expressing bigger energy than our family of origin enjoyed or was originally safe, we can shame ourselves into submission. The self-directed anger and contempt of self-hate are a handy, ever-available tool to make ourselves small enough so that we stay within our internalized window of welcome for emotion and expression.

The self-hate cycle is also a key player in anxiety, depression, addictions of all kinds, thinking about suicide, and actually committing suicide. The more we've been parented with acknowledgment and repair, the more resilient we are, and the less likely we are to self-destruct in these ways.

By letting the brain look at itself and think about itself, we start to create neural networks that support us to live in a new, gentler way, less driven by our implicit glaciers, with more choice, and more in relationship with the present moment. We have learned that when we name emotional experience we support our brain's well-being, and that we can harness our natural capacity to learn in ways that will help us heal.

And as we transform our inside voice, we start to change our outside voices, too, bringing new life to our families and communities and forming new connections with others who are transforming their inside voices. As we feel safe, we use words in ways that let others feel safe, too. Our bodies relax together as the patterns of communication shift and we learn to take more responsibility for our thoughts, our words, our actions.

At the same time, we are infinitely human and infinitely at play in the fields of the implicit, humbled by our not knowing, brought to our knees by our own fears, jealousies, and pettiness, and returned to standing and sustained by the timeless warmth that has been given to us by those who have loved us.

The very act of reading about these parts of your brain begins to invite connections to form between them, giving birth to your RSW, even if the possibility of self-compassion still feels very far away. This learning starts small in our brains and gradually becomes deeper and more complex as we live it. It becomes less and less possible to believe that we or other people are wrong or bad, and we start to see the aftereffects of trauma in the stamp of everyday life. We begin to notice that our old ideas about what people deserve and how life should be are more cramped and limited than we enjoy. Other people become more interesting; children become miracles again. Every time we touch on this learning, we uncover more implications and connections for the entirety of our lives.

When we catch people's life energy, and when ours is caught, a collective neuroception of safety arises (we know we're safe at the level of our cells). The lived experience of being safe and welcome with another person, not to mention being safe within a group, can be a completely foreign concept before we've ever read this material. It changes the way we talk to each other and how we listen. Our system moves into its truly social state, with warmth, gentleness, and delight. In this state, we are easily able to integrate, understand, and shift away from introducing stress into our language and gestures, allowing gentle and playful respect to take its place. Once this approach to being starts to catch hold, our relationships and communities are transformed.

Final Wondering About How It Was to Read This Book

I wonder if you feel some relief at reaching the end of this book. Is there a little delight at the hope you have found in these pages? Are you grateful to yourself for making the journey? Might there be a little overwhelm, too, and a longing for ease? Now that you have read the words, would you love to have all the knowing installed in your brain and your body without effort? If there is mourning for lost time and life energy from before you learned all of this, would you like to jump right over that grief? Do you need any time for grieving and releasing any anger, resentment, or helplessness? Do you need the enormity of your mourning to be acknowledged? And now, is there hope because you have a sense of being able to see the whole of the healing journey and you are starting to travel this road?

Self-Assessment Review

Here is a review for you, to take you back through what you have learned in this book. As you read the questions, let your body respond with a yes or a no to each item. The items you answer no to will let you know where to focus your guided meditations. There are no right or wrong answers, just a series of doors to open to see where they might lead. Let your resonating self-witness take your hand as you read:

Introduction
0.1 I know that my brain can change for the better.

Chapter 1
1.1 I know what a default mode network (DMN) is and how its tone impacts me.
1.2 I can hear the voice of my DMN.
1.3 Here are some of the things my DMN tells me: _____
1.4 I can invite my attention to come to my breath.
1.5 I understand that it is natural for my attention to wander away from whatever I ask it to do, as it is trying to make sure that I'm noticing what it thinks is important.
1.6 I can be gentle and warm with my attention, no matter what it does.

Chapter 2
2.1 I know that I have an amygdala, body sensations, and an emotional life.
2.2 I know that I have a prefrontal cortex (PFC) that can help me be capable of compassion and empathy.
2.3 I recognize that if I can have a flash of warmth for my attention, I might be able to start having some warmth for my whole self.
2.4 If self-warmth is hard, I can reduce the difficulty level by focusing on just one representative cell.

Chapter 3

3.1 I understand what a resonating self-witness (RSW) is and how this concept represents a web of associations that lets my PFC cradle my amygdala, calming, soothing, and regulating me.

3.2 I believe I am developing or will be able to develop an RSW.

3.3 I can make this pathway of self-compassion robust and capable of sustaining me through much of life's turbulence.

3.4 I understand that the sensations in my body help me know what emotions I'm feeling.

3.5 I can recognize gradations and nuances of my emotions.

3.6 I believe I am a complex person who feels every emotion, not just a few of them.

3.7 I understand how, if I feel an emotion every time I'm aware that I exist, that emotion can get tangled up with how I am. I can end up feeling like I was born angry, or ashamed, or anxious, or frightened.

3.8 I recognize that even if self-warmth is difficult, I, like all mammals, have a CARE circuit embedded in my brain patterns. I have the structure to support warmth for self and others here in my brain by virtue of being a mammal.

Chapter 4

4.1 I understand that my sense of self is made from every interaction I've ever had with other people, all combined.

4.2 I believe that it is possible that the voice of my savage DMN (if I have one) is trying to contribute.

4.3 It is possible to imagine that every emotion I have is linked to my deep longings and values.

4.4 If I cannot hear the voice of my body and my emotions, I may dismiss or discount my own experience and intuition.

4.5 I suspect that without an RSW, I might try to handle my emotional life by shaming and criticizing myself or by controlling my external or internal world.

4.6 I see that my inner critic is trying its best to contribute to my well-being. In other words, my inner judge wants to enrich my life, improve my circumstances, help me live up to my values, and help me stay true to my highest intentions—an integrity nag or bully.

4.7 I recognize how to work with my inner critic's voice by following my body sensations and making resonant feelings guesses and needs guesses.

Chapter 5

5.1 I have wondered about the roots of my anxiety, if I have it.

5.2 If I have anxiety, I have looked at my sense of my earliest experience of this deep worry.

5.3 I have wondered about what it was like to be in my mother's womb, and about my mother's experience when she was pregnant with me, and her mother's experience, and her mother's experience.

5.4 I understand that there are two roots of anxiety: fear and loneliness.

5.5 I have at least a handshake acquaintance with my anterior cingulate cortex (ACC), my brain's hamster wheel of anxiety.

5.6   I understand that as my RSW holds my anxious self with more and more power, gentleness, and understanding, my anxiety will start to calm, no matter what is happening in the outside world.

Chapter 6

6.1   I recognize that when a memory is painful and vivid, it is available for retrospective resonance.

6.2   I understand the value of making notes about any painful memories that I have.

6.3   I have begun to explore what it is like to time travel to these painful memories with resonance and bring them warm curiosity and understanding.

6.4   I understand that when my body relaxes in the presence of the memory that used to be painful, I have received the emotional information that was there for me.

6.5   I understand and hold with compassion the multiple blows that have created any posttraumatic stress for me, and I commit to bringing exquisite gentleness to the part of me that carries the aftereffects of trauma.

Chapter 7

7.1   I can tell there is life energy in my own and others' anger.

7.2   I can tell the difference between social engagement and fight-or-flight responses in myself and others.

7.3   I can be in the presence of anger and remember that I am safe.

7.4   I can recognize when I am in fight mode, rather than in real relationship with others.

7.5   I recognize the importance of making repairs with others who have been impacted by my anger.

7.6   I have begun using the posthearsal process to begin to change my responses to things and decrease the levels of everyday anger that I carry.

7.7   I am no longer afraid of my own and others' anger.

Chapter 8

8.1   I have compassion for my fear and can bring my RSW to stand beside me when I am scared.

8.2   I acknowledge the importance of having a safe place, even if I can't imagine one.

1.3   I understand how terrified children can be, and how terrified I might have been.

8.4   I recognize that both terror and rage stop the digestive system in its tracks, and that I need a neuroception of safety in order to have full health and well-being.

8.5   I am beginning to understand the implications of disorganized attachment and how terror might fracture a brain.

8.6   I recognize that, when I discount my terror, the dismissing voice is not connected to my body and my emotions.

8.7   I'm willing to try to imagine a safe place for myself.

Chapter 9

9.1   I am starting to comprehend the nonnegotiable need for belonging among humans.

9.2   I understand the concept of the window of welcome—the space that is open in a relationship for emotional expression and intensity.

9.3 I have started to see my own window of welcome in action for myself and others.

9.4 I see the relationship between not being acknowledged and the feeling of shame that can arise in social situations.

9.5 I know that we all can feel shame when our life energy is not acknowledged.

9.6 I understand how to bring gentle reassurance to my shamed self.

9.7 I recognize that dissociation has always been a protective strategy, even if it has become more difficult to live with now.

9.8 I have a fairly good idea about the ways that my childhood was not safe or did not provide the opportunities for hope, accompaniment, being supported, or a sense of agency that I want every child to have.

9.9 I know that if I do not feel safe, my nervous system will go first into fight-or-flight mode and then, if neither or those states is helpful, into the immobilization mode.

9.10 I understand that I can live predominantly in alarm (fight or flight) or dissociation (immobilization), and that as my RSW gains ground, I will begin to spend more time feeling safe, and my nervous system will spend more time in social engagement.

Chapter 10

10.1 I understand that the ways my parents used their brains to self-manage and self-regulate are likely the ways that I use my brain.

10.2 I have some warmth for the part of myself that believes I have to do it all alone (avoidant attachment).

10.3 I can bring tenderness and resonance to the part of me that goes into immediate alarm and distress (ambivalent attachment).

10.4 If I have the sense of starting from a different attachment style, I see myself reaching for earned secure attachment by accompanying myself with warmth, care, and understanding.

Chapter 11

11.1 I understand that the self-hate cycle is an attempt to survive.

11.2 I recognize that when I get angry at myself, I might make my life energy small and manageable by putting myself into immobilization (shaming myself into submission).

11.3 I recognize that I might use anger to try to beat myself up so that I will come out of immobilization (shame myself into action).

11.4 I have started to develop some skepticism about the veracity of the voice of my inner critic (the DMN).

Chapter 12

12.1 If I suffer from depression, I have begun to identify the role that my negative self-talk plays in my experience of remaining depressed.

12.2 I see that there are two forms of depression, one representing lifelong loneliness and the other representing negative self-image.

12.3 I am holding myself with compassion for either or both experiences, if they are mine.

12.4 I understand that the more warmth and resonance I can bring to any critical voices that are amplifying my depressive experiences, the more energy there will be to explore the healing avenues that will support regaining well-being.

Chapter 13

13.1 I understand that addictions or compulsions are our brain's attempts to self-regulate.

13.2 I see the impact that past traumas have on brains, especially the number of different kinds of traumas, and how they fracture brains, making addictions more compelling to keep brains functioning.

13.3 I see the impact that traumas from previous generations may have on the present experience of addiction in families.

13.4 It makes sense to me that the more resonance we can bring to transforming strategies for self-regulation, the more room we make to support recovery.

Chapter 14

14.1 I viscerally comprehend the importance of an empathetic, resonant response to pleasant emotions like joy, awe, delight, excitement, and happiness, as well as more traditionally difficult emotions.

14.2 I can make my warmth and caring for others visible, and I can begin to see myself as capable of attachment to others.

14.3 I recognize the importance of warm community.

14.4 I believe I can live a life of rich community and connection with self and others.

14.5 I am willing to turn to my community for help and support when I am overwhelmed, frozen, frightened, or enraged.

14.6 I can make decisions out of my sense of integrity and connection to self.

14.7 I am finding my meaning and purpose emerging from my sense of my true self.

14.8 I am becoming willing to respond with resonance to others as well as to myself.

Online Resources

To download the recordings of the guided meditations: http://www.yourresonantself.com

Sarah Peyton's website: http://www.empathybrain.com

For body-oriented therapy:
Body psychotherapy: http://usabp.org/
Hakomi: http://hakomi.com
Rosen Method: http://roseninstitute.net/
Somatic Experiencing: http://somaticexperiencing.com

To learn more about Nonviolent Communication:
Center for Nonviolent Communication: http://www.cnvc.org
Your Resonant Self Integration Program: http://www.yourresonantself.org

To find interpersonal neurobiology resources:
Bonnie Badenoch:http://www.nurturingtheheart.com (Bonnie Badenoch is the author
    of *Being a Brain-Wise Therapist: A Practical Guide to Interpersonal Neurobiology* and
    wrote the Foreword to this book. Although Bonnie's name is not mentioned on the
    homepage, persist! You have found her website.)
Global Association for Interpersonal Neurobiology Studies: http://www.mindgains.org
Daniel Siegel, M.D.: http://www.drdansiegel.com

To follow some of the researchers discussed in this book:
James Coan, Ph.D.: https://jamescoan.com
Matthew D. Lieberman, Ph.D.: http://www.scn.ucla.edu/people/lieberman.html
Jaak Panksepp, Ph.D.: https://ipn.vetmed.wsu.edu/people/faculty-ipn/panksepp-j
Stephen Porges, Ph.D.: http://stephenporges.com

Recommended Reading

Badenoch, B. (2008). *Being a brain-wise therapist: A practical guide to interpersonal neuro-biology.* New York, NY: Norton.

Badenoch, B. (2011). *The brain-savvy therapist's workbook.* New York, NY: Norton.

Bowers, E. (2016). *Meet me in hard-to-love places: The heart and science of relationship success.* Vancouver, BC: Eric Bowers.

Fogel, A. (2013). *Body sense: The science and practice of embodied self-awareness.* New York, NY: Norton.

Maté, G. (2010). *In the realm of hungry ghosts: Close encounters with addiction.* Berkeley, CA: North Atlantic Books.

McGilchrist, I. (2009). *The master and his emissary: The divided brain and the making of the Western world.* New Haven, CT: Yale University Press.

Morgan, B. (2015). *Coming home: A first step into the world of family constellations.* Bucharest: Editura Har Tios.

Perry, B. D., & Szalavitz, M. (2006). *The boy who was raised as a dog, and other stories from a child psychiatrist's notebook: What traumatized children can teach us about loss, love, and healing.* New York, NY: Basic Books.

Siegel, D. J. (2015). *The developing mind: Toward a neurobiology of interpersonal experience.* New York, NY: Guilford Press.

Van der Kolk, B. (2015). *The body keeps the score: Brain, mind and body in the healing of trauma.* New York, NY: Penguin Books.

Wolynn, M. (2016). *It didn't start with you: How inherited family trauma shapes who we are and how to end the cycle.* New York, NY: Viking.

Glossary

ACC: anterior cingulate cortex, or anterior cingulate; the forward part of a girdle-shaped bit of **cortex** tucked inside the **skull-brain** in front of the **posterior cingulate cortex**; especially important for the integration of emotions and thoughts and for consideration of our own autobiography. It helps us put ourselves into the past, present, and future social context of our world. A key player in anxiety, it is sometimes considered a part of the **DMN**.

Accompaniment: the real or imagined presence of a person who we feel cares about us; one of the forms of self-regulation.

ACE study: Adverse Childhood Experiences study, a huge study (17,000 participants) that correlated experiences of trauma with ill health, addiction, and early death.

Adult attachment styles: the categories that attachment researchers use when they are talking about patterns of adult attachment: secure, fearful avoidant, dismissive avoidant, and anxious/preoccupied.

Alexithymia: the inability to read the emotional messages of the body; body blindness.

Ambivalent attachment: a pattern of bonding in which people move directly into fight-or-flight response under stress; these people are continually trying to get resourced and sending behavioral signals of distress and are not easily soothed.

Amygdala: an organ in the **limbic system** responsible for emotional and **implicit memory** (nonconscious) that filters everything that comes in, automatically sorting present-day experience to identify similarities to difficult or dangerous situations from our past and sounding the alarm when it finds matches.

Anterior: a direction within the brain and body, toward the front; also **frontal**.

Anxiety: an emotion that the body interprets as a warning sign that something is wrong, a persistent feeling state of dread and anticipation; 50 percent of the time it is accompanied by depression.

Anxious-preoccupied attachment: an **adult attachment style** in which people want to be completely emotionally intimate with others but often find that others are reluctant to get as close as they would like. They are uncomfortable being without close relationships but sometimes worry that others don't value them.

Association: the linkage by thought patterns of neurons and brain areas that may not even be touching one another.

Attachment: learning about how to bond and what to expect from relationships.

Attunement: someone bringing their attention to rest on us with warmth, respect, and curiosity, and letting their whole body-brain system wonder what it is like to be us.

Avoidant attachment: a pattern of bonding in which people have learned to take care of themselves because they don't have the sense that others are a resource for them.

Axon: the root of a **neuron**.

Brain: the entire nervous system running throughout the body, including the brain in the skull.

CARE circuit: One of Panksepp's seven **circuits of emotion**, supporting warmth and affection and nurturing others and the self.

Cerebellum (Latin for "little brain): a small, low part of the **skull-brain**; coordinates thought and action; is affected by abuse.

Circuits of emotion: the seven basic emotional networks that carry our different life energies as mammals, as defined by neuroscientist Jaak Panksepp: **CARE, SEEKING, PANIC/GRIEF, RAGE, LUST, FEAR,** and **PLAY**.

Cortex: the part of our brain that thinks; it is like a skin covering the whole **skull-brain**. The cortex (Latin for "bark") is also called the gray matter.

Cortisol: a chemical that the brain and body work together to produce to mobilize resources when there is stress and to turn off the stress response when safety has returned.

Dendrite: a branch of a neuron.

Depression: a persistent feeling or state of sadness, loss of a sense of pleasure, and loss of interest in life; can be accompanied by fatigue and constant overwhelm; 50 percent of the time it is accompanied by **anxiety**.

Dismissive avoidant attachment: an **adult attachment style** in which people are comfortable without close emotional relationships; it is very important to them to feel independent and self-sufficient, and they prefer not to depend on others or have others depend on them.

Disorganized attachment: a pattern of bonding characterized by depression, overriding anxiety, addiction, mental illness, violence, abuse, neglect, outbursts of temper, and feelings of shame; the desperate need for intimacy while finding it alarming and responding to it unpredictably; reacting strangely and unpredictably to relationship and to intimacy.

Dissociation: the sense of no longer being connected with the body; a disconnection between the felt sense of being in the body and the sense of self.

Distraction: thinking about something else instead of what is bothering you; one of the forms of **self-regulation**.

Distributed nervous system: all the body's nerves, including the neurons of the **skull-brain**.

DMN: the default mode network, an automatic network of thought that integrates memory and creative thinking with the sense of self.

Dopamine: one of the **brain's** main **neurotransmitters**; very supportive of the **SEEKING circuit**; provides energy and pleasure.

Dorsal: a direction within the brain and body, toward the spine; also **posterior**. *Dorsal* also refers to a direction just within the **skull-brain**, which segments the PFC into two parts, forward and down, called **ventral**, and slightly back and up, also called **dorsal**.

Dorsal attention network: the **brain** network that comes online when we are doing novel tasks that demand our attention and that have nothing to do with the self. This is the pattern of thought that most completely turns off the **default mode network**.

Dorsal vagal complex: a set of **unmyelinated** nerve pathways in the **vagus nerve** system that primarily integrate information from our viscera (our guts), such as the intestines, the heart, and the lungs, bringing it up to the **skull-brain**. Activation of this complex initiates the **immobilized** state.

Dorsomedial PFC: an area of the **PFC** located along the midline of the **brain** and up and back from the forehead; part of the **DMN** especially important for consideration of our own autobiography and to help us put ourselves into the past, present, and future social context of our world.

Dysregulation: reactivity to and an unhealthy response to stress, including when people have temper tantrums, act out violently and abusively, or have to live with the aftereffects of unhealed **trauma** and **dissociation**.

Earned secure attachment: movement out of insecure attachment into more balance and an anticipation of warmth from others and for ourselves as a result of healing work or supportive relationships.

Embodied self-awareness network: the network that takes all the sensory information from where our body is in space, its boundaries, and interoceptive information (sensory input coming from inside the body, e.g., the gut, heart, and lungs), runs it up through the brain stem to the **limbic system**, and then links it in to **associations** in the **skull-brain** that let us read and understand this information to decipher our relationship to the world.

Emotional trauma: the moments when what is happening is too difficult, terrifying, or painful for the brain-body to bear and integrating the experience becomes impossible.

Emotional warmth: the experience of being met or meeting others with affection and welcome. On the body level, when we are close enough to feel one another's body heat, there is warmth, so this concept also encompasses closeness and the possibility of comfort with physical contact.

Endocannabinoids: one of the brain's primary chemical responses to support the healing of trauma.

Endogenous benzodiazepines: a set of brain chemicals that, like Valium, have antianxiety, muscle-relaxing, sedative, and hypnotic effects.

Endogenous opioids: also called endorphins; the brain's own morphine and heroin, they blunt pain and support a feeling of well-being.

Enteric nervous system: the gut brain; comprises around 500 million neurons embedded in the walls of the digestive system, from esophagus to anus.

Epigenetics: the study of the modification of gene expression, rather than alteration of the genetic code itself.

Ergoreceptors: nerve endings that sense pressure, tension, fatigue, temperature, pain, and all the other sensations coming from inside our bodies.

Explicit memory: memory we are conscious of—what we know that we know.

FEAR circuit: one of Panksepp's seven **circuits of emotion**, supporting running away, withdrawing, and hiding in the face of danger.

Fearful avoidant attachment: an **adult attachment style** in which people are uncomfortable getting close to others, want emotionally close relationships but find it difficult to trust others completely or to depend on them, and worry that they will be hurt if they allow themselves to become too close to others.

Frontal: a direction within the brain and body, toward the front; also **anterior**.

Frontal lobe: the forward-most division of the **skull-brain**.

Functional magnetic resonance imaging: a way to take pictures of the inner workings of the brain by detecting changes associated with blood flow.

GABA: gamma-aminobutyric acid, an amino acid that acts as a neurotransmitter in the skull- and body-brain. It limits nerve transmission, inhibiting nervous activity.

Heart rate variability: the varying tempo at which our heart beats.

Hemispheres: the two halves of the **skull-brain**.

Hippocampus: an organ in the **limbic system** involved in forming, storing, and processing memory, especially **explicit memory**.

Immobilization: the body's response if neither fight nor flight is effective; a shutdown of sympathetic activation and activation of the **dorsal vagal complex**, when there is helplessness during stress; includes shock, behavioral shutdown, feigning death, fainting, hopelessness, frozen immobility, and dissociation.

Implicit memory: memory we are not conscious of—what we don't know we know.

Inferior: a direction within the brain and body, down toward the feet.

Inferior frontal gyrus: an area of the **PFC**. Problems with connectivity between this area and the **DMN** lead to a linkage between negative thoughts and interpretations of life and the sense of self.

Insula: located in an inner layer of cortex, it takes the raw emotional charge that is coming from the amygdala and helps us name what we are feeling.

Interpersonal neurobiology (IPNB): the study of the relational **brain** (not just the brain by itself but how brains affect one another); synthesizes the fields of cognitive and social neuroscience, **attachment research**, complexity theory, and psychology.

Lateral: direction within the **brain** and body, away from the midline and out toward the sides.

Left hemisphere: the half of the **skull-brain** on the left side of the body.

Limbic system: brain tissue tucked deep inside the **skull-brain**, linking body and skull-brain, that helps us with emotions, memory, bonding, and watching for danger; a different kind of brain tissue from the cortex, it includes the **amygdala** and the **hippocampus**, among other organs and tissues.

Lobe: a division of the **skull-brain**.

LUST circuit: one of Panksepp's seven **circuits of emotion**, supporting sexuality.

Medial: a direction within the brain and body, toward the midline.

Medial PFC: an area of the **PFC** located along the midline of the brain; part of the

DMN; especially important for retrospective and prospective memory and for putting ourselves in others' shoes.

Medial temporal lobe: the part of the **temporal lobe** that is close to the midline of the brain; important for memory; part of the **DMN**.

Mirror neurons: neurons in the motor **cortex** that help us understand the actions of others.

Myelin: the insulation that forms on the outside of a **neuron** sheath, increasing the speed of transfer of energy and information. Myelin is white, which gives **white matter** its color.

Myelinated: covered with **myelin**.

Naming emotions: putting words to feelings; one of the forms of **self-regulation**.

Neuroception of safety: a sense of being safe that is happening at the level of the nervous system.

Neurogenesis: the growth of new **neurons**.

Neuron: a basic cell in the brain.

Neuronal remodeling: the growth or loss of neuronal spines.

Neuroplasticity: the scientific word for the **brain**'s capacity to change.

Neurotransmitter: one of a number of chemicals in the **brain** that communicate between **neurons**.

Occipital lobe: the division of the **skull-brain** located at the back of the head.

Oxytocin: a bonding hormone.

PANIC/GRIEF circuit: one of Panksepp's seven **circuits of emotion**, responding to abandonment, loneliness, loss, and mourning.

Parietal cortex: the outermost surface (the gray matter) of the **parietal lobe**; especially important for self recognition and self-tracking.

Parietal lobe: the division of the **skull-brain** located along each side of the head.

PFC: the prefrontal cortex, located in the front of the **frontal lobe**; the location of the intentional part of the **resonating self-witness**, because this is the area that helps the brain with **self-regulation**, planning, and carrying out the actions that make up our lives.

PLAY circuit: one of Panksepp's seven **circuits of emotion**, supporting active and mutual interaction that is fun and brings people and animals laughter.

Posterior: a direction within the brain and body, toward the spine; also **dorsal**.

Posterior cingulate cortex: the rear part of a girdle-shaped bit of cortex tucked inside the **skull-brain**, so deeply that some people consider it to be part of the **limbic system**, which helps us to integrate everything; part of the **DMN**.

Posthearsal: an intentional rerun of an experience that we feel triggered by or regret about, or both, to bring resonance to the part of the self that was overwhelmed and unaccompanied in that moment.

Precuneus: a wedge of **brain** tissue, located in the rear part of the **parietal lobe**, that holds memories of and reflections about the self and tracks what others do; part of the **DMN**.

PTSD: posttraumatic stress disorder, a brain state of continuing injury and disruption from **trauma** experiences, which can include intrusive memories of trauma and dissociation.

RAGE circuit: one of Panksepp's seven **circuits of emotion**, responding to frustration of needs for safety, respect, well-being, and effectiveness.

Receptor: the area on the end of the **dendrite** that receives chemical messages.

Reframing: thinking about a situation in a different way; one of the forms of **self-regulation**.

Resonance: the experience of sensing that another being fully understands us and sees us with emotional warmth and generosity. It is the sense that *we know* that they could try on our skin and that our feelings and longings would make sense to them.

Resonance skills: knowing how to use language in a way that brings one closer to others or to the self; being able to distinguish utilitarian from relational wording; being able to choose relational langluge.

Resonant language: language that shifts us into relational space and includes wondering about and naming emotion; dreams, longings, and needs; body sensations; what is happening in relationship; and fresh metaphor, visual imagery, and poetry.

Right hemisphere: the half of the **skull-brain** on the right side of the body.

RSW: resonating self-witness, a personification of the parts of the brain that are capable of self-warmth and **self-regulation.**

Secure attachment: a pattern of bonding that embodies the anticipation that the other can be depended upon for predictable warmth, responsiveness, and resonance.

SEEKING circuit: one of Panksepp's seven **circuits of emotion**, supporting taking action to get what is needed and to explore and discover.

Self-management: externalized strategies that we use to respond to stress, including addictions, compulsions, and controlling others and the environment, as well as standing outside ourselves to judge and criticize ourselves.

Self-regulation: having the ability to control bodily functions, come back to balance after experiencing powerful emotions, and to maintain focus and attention.

Skull-brain: the **brain** tissue that is inside the skull.

Social engagement: the nervous system state that makes use of the **ventral vagal complex**, which occurs when people have a **neuroception of safety**. In this state they start to run on oxygen as their main fuel, and their brain and body shift into the capacity for nuanced reading and expression of social cues.

Spine: site on a **dendrite** that can receive information from an **axon** of another **neuron** to form a new connection and that can grow into a new **dendrite** if it receives enough use.

Superior: a direction within the brain and body, up toward the crown of the head.

Sympathetic activation: refers to fight-or-flight response; activation of the body's response to stress with increased heart rate and the need either to take action to protect or defend or to get away from the source of danger.

Synapse: a connection site between **neurons**.

Temporal lobe: the part of the skull-brain that is located inside a person's temples. Much of our memory is stored here.

Transgenerational trauma: when the effects of difficult historical and personal events show up in the neurobiology of the survivors' children and grandchildren.

Traumatic dissociation: a disconnected state of being; a state in which connection between the inner world and the outer world and between the sense of self and the sense of body become fractured.

Unmyelinated: lacking **myelin**.

Vagus nerve complex: the nerve bundles that run up from the inside of the body to the skull-brain and back (~80 percent to the brain and ~20 percent to the body), mostly carrying information from all of the organs and digestive system.

Ventral: a direction within the brain and body, toward the front of the body. Ventral also refers to a direction just within the **skull-brain**, which segments the **prefrontal cortex** into two parts, forward and down, called **ventral**, and slightly back and up, also called **dorsal**.

Ventral vagal complex: the myelinated portion of the **vagus nerve complex**, used when the nervous system has a **neuroception of safety**. In this **social engagement** state, people start to run on oxygen as their main fuel, and their brain and body shift into the capacity for nuanced reading and expression of social cues.

Ventrolateral PFC: a part of the **inferior frontal gyrus** in the **PFC**, located away from the midline of the brain, moving down and forward from the dorsal-ventral line; part of the **DMN** especially important for making decisions to stop doing things and reorienting attention to perceptual events that occur outside the current focus of attention.

Ventromedial PFC: an area of the **PFC** located along the midline of the brain, moving down and forward from the dorsal-ventral line; part of the **DMN** especially important for connecting the body and emotional awareness and managing emotion.

Window of tolerance: the amount of stress that an animal or human can experience and recover from without moving into the fight-or-flight or immobilization response.

Window of welcome: the emotional expression and intensity that can actually be met with warmth and understanding and is easily reflected and resonated with within a relationship.

References

Introduction

1. Wilson, T. D., Reinhard, D. A., Westgate, E. C., Gilbert, D. T., Ellerbeck, N., Hahn, C., . . . Shaked, A. (2014). Just think: The challenges of the disengaged mind. *Science, 345*(6192), 75–77. doi:10.1126/science.1250830

2. Lieberman, M. D. (2013). *Social: Why our brains are wired to connect.* New York, NY: Broadway Books, p. 21.

3. Buchheim, A. (2000). The relationship among attachment representation, emotion-abstraction patterns, and narrative style: A computer-based text analysis of the adult attachment interview. *Psychotherapy Research, 10*(4), 390–407. doi:10.1093/ptr/10.4.390

4. Pelvig, D., Pakkenberg, H., Stark, A., & Pakkenberg, B. (2008). Neocortical glial cell numbers in human brains. *Neurobiology of Aging, 29*(11), 1754–1762. doi:10.1016/j.neurobiolaging.2007.04.013

5. Yuan, T., Li, J., Ding, F., & Arias-Carrion, O. (2014). Evidence of adult neurogenesis in nonhuman primates and human. *Cell and Tissue Research, 358*(1), 17–23. doi:10.1007/s00441-014-1980-z

6. Fukazawa, Y., Saitoh, Y., Ozawa, F., Ohta, Y., Mizuno, K., & Inokuchi, K. (2003). Hippocampal LTP is accompanied by enhanced F-actin content within the dendritic spine that is essential for late LTP maintenance in vivo. *Neuron, 38*(3), 447–460. doi:10.1016/s0896-6273(03)00206-x

7. Kiebel, S. J., & Friston, K. J. (2011). Free energy and dendritic self-organization. *Frontiers in Systems Neuroscience, 5.* doi:10.3389/fnsys.2011.00080

8. Coan, J. A., Beckes, L., & Allen, J. P. (2013). Childhood maternal support and social capital moderate the regulatory impact of social relationships in adulthood. *International Journal of Psychophysiology, 88*(3), 224–231. doi:10.1016/j.ijpsycho.2013.04.006

9. Ibid.

10. Saunders, R., Jacobvitz, D., Zaccagnino, M., Beverung, L. M., & Hazen, N. (2011). Pathways to earned-security: The role of alternative support figures. *Attachment and Human Development, 13*(4), 403–420. doi:10.1080/14616734.2011.584405

Chapter One

1. Raichle, M. E. (2015). The restless brain: How intrinsic activity organizes brain function. *Philosophical Transactions of the Royal Society B: Biological Sciences, 370*(1668). doi:10.1098/rstb.2014.0172

2. Lieberman, M. D. (2013). *Social: Why our brains are wired to connect.* New York, NY: Crown, p. 21.

3. Ostby, Y., Walhovd, K. B., Tamnes, C. K., Grydeland, H., Westlye, L. T., & Fjell, A. M. (2012). Mental time travel and default-mode network functional connectivity in the developing brain. *Proceedings of the National Academy of Sciences of the USA, 109*(42), 16800–16804. doi:10.1073/pnas.1210627109

4. Greicius, M. D., Kiviniemi, V., Tervonen, O., Vainionpää, V., Alahuhta, S., Reiss, A. L., & Menon, V. (2008). Persistent default-mode network connectivity during light sedation. *Human Brain Mapping, 29*(7), 839–847. doi:10.1002/hbm.20537

5. Raichle (2015).

6. Shannon, B. J., Dosenbach, R. A., Su, Y., Vlassenko, A. G., Larson-Prior, L. J., Nolan, T. S., . . . Raichle, M. E. (2012). Morning-evening variation in human brain metabolism and memory circuits. *Journal of Neurophysiology, 109*(5), 1444–1456. doi:10.1152/jn.00651.2012

7. Shamloo, F., & Helie, S. (2016). Changes in default mode network as automaticity develops in a categorization task. *Behavioural Brain Research, 313,* 324–333. doi:10.1016/j.bbr.2016.07.029

8. Raichle (2015).

9. Howard-Jones, P. A., Jay, T., Mason, A., & Jones, H. (2016). Gamification of learning deactivates the default mode network. *Frontiers in Psychology, 6.* doi:10.3389/fpsyg.2015.01891

10. Welborn, B. L., & Lieberman, M. D. (2015). Person-specific theory of mind in medial PFC. *Journal of Cognitive Neuroscience, 27*(1), 1–12. doi:10.1162/jocn_a_00700

11. Bado, P., Engel, A., Oliveira-Souza, R. D., Bramati, I. E., Paiva, F. F., Basilio, R., . . . Moll, J. (2013). Functional dissociation of ventral frontal and dorsomedial default mode network components during resting state and emotional autobiographical recall. *Human Brain Mapping, 35*(7), 3302–3313. doi:10.1002/hbm.22403

12. Spunt, R. P., Meyer, M. L., & Lieberman, M. D. (2015). The default mode of human brain function primes the intentional stance. *Journal of Cognitive Neuroscience, 27*(6), 1116–1124. doi:10.1162/jocn_a_00785

13. Carvalho, F. M., Chaim, K. T., Sanchez, T. A., & Araujo, D. B. (2016). Time-perception network and default mode network are associated with temporal prediction in a periodic motion task. *Frontiers in Human Neuroscience, 10.* doi:10.3389/fnhum.2016.00268

14. Sheline, Y. I., Barch, D. M., Price, J. L., Rundle, M. M., Vaishnavi, S. N., Snyder, A. Z., . . . Raichle, M. E. (2009). The default mode network and self-referential processes in depression. *Proceedings of the National Academy of Sciences of the USA, 106*(6), 1942–1947. doi:10.1073/pnas.0812686106

15. Soch, J., Deserno, L., Assmann, A., Barman, A., Walter, H., Richardson-Klavehn, A., & Schott, B. H. (2016). Inhibition of information flow to the default mode network during self-reference versus reference to others. *Cerebral Cortex.* Advance online publication. doi:10.1093/cercor/bhw206

16. Lieberman, M. D. (2007). Social cognitive neuroscience: A review of core processes. *Annual Review of Psychology, 58*(1), 259–289. doi:10.1146/annurev.psych.58.110405.085654

17. Spreng, R., & Andrews-Hanna, J. (2015). The default network and social cognition. *Brain Mapping,* 165–169. doi:10.1016/b978-0-12-397025-1.00173-1

18. Yang, R., Gao, C., Wu, X., Yang, J., Li, S., & Cheng, H. (2016). Decreased functional connectivity to posterior cingulate cortex in major depressive disorder. *Psychiatry Research: Neuroimaging, 255,* 15–23. doi:10.1016/j.pscychresns.2016.07.010

19. Devinsky, O., Morrell, M. J., & Vogt, B. A. (1995). Contributions of anterior cingulate cortex to behaviour. *Brain, 118*(1), 279–306. doi:10.1093/brain/118.1.279

20. Soch et al. (2016).

21. Spreng, R. N., & Mar, R. A. (2012). I remember you: A role for memory in social cognition and the functional neuroanatomy of their interaction. *Brain Research, 1428,* 43–50. doi:10.1016/j.brainres.2010.12.024

22. Turner, G. R., & Spreng, R. N. (2015). Prefrontal engagement and reduced default network suppression co-occur and are dynamically coupled in older adults: The default-executive coupling hypothesis of aging. *Journal of Cognitive Neuroscience, 27*(12), 2462–2476. doi:10.1162/jocn_a_00869

23. Daniels, J. (2011). Default mode alterations in posttraumatic stress disorder related to early-life trauma: A developmental perspective. *Journal of Psychiatry and Neuroscience, 36*(1), 56–59. doi:10.1503/jpn.100050

24. Ibid.

25. Hao, L., Yang, J., Wang, Y., Zhang, S., Xie, P., Luo, Q., . . . Qiu, J. (2015). Neural correlates of causal attribution in negative events of depressed patients: Evidence from an fMRI study. *Clinical Neurophysiology, 126*(7), 1331–1337. doi:10.1016/j.clinph.2014.10.146

26. Cha, J., Dedora, D., Nedic, S., Ide, J., Greenberg, T., Hajcak, G., & Mujica-Parodi, L. R. (2016). Clinically anxious individuals show disrupted feedback between inferior frontal gyrus and prefrontal-limbic control circuit. *Journal of Neuroscience, 36*(17), 4708–4718. doi:10.1523/jneurosci.1092-15.2016

27. Wilson, T. D., Reinhard, D. A., Westgate, E. C., Gilbert, D. T., Ellerbeck, N., Hahn, C., . . . Shaked, A. (2014). Just think: The challenges of the disengaged mind. *Science, 345*(6192), 75–77. doi:10.1126/science.1250830

28. Howard-Jones et al. (2016).

29. Hahn, B., Ross, T. J., Yang, Y., Kim, I., Huestis, M. A., & Stein, E. A. (2007). Nicotine enhances visuospatial attention by deactivating areas of the resting brain default network. *Journal of Neuroscience, 27*(13), 3477–3489. doi:10.1523/jneurosci.5129-06.2007

30. Simon, R., & Engstrã, M. M. (2015). The default mode network as a biomarker for monitoring the therapeutic effects of meditation. *Frontiers in Psychology, 6.* doi:10.3389/fpsyg.2015.00776

31. Mantovani, A. M., Fregonesi, C. E., Lorençoni, R. M., Savian, N. U., Palma, M. R., Salgado, A. S., . . . Parreira, R. B. (2016). Immediate effect of basic body awareness therapy on heart rate variability. *Complementary Therapies in Clinical Practice, 22,* 8–11. doi:10.1016/j.ctcp.2015.10.003

32. Tamir, D. I., Bricker, A. B., Dodell-Feder, D., & Mitchell, J. P. (2015). Reading fiction

and reading minds: The role of simulation in the default network. *Social Cognitive and Affective Neuroscience, 11*(2), 215–224. doi:10.1093/scan/nsv114

33. Goldstein, T. R., & Winner, E. (2012). Enhancing empathy and theory of mind. *Journal of Cognition and Development, 13*(1), 19–37. doi:10.1080/15248372.2011.573514

34. Lutz, J., Brühl, A., Doerig, N., Scheerer, H., Achermann, R., Weibel, A., . . . Herwig, U. (2016). Altered processing of self-related emotional stimuli in mindfulness meditators. *NeuroImage, 124*, 958–967. doi:10.1016/j.neuroimage.2015.09.057

35. Kornfield, J. (n.d.). Even the best meditators have old wounds to heal. Retrieved August 28, 2016, from http://www.buddhanet.net/psymed1.htm

36. Lanius, R. A., Bluhm, R. L., Coupland, N. J., Hegadoren, K. M., Rowe, B., Théberge, J., . . . Brimson, M. (2010). Default mode network connectivity as a predictor of post-traumatic stress disorder symptom severity in acutely traumatized subjects. *Acta Psychiatrica Scandinavica, 121*(1), 33–40. doi:10.1111/j.1600-0447.2009.01391.x

37. Modi, S., Kumar, M., Kumar, P., & Khushu, S. (2015). Aberrant functional connectivity of resting state networks associated with trait anxiety. *Psychiatry Research: Neuroimaging, 234*(1), 25–34. doi:10.1016/j.pscychresns.2015.07.006

38. Beaty, R. E., Kaufman, S. B., Benedek, M., Jung, R. E., Kenett, Y. N., Jauk, E., . . . Silvia, P. J. (2015). Personality and complex brain networks: The role of openness to experience in default network efficiency. *Human Brain Mapping, 37*(2), 773–779. doi:10.1002/hbm.23065

Chapter Two

1. Siegel, D. J. (2012). *The developing mind: How relationships and the brain interact to shape who we are.* New York, NY: Guilford Press, p. 20.

2. Lalo, E., Gilbertson, T., Doyle, L., Di Lazzaro, V., Cioni, B., & Brown, P. (2007). Phasic increases in cortical beta activity are associated with alterations in sensory processing in the human. *Experimental Brain Research, 177*(1), 137–45. doi:10.1007/s00221-006-0655-8.

3. Hughes, J. R. (2008). Gamma, fast, and ultrafast waves of the brain: Their relationships with epilepsy and behavior. *Epilepsy and Behavior, 13*(1), 25–31. doi:10.1016/j.yebeh.2008.01.011

4. Shafer, A. T., & Dolcos, F. (2014). Dissociating retrieval success from incidental encoding activity during emotional memory retrieval, in the medial temporal lobe. *Frontiers in Behavioral Neuroscience, 8* (177), 1–15. doi:10.3389/fnbeh.2014.00177

5. Bisby, J. A., Horner, A. J., Hørlyck, L. D., & Burgess, N. (2016). Opposing effects of negative emotion on amygdalar and hippocampal memory for items and associations. *Social Cognitive and Affective Neuroscience, 11*(6), 981–990. doi:10.1093/scan/nsw028

6. Coan, J. A., Beckes, L., & Allen, J. P. (2013). Childhood maternal support and social capital moderate the regulatory impact of social relationships in adulthood. *International Journal of Psychophysiology, 88*(3), 224–231. doi:10.1016/j.ijpsycho.2013.04.006

7. Vrtička, P., Sander, D., Anderson, B., Badoud, D., Eliez, S., & Debbané, M. (2014). Social feedback processing from early to late adolescence: Influence of sex, age, and attachment style. *Brain and Behavior, 4*(5), 703–720. doi:10.1002/brb3.251

8. Sakaki, M., Yoo, H. J., Nga, L., Lee, T., Thayer, J. F., & Mather, M. (2016). Heart

rate variability is associated with amygdala functional connectivity with MPFC across younger and older adults. *NeuroImage, 139*, 44–52. doi:10.1016/j.neuroimage .2016.05.076

9. Lanius, R. A., Frewen, P. A., Tursich, M., Jetly, R., & McKinnon, M. C. (2015). Restoring large-scale brain networks in PTSD and related disorders: A proposal for neuroscientifically-informed treatment interventions. *European Journal of Psycho-traumatology, 6*. doi:10.3402/ejpt.v6.27313

10. Szyf, M. (2013, July). *Epigenetics.* Paper presented at the Brain Development and Learning Conference, Vancouver, British Columbia, Canada.

11. Lieberman, M. D., Inagaki, T. K., Tabibnia, G., & Crockett, M. J. (2011). Subjective responses to emotional stimuli during labeling, reappraisal, and distraction. *Emotion, 11*(3), 468–480. doi:10.1037/a0023503

12. Coan, J. A., Schaefer, H. S., & Davidson, R. J. (2006). Lending a hand: Social regulation of the neural response to threat. *Psychological Science, 17*(12), 1032–1039. doi:10.1111/j.1467-9280.2006.01832.x

13. Lieberman et al. (2011).

14. Coan, J. A. (2011). The social regulation of emotion. In J. Decety & J. T. Cacioppo (Eds.), *The Oxford Handbook of Social Neuroscience.* Oxford Handbooks Online. doi:10.1093/oxfordhb/9780195342161.013.0041

15. Coan et al. (2013).

16. Hopper, J. W., Frewen, P. A., Kolk, B. A., & Lanius, R. A. (2007). Neural correlates of reexperiencing, avoidance, and dissociation in PTSD: Symptom dimensions and emotion dysregulation in responses to script-driven trauma imagery. *Journal of Traumatic Stress, 20*(5), 713–725. doi:10.1002/jts.20284

17. Tabibnia, G., Lieberman, M. D., & Craske, M. G. (2008). The lasting effect of words on feelings: Words may facilitate exposure effects to threatening images. *Emotion,* 8(3), 307–317. doi:10.1037/1528-3542.8.3.307

18. Park, E. R., Traeger, L., Vranceanu, A., Scult, M., Lerner, J. A., Benson, H., . . . Fricchione, G. L. (2013). The development of a patient-centered program based on the relaxation response: The Relaxation Response Resiliency Program (3RP). *Psychosomatics, 54*(2), 165–174. doi:10.1016/j.psym.2012.09.001

19. Uher, T. (2010). Alexithymia and immune dysregulation: A critical review. *Activitas Nervosa Superior, 52*(1), 40–44. doi:10.1007/bf03379564

20. Foran, H. M., & O'Leary, K. D. (2012). The role of relationships in understanding the alexithymia-depression link. *European Journal of Personality, 27*(5). doi:10.1002/per.1887

21. Frewen, P.A., Lanius, R.A., Dozois, D.J.A., Neufeld, R.W.J., Pain, C., Hopper, J.W., . . . (2008). Clinical and neural correlates of alexithymia in posttraumatic stress disorder. *Journal of Abnormal Psychology, 117*(1):171-181. doi:10.1037/0021–843x. 117.1.171

22. Teicher, M. H., & Samson, J. A. (2016). Annual research review: Enduring neurobiological effects of childhood abuse and neglect. *Journal of Child Psychology and Psychiatry, 57*(3), 241–266. doi:10.1111/jcpp.12507

23. Coan et al. (2006).

24. Telzer, E. H., Qu, Y., Goldenberg, D., Fuligni, A. J., Galván, A., & Lieberman, M. D. (2014). Adolescents' emotional competence is associated with parents' neural sensitivity to emotions. *Frontiers in Human Neuroscience, 8*(558), 1–12. doi:10.3389/fnhum.2014.00558

25. Natalie, E., & Fischer, H. (2015). *Emotion and aging: Recent evidence from brain and behavior.* Frontiers Media. doi:10.3389/978-2-88919-425-4

Chapter Three

1. Siegel, D. J. (2012). *Pocket guide to interpersonal neurobiology: An integrative handbook of the mind.* New York, NY: Norton, p. 6-5.

2. Ibid., p. 19-3.

3. Panksepp, J. (1998). *Affective neuroscience: The foundations of human and animal emotions.* New York, NY: Oxford University Press, pp. 246–260.

4. Salat, D. H., Kaye, J. A., & Janowsky, J. S. (2001). Selective preservation and degeneration within the prefrontal cortex in aging and Alzheimer disease. *Archives of Neurology, 58,* 1403–1408. doi:10.1001/archneur.58.9.1403

5. Dolcos, S., Katsumi, Y., & Dixon, R. A. (2014). The role of arousal in the spontaneous regulation of emotions in healthy aging: A fMRI investigation. *Frontiers in Psychology, 5.* doi:10.3389/fpsyg.2014.00681

6. Hecht, D. (2014). Cerebral lateralization of pro- and anti-social tendencies. *Experimental Neurobiology, 23*(1), 1. doi:10.5607/en.2014.23.1.1

7. Coan, J. A., Beckes, L., & Allen, J. P. (2013). Childhood maternal support and social capital moderate the regulatory impact of social relationships in adulthood. *International Journal of Psychophysiology, 88*(3), 224–231. doi:10.1016/j.ijpsycho.2013.04.006

8. Lewis, M., Haviland-Jones, J. M., & Barrett, L. F. (2008). *Handbook of emotions.* New York, NY: Guilford Press. pp. 116–119.

9. Hebb, D. O. (1949). *The organization of behavior.* New York, NY: Wiley.

10. The mnemonic phrase is usually attributed to Carla Shatz at Stanford University, referenced, for example, in Doidge, N. (2007). *The brain that changes itself.* New York: Viking Press, p. 427.

11. Longe, O., Maratos, F. A., Gilbert, P., Evans, G., Volker, F., Rockliff, H., & Rippon, G. (2010). Having a word with yourself: Neural correlates of self-criticism and self-reassurance. *NeuroImage, 49*(2), 1849–1856. doi:10.1016/j.neuroimage.2009.09.019

Chapter Four

1. Peasley-Miklus, C. E., Panayiotou, G., & Vrana, S. R. (2016). Alexithymia predicts arousal-based processing deficits and discordance between emotion response systems during emotional imagery. *Emotion, 16*(2), 164–174. doi:10.1037/emo0000086

2. Thoma, P., & Bellebaum, C. (2012). Your error's got me feeling — How empathy relates to the electrophysiological correlates of performance monitoring. *Frontiers in Human Neuroscience, 6.* doi:10.3389/fnhum.2012.00135

3. Cauda, F., D'agata, F., Sacco, K., Duca, S., Geminiani, G., & Vercelli, A. (2011). Functional connectivity of the insula in the resting brain. *NeuroImage, 55*(1), 8–23. doi:10.1016/j.neuroimage.2010.11.049

4. Joseph, R. (1988). The right cerebral hemisphere: Emotion, music, visual-spatial skills, body-image, dreams, and awareness. *Journal of Clinical Psychology, 44*(5), 630–673. doi:10.1002/1097-4679(198809)44:53.0.co;2-v

5. Godfrey, H. K., & Grimshaw, G. M. (2015). Emotional language is all right: Emotional prosody reduces hemispheric asymmetry for linguistic processing. *Laterality: Asymmetries of Body, Brain and Cognition, 21*(4–6), 568-584. doi:10.1080/1357650x.2015.1096940

6. Jackson, P. L., Brunet, E., Meltzoff, A. N., & Decety, J. (2006). Empathy examined through the neural mechanisms involved in imagining how I feel versus how you feel pain. *Neuropsychologia, 44*(5), 752–761. doi:10.1016/j.neuropsychologia.2005.07.015

7. Laeng, B., Zarrinpar, A., & Kosslyn, S. M. (2003). Do separate processes identify objects as exemplars versus members of basic-level categories? Evidence from hemispheric specialization. *Brain and Cognition, 53*(1), 15–27. doi:10.1016/s0278-2626(03)00184-2

8. Perani, D., Cappa, S. F., Bettinardi, V., Bressi, S., Gorno-Tempini, M., Matarrese, M., & Fazio, F. (1995). Different neural systems for the recognition of animals and man-made tools. *NeuroReport, 6*(12), 1637–1641. doi:10.1097/00001756-199508000-00012

9. Balconi, M., & Pagani, S. (2014). Social hierarchies and emotions: Cortical prefrontal activity, facial feedback (EMG), and cognitive performance in a dynamic interaction. *Social Neuroscience, 10*(2), 166–178. doi:10.1080/17470919.2014.977403

10. Ocklenburg, S., Friedrich, P., Güntürkün, O., & Genç, E. (2016). Intrahemispheric white matter asymmetries: The missing link between brain structure and functional lateralization? *Reviews in the Neurosciences, 27*(5). doi:10.1515/revneuro-2015-0052

11. Chance, S. A. (2014). The cortical microstructural basis of lateralized cognition: A review. *Frontiers in Psychology, 5.* doi:10.3389/fpsyg.2014.00820

12. Lamb, M. R., Robertson, L. C., & Knight, R. T. (1989). Attention and interference in the processing of global and local information: Effects of unilateral temporal-parietal junction lesions. *Neuropsychologia, 27*(4), 471–483. doi:10.1016/0028-3932(89)90052-3

13. Exchange of views. (n.d.). Retrieved December 27, 2016, from http://iainmcgilchrist.com/exchange-of-views/

14. Faust, M., & Mashal, N. (2007). The role of the right cerebral hemisphere in processing novel metaphoric expressions taken from poetry: A divided visual field study. *Neuropsychologia, 45*(4), 860–870. doi:10.1016/j.neuropsychologia.2006.08.010

15. Foldi, N. S. (1987). Appreciation of pragmatic interpretations of indirect commands: Comparison of right and left hemisphere brain-damaged patients. *Brain and Language, 31*(1), 88–108. doi:10.1016/0093-934x(87)90062-9

16. Sidtis, D. V., & Postman, W. A. (2006). Formulaic expressions in spontaneous speech of left- and right-hemisphere-damaged subjects. *Aphasiology, 20*(5), 411–426. doi:10.1080/02687030500538148

17. Huth, A. G., Heer, W. A., Griffiths, T. L., Theunissen, F. E., & Gallant, J. L. (2016). Natural speech reveals the semantic maps that tile human cerebral cortex. *Nature, 532*(7600), 453–458. doi:10.1038/nature17637

18. Foldi (1987).

19. Tranel, D., Bechara, A., & Denburg, N. L. (2002). Asymmetric functional roles of right and left ventromedial prefrontal cortices in social conduct, decision-making, and emotional processing. *Cortex, 38*(4), 589–612. doi:10.1016/s0010-9452(08)70024-8

20. Rosenberg, M. B. (2015). *Nonviolent communication: A language of life: Life-changing tools for healthy relationships.* Encinitas, CA: Puddle Dancer Press. p. 52.

21. Ibid. p. 52.

Chapter Five

1. Ball, T. M., Ramsawh, H. J., Campbell-Sills, L., Paulus, M. P., & Stein, M. B. (2012). Prefrontal dysfunction during emotion regulation in generalized anxiety and panic disorders. *Psychological Medicine, 43*(7), 1475–1486. doi:10.1017/s0033291712002383

2. Panksepp, J. (2007). Neuroevolutionary sources of laughter and social joy: Modeling primal human laughter in laboratory rats. *Behavioural Brain Research, 182*(2), 231–244. doi:10.1016/j.bbr.2007.02.015

3. Panksepp, J. (2011). What is an emotional feeling? Lessons about affective origins from cross-species neuroscience. *Motivation and Emotion, 36*(1), 4–15. doi:10.1007/s11031-011-9232-y

4. Panksepp, J., & Biven, L. (2012). *The archaeology of mind: Neuroevolutionary origins of human emotions.* New York, NY: Norton, p. 189.

5. Ibid. p. 333.

6. Ibid., p. 333.

7. Ibid., p. 333.

8. Ibid., p. 335.

9. Kidd, T., Hamer, M., & Steptoe, A. (2013). Adult attachment style and cortisol responses across the day in older adults. *Psychophysiology, 50*(9), 841–847. doi:10.1111/psyp.12075

10. Panksepp & Biven (2012), p. 335.

11. Kazi, A., & Oommen, A. (2014). Chronic noise stress-induced alterations of glutamate and gamma-aminobutyric acid and their metabolism in the rat brain. *Noise Health, 16*(73), 343. doi:10.4103/1463-1741.144394

12. Bowers, M. E., Choi, D. C., & Ressler, K. J. (2012). Neuropeptide regulation of fear and anxiety: Implications of cholecystokinin, endogenous opioids, and neuropeptide Y. *Physiology and Behavior, 107*(5), 699–710. doi:10.1016/j.physbeh.2012.03.004

13. Laeger, I., Dobel, C., Radenz, B., Kugel, H., Keuper, K., Eden, A., . . . Zwanzger, P. (2014). Of "disgrace" and "pain" – Corticolimbic interaction patterns for disorder-relevant and emotional words in social phobia. *PLoS ONE, 9*(11). doi:10.1371/journal.pone.0109949

14. Giebels, V., Repping-Wuts, H., Bleijenberg, G., Kroese, J. M., Stikkelbroeck, N., & Hermus, A. (2014). Severe fatigue in patients with adrenal insufficiency: Physical, psychosocial and endocrine determinants. *Journal of Endocrinological Investigation, 37*(3), 293–301. doi:10.1007/s40618-013-0042-9

15. Oliveira, J. F., Dias, N. S., Correia, M., Gama-Pereira, F., Sardinha, V. M., Lima, A., . . . Sousa, N. (2013). Chronic stress disrupts neural coherence between cortico-limbic structures. *Frontiers in Neural Circuits, 7.* doi:10.3389/fncir.2013.00010

16. Bierer, L. M., Bader, H. N., Daskalakis, N. P., Lehrner, A. L., Makotkine, I., Seckl, J. R., & Yehuda, R. (2014). Elevation of 11β-hydroxysteroid dehydrogenase type 2 activity in Holocaust survivor offspring: Evidence for an intergenerational effect of maternal trauma exposure. *Psychoneuroendocrinology, 48*, 1–10. doi:10.1016/j.psyneuen.2014.06.001

17. Olsson, A., Kross, E., Nordberg, S. S., Weinberg, A., Weber, J., Schmer-Galunder, S., . . . Ochsner, K. N. (2014). Neural and genetic markers of vulnerability to post-traumatic stress symptoms among survivors of the World Trade Center attacks. *Social Cognitive and Affective Neuroscience, 10*(6), 863–868. doi:10.1093/scan/nsu125

18. Robinson, O. J., Krimsky, M., Lieberman, L., Allen, P., Vytal, K., & Grillon, C. (2014). The dorsal medial prefrontal (anterior cingulate) cortex–amygdala aversive amplification circuit in unmedicated generalised and social anxiety disorders: An observational study. *Lancet Psychiatry, 1*(4), 294–302. doi:10.1016/s2215-0366(14)70305-0

19. Vogt, B. A., & Peters, A. (1981). Form and distribution of neurons in rat cingulate cortex: Areas 32, 24, and 29. *Journal of Comparative Neurology, 195*(4), 603–625. doi:10.1002/cne.901950406

20. King, A. P., Block, S. R., Sripada, R. K., Rauch, S., Giardino, N., Favorite, T., . . . Liberzon, I. (2016). Altered default mode network (DMN) resting state functional connectivity following a mindfulness-based exposure therapy for posttraumatic stress disorder (PTSD) in combat veterans of Afghanistan and Iraq. *Depression and Anxiety Depress Anxiety, 33*(4), 289–299. doi:10.1002/da.22481

21. Liu, T., Li, J., Zhao, Z., Zhong, Y., Zhang, Z., Xu, Q., . . . Chen, F. (2016). Betel quid dependence is associated with functional connectivity changes of the anterior cingulate cortex: A resting-state fMRI study. *Journal of Translational Medicine, 14*(1). doi:10.1186/s12967-016-0784-1

22. Jahn, A., Nee, D. E., Alexander, W. H., & Brown, J. W. (2014). Distinct regions of anterior cingulate cortex signal prediction and outcome evaluation. *NeuroImage, 95*, 80–89. doi:10.1016/j.neuroimage.2014.03.050

23. Smith, R., Alkozei, A., & Killgore, W. D. (2016). Contributions of self-report and performance-based individual differences measures of social cognitive ability to large-scale neural network functioning. *Brain Imaging and Behavior.* Advance online publication. doi:10.1007/s11682-016-9545-2

24. Zendehrouh, S., Gharibzadeh, S., & Towhidkhah, F. (2014). Reinforcement-conflict based control: An integrative model of error detection in anterior cingulate cortex. *Neurocomputing, 123*, 140–149. doi:10.1016/j.neucom.2013.06.020

25. Marcus, S., Lopez, J. F., Mcdonough, S., Mackenzie, M. J., Flynn, H., Neal, C. R., . . . Vazquez, D. M. (2011). Depressive symptoms during pregnancy: Impact on neuroendocrine and neonatal outcomes. *Infant Behavior and Development, 34*(1), 26–34. doi:10.1016/j.infbeh.2010.07.002

26. Veenendaal, M., Painter, R., Rooij, S. D., Bossuyt, P., Post, J. V., Gluckman, P., . . . Roseboom, T. (2013). Transgenerational effects of prenatal exposure to the 1944–45 Dutch famine. *BJOG: An International Journal of Obstetrics and Gynaecology, 120*(5), 548–554. doi:10.1111/1471-0528.12136

27. Yehuda, R., Daskalakis, N. P., Bierer, L. M., Bader, H. N., Klengel, T.,Holsbuer, F., & Binder, E. B. (2016) Holocaust exposure induced intergenerational effects on FKBPS methylation. *Biological Psychology, 80*(5), 375–380. doi:10/1016/j.piopsych.2015.08.005

28. Vukojevic, V., Kolassa, I., Fastenrath, M., Gschwind, L., Spalek, K., Milnik, A., . . . Quervain, D. J. (2014). Epigenetic modification of the glucocorticoid receptor gene is linked to transmatic memory and post-traumatic stress disorder risk in genocide survivors. *Journal of Neuroscience, 34*(31), 10274–10284. doi:10.1523/jneurosci.1526-14.2014

29. Stalder, T., Evans, P., Hucklebridge, F., & Clow, A. (2011). Associations between the cortisol awakening response and heart rate variability. *Psychoneuroendocrinology, 36*(4), 454–462. doi:10.1016/j.psyneuen.2010.07.020

30. Kao, L., Liu, Y., Tzeng, N., Kuo, T. B., Huang, S., Chang, C., & Chang, H. (2016). Linking an anxiety-related personality trait to cardiac autonomic regulation in well-defined healthy adults: Harm avoidance and resting heart rate variability. *Psychiatry Investigation, 13*(4), 397. doi:10.4306/pi.2016.13.4.397

31. Lehman, B. J., Cane, A. C., Tallon, S. J., & Smith, S. F. (2014). Physiological and emotional responses to subjective social evaluative threat in daily life. *Anxiety, Stress, and Coping, 28*(3), 321–339. doi:10.1080/10615806.2014.968563

32. Kolesnikov, O. L., Dolgushin, I. I., Selyanina, G. A., Shadrina, I. V., Shalashova, M. A., & Kolesnikova, A. A. (2006). Dependence of immune system function and metabolism on reactive anxiety. *Bulletin of Experimental Biology and Medicine, 142*(2), 219–221. doi:10.1007/s10517-006-0332-8

33. Smith, A. P. (2011). Breakfast cereal, digestive problems and well-being. *Stress and Health, 27*(5), 388–394. doi:10.1002/smi.1390

34. McAuley, M. T., Kenny, R., Kirkwood, T. B., Wilkinson, D. J., Jones, J. J., & Miller, V. M. (2009). A mathematical model of aging-related and cortisol induced hippocampal dysfunction. BMC *Neuroscience, 10*(1), 26. doi:10.1186/1471-2202-10-26

35. Laar, M. V., Pevernagie, D., Mierlo, P. V., & Overeem, S. (2014). Subjective sleep characteristics in primary insomnia versus insomnia with comorbid anxiety or mood disorder. *Sleep and Biological Rhythms, 13*(1), 41–48. doi:10.1111/sbr.12100

36. Coan, J. A., Beckes, L., & Allen, J. P. (2013). Childhood maternal support and social capital moderate the regulatory impact of social relationships in adulthood. *International Journal of Psychophysiology, 88*(3), 224–231. doi:10.1016/j.ijpsycho.2013.04.006

Chapter Six

1. Bailey, C. H., Kandel, E. R., & Harris, K. M. (2015). Structural components of synaptic plasticity and memory consolidation. *Cold Spring Harbor Perspectives in Biology, 7*(7). doi:10.1101/cshperspect.a021758

2. Ritov, G., Ardi, Z., & Richter-Levin, G. (2014). Differential activation of amygdala, dorsal and ventral hippocampus following an exposure to a reminder of underwater trauma. *Frontiers in Behavioral Neuroscience, 8.* doi:10.3389/fnbeh.2014.00018

3. Kensinger, E. A., Addis, D. R., & Atapattu, R. K. (2011). Amygdala activity at encoding corresponds with memory vividness and with memory for select episodic details. *Neuropsychologia, 49*(4), 663–673. doi:10.1016/j.neuropsychologia.2011.01.017

4. Ge, R., Fu, Y., Wang, D., Yao, L., & Long, Z. (2012). Neural mechanism underlying autobiographical memory modulated by remoteness and emotion [Abstract]. *Proceedings of the SPIE, 8317.* doi:10.1117/12.910870

5. Zelikowsky, M., Hersman, S., Chawla, M. K., Barnes, C. A., & Fanselow, M. S. (2014). Neuronal ensembles in amygdala, hippocampus, and prefrontal cortex track differential components of contextual fear. *Journal of Neuroscience, 34*(25), 8462–8466. doi:10.1523/jneurosci.3624-13.2014

6. Kensinger et al. (2011).

7. Roy-Byrne, P., Arguelles, L., Vitek, M. E., Goldberg, J., Keane, T. M., True, W. R., & Pitman, R. K. (2004). Persistence and change of PTSD symptomatology. *Social Psychiatry and Psychiatric Epidemiology, 39*(9), 681–685. doi:10.1007/s00127-004-0810-0

8. Lonsdorf, T. B., Haaker, J., & Kalisch, R. (2014). Long-term expression of human contextual fear and extinction memories involves amygdala, hippocampus and

ventromedial prefrontal cortex: A reinstatement study in two independent samples. *Social Cognitive and Affective Neuroscience, 9*(12), 1973–1983. doi:10.1093/scan/nsu018

9. Lanius, R. A., Frewen, P. A., Tursich, M., Jetly, R., & Mckinnon, M. C. (2015). Restoring large-scale brain networks in PTSD and related disorders: A proposal for neuroscientifically-informed treatment interventions. *European Journal of Psychotraumatology, 6.* doi:10.3402/ejpt.v6.27313

10. Nader, K. (2015). Reconsolidation and the dynamic nature of memory. In K. P. Giese & K. Radwanska (Eds.), *Novel mechanisms of memory* (pp. 1–20). doi:10.1007/978-3-319-24364-1_1

11. Tranel, D., Bechara, A., & Denburg, N. L. (2002). Asymmetric functional roles of right and left ventromedial prefrontal cortices in social conduct, decision-making, and emotional processing. *Cortex, 38*(4), 589–612. doi:10.1016/s0010-9452(08)70024-8

12. Sheline, Y. I., Barch, D. M., Price, J. L., Rundle, M. M., Vaishnavi, S. N., Snyder, A. Z., . . . Raichle, M. E. (2009). The default mode network and self-referential processes in depression. *Proceedings of the National Academy of Sciences of the USA, 106*(6), 1942–1947. doi:10.1073/pnas.0812686106

13. Furini, C., Myskiw, J., & Izquierdo, I. (2014). The learning of fear extinction. *Neuroscience and Biobehavioral Reviews, 47*, 670–683. doi:10.1016/j.neubiorev.2014.10.016

14. Kohrt, B. A., Jordans, M. J., Tol, W. A., Perera, E., Karki, R., Koirala, S., & Upadhaya, N. (2010). Social ecology of child soldiers: Child, family, and community determinants of mental health, psychosocial well-being, and reintegration in Nepal. *Transcultural Psychiatry, 47*(5), 727–753. doi:10.1177/1363461510381290

15. Danese, A., & Mcewen, B. S. (2012). Adverse childhood experiences, allostasis, allostatic load, and age-related disease. *Physiology and Behavior, 106*(1), 29–39. doi:10.1016/j.physbeh.2011.08.019

16. BRFSS Adverse Childhood Experience (ACE) Module. (n.d.). Retrieved December 29, 2016, from https://www.bing.com/cr?IG=A16C959918EC45FFB92BF67738ED00C9&CID=276E50666D956BDD04EE599C6CA46AB3&rd=1&h=LIP9HQeb4wZVKF86RdJ2yVXGtp0iIpPQ1fEWGK11uo&v=1&r=https%3a%2f%2fwww.cdc.gov%2fviolenceprevention%2facestudy%2fpdf%2fbrfss_adverse_module.pdf&p=DevEx,5084.1

17. Child Abuse and Neglect: Consequences. (2016). Retrieved December 29, 2016, from https://www.cdc.gov/violenceprevention/childmaltreatment/consequences.html

18. Seedall, R. B., Butler, M. H., Zamora, J. P., & Yang, C. (2015). Attachment change in the beginning stages of therapy: Examining change trajectories for avoidance and anxiety. *Journal of Marital and Family Therapy, 42*(2), 217–230. doi:10.1111/jmft.12146

19. Bhasin, M. K., Dusek, J. A., Chang, B., Joseph, M. G., Denninger, J. W., Fricchione, G. L., . . . Libermann, T. A. (2013). Relaxation response induces temporal transcriptome changes in energy metabolism, insulin secretion and inflammatory pathways. *PLoS ONE, 8*(5). doi:10.1371/journal.pone.0062817

20. Roisman, G. I., Padron, E., Sroufe, L. A., & Egeland, B. (2002). Earned-secure attachment status in retrospect and prospect. *Child Development, 73*(4), 1204–1219. doi:10.1111/1467-8624.00467

21. Ramo-Fernández, L., Schneider, A., Wilker, S., & Kolassa, I. (2015). Epigenetic

alterations associated with war trauma and childhood maltreatment. *Behavioral Sciences and the Law, 33*(5), 701–721. doi:10.1002/bsl.2200

22. Teicher, M. H., Samson, J. A., Sheu, Y., Polcari, A., & Mcgreenery, C. E. (2010). Hurtful words: Association of exposure to peer verbal abuse with elevated psychiatric symptom scores and corpus callosum abnormalities. *American Journal of Psychiatry, 167*(12), 1464–1471. doi:10.1176/appi.ajp.2010.10010030

23. Ibid.

24. Cancel, A., Comte, M., Truillet, R., Boukezzi, S., Rousseau, P., Zendjidjian, X. Y., . . . Fakra, E. (2015). Childhood neglect predicts disorganization in schizophrenia through grey matter decrease in dorsolateral prefrontal cortex. *Acta Psychiatrica Scandinavica, 132*(4), 244–256. doi:10.1111/acps.12455

25. Parks, R. W., Stevens, R. J., & Spence, S. A. (2007). A systematic review of cognition in homeless children and adolescents. *Journal of the Royal Society of Medicine, 100*(1), 46–50. doi:10.1258/jrsm.100.1.46

26. Sheikh, T. L., Mohammed, A., Agunbiade, S., Ike, J., Ebiti, W. N., & Adekeye, O. (2014). Psycho-trauma, psychosocial adjustment, and symptomatic posttraumatic stress disorder among internally displaced persons in Kaduna, northwestern Nigeria. *Frontiers in Psychiatry, 5*. doi:10.3389/fpsyt.2014.00127

27. Lanius, R. A., Hopper, J. W., & Menon, R. S. (2003). Individual differences in a husband and wife who developed PTSD after a motor vehicle accident: A functional MRI case study. *American Journal of Psychiatry, 160*(4), 667–669. doi:10.1176/appi. ajp.160.4.667

28. Cain, A. C. (2006). Parent suicide: Pathways of effects into the third generation. *Psychiatry: Interpersonal and Biological Processes, 69*(3), 204–227. doi:10.1521/ psyc.2006.69.3.204

29. Benjet, C., Bromet, E., Karam, E. G., Kessler, R. C., Mclaughlin, K. A., Ruscio, A. M., . . . Koenen, K. C. (2015). The epidemiology of traumatic event exposure worldwide: Results from the World Mental Health Survey Consortium. *Psychological Medicine, 46*(2), 327–343. doi:10.1017/s0033291715001981

30. Ibid.

31. Jenkins, E. J., Wang, E., & Turner, L. (2014). Beyond community violence: Loss and traumatic grief in African American elementary school children. *Journal of Child and Adolescent Trauma, 7*(1), 27–36. doi:10.1007/s40653-014-0001-4

32. Kousha, M., & Kiani, S. (2012). Normative life events and PTSD in children: How easy stress can affect children's brain? *Neuropsychiatrie de l'Enfance et de l'Adolescence, 60*(5). doi:10.1016/j.neurenf.2012.04.627

33. Tomoda, A., Polcari, A., Anderson, C. M., & Teicher, M. H. (2012). Reduced visual cortex gray matter volume and thickness in young adults who witnessed domestic violence during childhood. *PLoS ONE, 7*(12). doi:10.1371/journal.pone.0052528

34. Benjet et al. (2015).

35. May, C. L., & Wisco, B. E. (2016). Defining trauma: How level of exposure and proximity affect risk for posttraumatic stress disorder. *Psychological Trauma: Theory, Research, Practice, and Policy, 8*(2), 233–240. doi:10.1037/tra0000077

36. Kun, P., Chen, X., Han, S., Gong, X., Chen, M., Zhang, W., & Yao, L. (2009). Prevalence of posttraumatic stress disorder in Sichuan Province, China after the

2008 Wenchuan earthquake. *Public Health, 123*(11), 703–707. doi:10.1016/j.puhe.2009.09.017

37. Burri, A., & Maercker, A. (2014). Differences in prevalence rates of PTSD in various European countries explained by war exposure, other trauma and cultural value orientation. *BMC Research Notes, 7*(1), 407. doi:10.1186/1756-0500-7-407

38. Loo, C. M., Fairbank, J. A., Scurfield, R. M., Ruch, L. O., King, D. W., Adams, L. J., & Chemtob, C. M. (2001). Measuring exposure to racism: Development and validation of a Race-Related Stressor Scale (RRSS) for Asian American Vietnam veterans. *Psychological Assessment, 13*(4), 503–520. doi:10.1037/1040-3590.13.4.503

39. Liberzon, I., Ma, S. T., Okada, G., Ho, S. S., Swain, J. E., & Evans, G. W. (2015). Childhood poverty and recruitment of adult emotion regulatory neurocircuitry. *Social Cognitive and Affective Neuroscience, 10*(11), 1596–1606. doi:10.1093/scan/nsv045

40. Ritchwood, T. D., Traylor, A. C., Howell, R. J., Church, W. T., & Bolland, J. M. (2014). Socio-ecological predictors of intercourse frequency and number of sexual partners among male and female African American adolescents. *Journal of Community Psychology, 42*(7), 765–781. doi:10.1002/jcop.21651

41. Langlois, K. A. & Garner, R. (2013). Trajectories of psychological distress among Canadian adults who experienced parental addiction in childhood. *Health Reports, 24*(3), 14–21.

42. Walsh, K., Wells, J. B., Lurie, B., & Koenen, K. C. (2015). Trauma and stressor-related disorders. *Anxiety Disorders and Gender,* 113–135. doi:10.1007/978-3-319-13060-6_6

43. Levinson, C. A., Rodebaugh, T. L., & Bertelson, A. D. (2013). Prolonged exposure therapy following awareness under anesthesia: A case study. *Cognitive and Behavioral Practice, 20*(1), 74–80. doi:10.1016/j.cbpra.2012.02.003

44. Elmir, R., & Schmied, V. (2016). A meta-ethnographic synthesis of fathers' experiences of complicated births that are potentially traumatic. *Midwifery, 32,* 66–74. doi:10.1016/j.midw.2015.09.008

45. Benjet et al. (2015).

46. Hansson, J., Hurtig, A., Lauritz, L., & Padyab, M. (2016). Swedish police officers' job strain, work-related social support and general mental health. *Journal of Police and Criminal Psychology.* Advance online publication. doi:10.1007/s11896-016-9202-0

47. Benjet et al. (2015).

48. Maybery, D., Reupert, A., Goodyear, M., Ritchie, R., & Brann, P. (2009). Investigating the strengths and difficulties of children from families with a parental mental illness. *Advances in Mental Health, 8*(2), 165–174. doi:10.5172/jamh.8.2.165

49. Benjet et al. (2015).

50. Ibid.

51. Chan, K. L. (2011). Correlates of childhood sexual abuse and intimate partner sexual victimization. *Partner Abuse, 2*(3), 365–381. doi:10.1891/1946-6560.2.3.365

52. Briere, J., & Runtz, M. (1988). Multivariate correlates of childhood psychological and physical maltreatment among university women. *Child Abuse and Neglect, 12*(3), 331–341. doi:10.1016/0145-2134(88)90046-4

53. Teicher, M. (2006). Sticks, stones, and hurtful words: Relative effects of various forms of childhood maltreatment. *American Journal of Psychiatry, 163*(6), 993. doi:10.1176/appi.ajp.163.6.993

54. Lanius et al. (2015).

Chapter Seven

1. Sato, W., Kochiyama, T., Uono, S., Matsuda, K., Usui, K., Inoue, Y., & Toichi, M. (2011). Rapid amygdala gamma oscillations in response to fearful facial expressions. *Neuropsychologia, 49*(4), 612–617. doi:10.1016/j.neuropsychologia.2010.12.025

2. Lieberman, M. D., Eisenberger, N. I., Crockett, M. J., Tom, S. M., Pfeifer, J. H., & Way, B. M. (2007). Putting feelings into words: Affect labeling disrupts amygdala activity in response to affective stimuli. *Psychological Science, 18*(5), 421–428. doi:10.1111/j.1467-9280.2007.01916.x

3. Ibid.

4. Couppis, M. H., & Kennedy, C. H. (2008). The rewarding effect of aggression is reduced by nucleus accumbens dopamine receptor antagonism in mice. *Psychopharmacology, 197*(3), 449–456. doi:10.1007/s00213-007-1054-y

5. Goldstein, R. Z., & Volkow, N. D. (2011). Dysfunction of the prefrontal cortex in addiction: Neuroimaging findings and clinical implications. *Nature Reviews Neuroscience 12*(11), 652–659. doi:10.1038/nrn3119

6. Fulwiler, C. E., King, J. A., & Zhang, N. (2012). Amygdala-orbitofrontal resting-state functional connectivity is associated with trait anger. *NeuroReport, 23*(10), 606–610. doi:10.1097/wnr.0b013e3283551cfc

7. Keay, K. A., & Bandler, R. (2001). Parallel circuits mediating distinct emotional coping reactions to different types of stress. *Neuroscience and Biobehavioral Reviews, 25*(7–8), 669–678. doi:10.1016/s0149-7634(01)00049-5

8. Porges, S. W. (2009). The polyvagal theory: New insights into adaptive reactions of the autonomic nervous system. *Cleveland Clinic Journal of Medicine, 76*(Suppl. 2). doi:10.3949/ccjm.76.s2.17

9. Ibid.

10. Porges, S. W., Bazhenova, O. V., Bal, E., Carlson, N., Sorokin, Y., Heilman, K. J., . . . Lewis, G. F. (2014). Reducing auditory hypersensitivities in autistic spectrum disorder: Preliminary findings evaluating the Listening Project Protocol. *Frontiers in Pediatrics, 2.* doi:10.3389/fped.2014.00080

11. Porges (2009).

12. Wang, Z., Deater-Deckard, K., & Bell, M. A. (2016). The role of negative affect and physiological regulation in maternal attribution. *Parenting, 16*(3), 206–218. doi:10.1080/15295192.2016.1158604

13. Porges (2009).

14. Soussignan, R., Chadwick, M., Philip, L., Conty, L., Dezecache, G., & Grèzes, J. (2013). Self-relevance appraisal of gaze direction and dynamic facial expressions: Effects on facial electromyographic and autonomic reactions. *Emotion, 13*(2), 330–337. doi:10.1037/a0029892

15. Geisler, F. C., Kubiak, T., Siewert, K., & Weber, H. (2013). Cardiac vagal tone is associated with social engagement and self-regulation. *Biological Psychology, 93*(2), 279–286. doi:10.1016/j.biopsycho.2013.02.013

16. Sinha, R., Lovallo, W. R., & Parsons, O. A. (1992). Cardiovascular differentiation of emotions. *Psychosomatic Medicine, 54*(4), 422–435. doi:10.1097/00006842-199207000-00005

17. Swartz, J. R., Williamson, D. E., & Hariri, A. R. (2015). Developmental change in amygdala reactivity during adolescence: Effects of family history of depression and stressful life events. *American Journal of Psychiatry, 172*(3), 276–283. doi:10.1176/appi.ajp.2014.14020195

18. Siegel, D. J. (2010). *The mindful therapist: A clinician's guide to mindsight and neural integration.* New York, NY: Norton, p. 50.

Chapter Eight

1. Porges, S. W. (2009). The polyvagal theory: New insights into adaptive reactions of the autonomic nervous system. *Cleveland Clinic Journal of Medicine, 76*(Suppl. 2). doi:10.3949/ccjm.76.s2.17

2. Beissner, F., Meissner, K., Bar, K., & Napadow, V. (2013). The autonomic brain: An activation likelihood estimation meta-analysis for central processing of autonomic function. *Journal of Neuroscience, 33*(25), 10503–10511. doi:10.1523/jneurosci.1103-13.2013

3. Salz, D. M., Tiganj, Z., Khasnabish, S., Kohley, A., Sheehan, D., Howard, M. W., & Eichenbaum, H. (2016). Time cells in hippocampal area CA3. *Journal of Neuroscience, 36*(28), 7476–7484. doi:10.1523/jneurosci.0087-16.2016

4. Lalo, E., Gilbertson, T., Doyle, L., Lazzaro, V. D., Cioni, B., & Brown, P. (2006). Phasic increases in cortical beta activity are associated with alterations in sensory processing in the human. *Experimental Brain Research, 177*(1), 137–145. doi:10.1007/s00221-006-0655-8

5. Hughes, J. R. (2008). Gamma, fast, and ultrafast waves of the brain: Their relationships with epilepsy and behavior. *Epilepsy and Behavior, 13*(1), 25–31. doi:10.1016/j.yebeh.2008.01.011

6. Piccolo, L. D., Sbicigo, J. B., Grassi-Oliveira, R., & Salles, J. F. (2014). Do socioeconomic status and stress reactivity really impact neurocognitive performance? *Psychology and Neuroscience, 7*(4), 567–575. doi:10.3922/j.psns.2014.4.16

7. Young, E. (2012). Gut instincts: The secrets of your second brain. *New Scientist, 216*(2895), 38–42. doi:10.1016/s0262-4079(12)63204-7

8. Bonnet, M. S., Ouelaa, W., Tillement, V., Trouslard, J., Jean, A., Gonzalez, B. J., . . . Mounien, L. (2013). Gastric distension activates NUCB2/nesfatin-1-expressing neurons in the nucleus of the solitary tract. *Regulatory Peptides, 187*, 17–23. doi:10.1016/j.regpep.2013.10.001

9. Dockray, G. J. (2013). Enteroendocrine cell signaling via the vagus nerve. *Current Opinion in Pharmacology, 13*(6), 954–958. doi:10.1016/j.coph.2013.09.007

10. Bonnet et al. (2013).

11. Ibid.

12. Ibid.

13. Ibid.

14. Panksepp, J. (1998). *Affective neuroscience: The foundations of human and animal emotions.* New York, NY: Oxford University Press, p. 208.

15. Nardone, G., & Compare, D. (2014). The psyche and gastric functions. *Digestive Diseases, 32*(3), 206–212. doi:10.1159/000357851

16. Panksepp (1998), p. 340.

Chapter Nine

1. Schneider-Hassloff, H., Straube, B., Jansen, A., Nuscheler, B., Wemken, G., Witt, S., . . . Kircher, T. (2016). Oxytocin receptor polymorphism and childhood social experiences shape adult personality, brain structure and neural correlates of mentalizing. *NeuroImage, 134*, 671–684. doi:10.1016/j.neuroimage.2016.04.009

2. Fogel, A. (2011). Embodied awareness: Neither implicit nor explicit, and not necessarily nonverbal. *Child Development Perspectives, 5*(3), 183–186. doi:10.1111/j.1750-8606.2011.00177.x

3. Ibid.

4. Craig, A. D. (2002). How do you feel? Interoception: The sense of the physiological condition of the body. *Nature Reviews Neuroscience, 3*(8), 655–666. doi:10.1038/nrn894

5. Mickleborough, M. (2011). Effects of trauma-related cues on pain processing in post-traumatic stress disorder: An fMRI investigation. *Journal of Psychiatry and Neuroscience, 36*(1), 6–14. doi:10.1503/jpn.080188

6. Craig (2002).

7. Daniels, J. K., Coupland, N. J., Hegadoren, K. M., Rowe, B. H., Densmore, M., Neufeld, R. W., & Lanius, R. A. (2012). Neural and behavioral correlates of peritraumatic dissociation in an acutely traumatized sample. *Journal of Clinical Psychiatry, 73*(4), 420–426. doi:10.4088/jcp.10m06642

8. Pfeiffer, A., Brantl, V., Herz, A., & Emrich, H. (1986). Psychotomimesis mediated by kappa opiate receptors. *Science, 233*(4765), 774–776. doi:10.1126/science.3016896

9. Minshew, R., & D'Andrea, W. (2015). Implicit and explicit memory in survivors of chronic interpersonal violence. *Psychological Trauma: Theory, Research, Practice, and Policy, 7*(1), 67–75. doi:10.1037/a0036787

10. Frewen, P. A. (2006). Toward a psychobiology of posttraumatic self-dysregulation: Reexperiencing, hyperarousal, dissociation, and emotional numbing. *Annals of the New York Academy of Sciences, 1071*(1), 110–124. doi:10.1196/annals.1364.010

11. Whitlock, E. L., Rodebaugh, T. L., Hassett, A. L., Shanks, A. M., Kolarik, E., Houghtby, J., . . . Avidan, M. S. (2015). Psychological sequelae of surgery in a prospective cohort of patients from three intraoperative awareness prevention trials. *Survey of Anesthesiology, 59*(3), 147–148. doi:10.1097/01.sa.0000464111.57640.a7

12. Mooren, N., & Minnen, A. V. (2014). Feeling psychologically restrained: The effect of social exclusion on tonic immobility. *European Journal of Psychotraumatology, 5.* doi:10.3402/ejpt.v5.22928

13. Porges, S. W. (2015). Making the world safe for our children: Down-regulating defence and up-regulating social engagement to 'optimise' the human experience. *Children Australia, 40*(2), 114-123. doi:10.1017/cha.2015.12

14. Porges, S. W. (2009). The polyvagal theory: New insights into adaptive reactions of the autonomic nervous system. *Cleveland Clinic Journal of Medicine, 76*(Suppl. 2). doi:10.3949/ccjm.76.s2.17

15. Ibid.

16. Ibid.

17. Hsu, K., & Terakawa, S. (1996). Fenestration in the myelin sheath of nerve fibers of the shrimp: A novel node of excitation for saltatory conduction. *Journal of Neurobiology, 30*(3), 397–409. doi:10.1002/(sici)1097-4695(199607)30:33.0.co;2-

18. Mussa, B. M., Sartor, D. M., & Verberne, A. J. (2010). Dorsal vagal preganglionic neurons: Differential responses to CCK1 and 5-HT3 receptor stimulation. *Autonomic Neuroscience, 156*(1–2), 36–43. doi:10.1016/j.autneu.2010.03.001

19. Daniels et al. (2012).

20. Lemche, E., Surguladze, S. A., Brammer, M. J., Phillips, M. L., Sierra, M., David, A. S., . . . Giampietro, V. P. (2013). Dissociable brain correlates for depression, anxiety, dissociation, and somatization in depersonalization-derealization disorder. *CNS Spectrums, 21*(01), 35–42. doi:10.1017/s1092852913000588

21. Frewen (2006).

22. Batey, H., May, J., & Andrade, J. (2010). Negative intrusive thoughts and dissociation as risk factors for self-harm. *Suicide and Life-Threatening Behavior, 40*(1), 35–49. doi:10.1521/suli.2010.40.1.35

23. Vermetten, E. (2015). Fear, helplessness, and horror—if it does not stop: Reflections on the evolving concept of impact of trauma. *European Journal of Psychotraumatology, 6.* doi:10.3402/ejpt.v6.27634

24. Dykema, R. (2006). How your nervous system sabotages your ability to relate: An interview with Stephen Porges about his polyvagal theory. Retrieved March 8, 2015, from http:/www.nexuspub.com/articles_2006/interview_porges_06_ma.php

24. Ibid.

25. Ibid.

26. Ibid.

27. Ibid.

28. Ibid.

29. Ibid.

30. Ibid.

31. Ibid.

32. Kensinger, E. A., Addis, D. R., & Atapattu, R. K. (2011). Amygdala activity at encoding corresponds with memory vividness and with memory for select episodic details. *Neuropsychologia, 49*(4), 663–673. doi:10.1016/j.neuropsychologia.2011.01.017

33. Ritchey, M., Dolcos, F., & Cabeza, R. (2008). Role of amygdala connectivity in the persistence of emotional memories over time: An event-related fMRI investigation. *Cerebral Cortex, 18*(11), 2494–2504. doi:10.1093/cercor/bhm262

34. Daniels et al. (2012).

35. Nazarov, A., Frewen, P., Parlar, M., Oremus, C., Macqueen, G., Mckinnon, M., & Lanius, R. (2013). Theory of mind performance in women with posttraumatic stress disorder related to childhood abuse. *Acta Psychiatrica Scandinavica, 129*(3), 193–201. doi:10.1111/acps.12142

36. Porges, S. W. (2003). Social engagement and attachment. *Annals of the New York Academy of Sciences, 1008*(1), 31–47. doi:10.1196/annals.1301.004

37. Becker-Blease, K., & Freyd, J. J. (2007). Dissociation and memory for perpetration among convicted sex offenders. *Journal of Trauma and Dissociation, 8*(2), 69–80. doi:10.1300/j229v08n02_05

11. Coan, J. A., & Sbarra, D. A. (2015). Social baseline theory: The social regulation of risk and effort. *Current Opinion in Psychology, 1*, 87–91. doi:10.1016/j.copsyc.2014.12.021

12. Ibid.

13. Odgen, P., & Fisher, J. (2015). Neuroception and the window of tolerance. *Neuropsychotherapist*, (12), 6–19. doi:10.12744/tnpt(12)006-019

14. Teicher, M. H., & Samson, J. A. (2016). Annual research review: Enduring neurobiological effects of childhood abuse and neglect. *Journal of Child Psychology and Psychiatry, 57*(3), 241–266. doi:10.1111/jcpp.12507

15. Teicher, M. H., & Parigger, A. (2015). The "Maltreatment and Abuse Chronology of Exposure" (MACE) scale for the retrospective assessment of abuse and neglect during development. *PLoS ONE, 10*(2). doi:10.1371/journal.pone.0117423

16. Teicher, M. H., & Samson, J. A. (2016). Annual research review: Enduring neurobiological effects of childhood abuse and neglect. *Journal of Child Psychology and Psychiatry, 57*(3), 241–266. doi:10.1111/jcpp.12507

17. Ibid.

18. Ibid.

19. Dickerson, S. S. (2008). Emotional and physiological responses to social-evaluative threat. *Social and Personality Psychology Compass, 2*(3), 1362–1378. doi:10.1111/j.1751-9004.2008.00095.x

20. Dube, S. R., Anda, R. F., Felitti, V. J., Chapman, D. P., Williamson, D. F., & Giles, W. H. (2001). Childhood abuse, household dysfunction, and the risk of attempted suicide throughout the life span. *JAMA, 286*(24), 3089. doi:10.1001/jama.286.24.3089

21. Nanayakkara, S., Misch, D., Chang, L., & Henry, D. (2013). Depression and exposure to suicide predict suicide attempt. *Depression and Anxiety, 10*, 991–996. doi:10.1002/da.22143

Chapter Twelve

1. Burgdorf, J., Colechio, E., Stanton, P., & Panksepp, J. (2016). Positive emotional learning induces resilience to depression: A role for NMDA receptor-mediated synaptic plasticity. *Current Neuropharmacology, 14*. Advance online publication. doi:10.2174/1570159x14666160422110344

2. Chapman, D. P., Whitfield, C. L., Felitti, V. J., Dube, S. R., Edwards, V. J., & Anda, R. F. (2004). Adverse childhood experiences and the risk of depressive disorders in adulthood. *Journal of Affective Disorders, 82*(2), 217–225. doi:10.1016/j.jad.2003.12.013

3. Zeugmann, S., Buehrsch, N., Bajbouj, M., Heuser, I., Anghelescu, I., & Quante, A. (2013). Childhood maltreatment and adult proinflammatory status in patients with major depression. *Psychiatria Danubina, 25*(3), 227–235.

4. Satterthwaite, T. D., Cook, P. A., Bruce, S. E., Conway, C., Mikkelsen, E., Satchell, E., . . . Sheline, Y. I. (2015). Dimensional depression severity in women with major depression and post-traumatic stress disorder correlates with fronto-amygdalar hypoconnectivity. *Molecular Psychiatry, 21*(7), 894–902. doi:10.1038/mp.2015.149

5. Reser, J. E. (2016). Chronic stress, cortical plasticity and neuroecology. *Behavioural Processes, 129*, 105–115. doi:10.1016/j.beproc.2016.06.010

6. Renner, F., Siep, N., Lobbestael, J., Arntz, A., Peeters, F. P., & Huibers, M. J. (2015). Neural correlates of self-referential processing and implicit self-associations in chronic depression. *Journal of Affective Disorders, 186*, 40–47. doi:10.1016/j.jad.2015.07.008

7. Gradin, V. B., Pérez, A., Macfarlane, J. A., Cavin, I., Waiter, G., Tone, E. B., . . . Steele, J. D. (2016). Neural correlates of social exchanges during the prisoner's dilemma game in depression. *Psychological Medicine, 46*(6), 1289–1300. doi:10.1017/s0033291715002834

8. Hao, L., Yang, J., Wang, Y., Zhang, S., Xie, P., Luo, Q., . . . Qiu, J. (2015). Neural correlates of causal attribution in negative events of depressed patients: Evidence from an fMRI study. *Clinical Neurophysiology, 126*(7), 1331–1337. doi:10.1016/j.clinph.2014.10.146

9. Ebdlahad, S., Nofzinger, E. A., James, J. A., Buysse, D. J., Price, J. C., & Germain, A. (2013). Comparing neural correlates of REM sleep in posttraumatic stress disorder and depression: A neuroimaging study. *Psychiatry Research: Neuroimaging, 214*(3), 422–428. doi:10.1016/j.pscychresns.2013.09.007

10. Wang, K., Wei, D., Yang, J., Xie, P., Hao, X., & Qiu, J. (2015). Individual differences in rumination in healthy and depressive samples: Association with brain structure, functional connectivity and depression. *Psychological Medicine, 45*(14), 2999–3008. doi:10.1017/s0033291715000938

11. Wimalawansa, S. J. (2016). Endocrinological mechanisms of depressive disorders and ill health. *Expert Review of Endocrinology and Metabolism, 11*(1), 3–6. doi:10.1586/17446651.2016.1127755

12. Mccabe, C. (2014). Neural correlates of anhedonia as a trait marker for depression. In M. S. Ritsner (Ed.), *Anhedonia: A comprehensive handbook* (Vol. 2, pp. 159–174). doi:10.1007/978-94-017-8610-2_6

13. Panksepp, J., & Yovell, Y. (2014). Preclinical modeling of primal emotional affects (SEEKING, PANIC and PLAY): Gateways to the development of new treatments for depression. *Psychopathology, 47*(6), 383–393. doi:10.1159/000366208

14. Panksepp, J. (2016). The cross-mammalian neurophenomenology of primal emotional affects: From animal feelings to human therapeutics. *Journal of Comparative Neurology, 524*(8), 1624–1635. doi:10.1002/cne.23969

Chapter Thirteen

1. Hill-Soderlund, A. L., Mills-Koonce, W. R., Propper, C., Calkins, S. D., Granger, D. A., Moore, G. A., . . . Cox, M. J. (2008). Parasympathetic and sympathetic responses to the strange situation in infants and mothers from avoidant and securely attached dyads. *Developmental Psychobiology, 50*(4), 361–376. doi:10.1002/dev.20302

2. Hughes, C. E., & Stevens, A. (2010). What can we learn from the Portuguese decriminalization of illicit drugs? *British Journal of Criminology, 50*(6), 999–1022. doi:10.1093/bjc/azq038

3. Dube, S. R., Felitti, V. J., Dong, M., Chapman, D. P., Giles, W. H., & Anda, R. F. (2003). Childhood abuse, neglect, and household dysfunction and the risk of illicit drug use: The Adverse Childhood Experiences study. *Pediatrics, 111*(3), 564–572. doi:10.1542/peds.111.3.564

4. Robins, L. N. (1993). Vietnam veterans' rapid recovery from heroin addiction:

A fluke or normal expectation? *Addiction, 88*(8), 1041–1054. doi:10.1111/j.1360-0443.1993.tb02123.x

5. Lopez-Quintero, C., Cobos, J. P., Hasin, D. S., Okuda, M., Wang, S., Grant, B. F., & Blanco, C. (2011). Probability and predictors of transition from first use to dependence on nicotine, alcohol, cannabis, and cocaine: Results of the National Epidemiologic Survey on Alcohol and Related Conditions (NESARC). *Drug and Alcohol Dependence, 115*(1–2), 120–130. doi:10.1016/j.drugalcdep.2010.11.004

6. Alexander, B. K. (2008). *The globalisation of addiction: A study in poverty of the spirit.* Oxford, UK: Oxford University Press, pp. 193–195.

7. Dennis, M. L., Foss, M. A., & Scott, C. K. (2007). An eight-year perspective on the relationship between the duration of abstinence and other aspects of recovery. *Evaluation Review, 31*(6), 585–612. doi:10.1177/0193841x07307771

8. Cao-Lei, L., Massart, R., Suderman, M. J., Machnes, Z., Elgbeili, G., Laplante, D. P., . . . King, S. (2014). DNA methylation signatures triggered by prenatal maternal stress exposure to a natural disaster: Project Ice Storm. *PLoS ONE, 9*(9). doi:10.1371/journal.pone.0107653

Chapter Fourteen

1. Porges, S. W. (2009). The polyvagal theory: New insights into adaptive reactions of the autonomic nervous system. *Cleveland Clinic Journal of Medicine, 76*(Suppl. 2). doi:10.3949/ccjm.76.s2.17

2. Porges, S. W. (1998). Love: An emergent property of the mammalian autonomic nervous system. *Psychoneuroendocrinology, 23*(8), 837–861. doi:10.1016/s0306-4530(98)00057-2

3. Ibid.

4. Porges, S. W., Bazhenova, O. V., Bal, E., Carlson, N., Sorokin, Y., Heilman, K. J., . . . Lewis, G. F. (2014). Reducing auditory hypersensitivities in autistic spectrum disorder: Preliminary findings evaluating the Listening Project Protocol. *Frontiers in Pediatrics, 2.* doi:10.3389/fped.2014.00080

5. Porges (1998).

6. Porges (2009).

7. Porges (1998).

8. Porges (2009).

9. Coan, J. A. (2011). The social regulation of emotion. In J. Decety & J. T. Cacioppo (Eds.), *The Oxford Handbook of Social Neuroscience.* Oxford Handbooks Online. doi:10.1093/oxfordhb/9780195342161.013.0041

10. Collins, N. L., & Ford, M. B. (2010). Responding to the needs of others: The caregiving behavioral system in intimate relationships. *Journal of Social and Personal Relationships, 27*(2), 235-244. doi:10.1177/0265407509360907

11. Rotge, J., Lemogne, C., Hinfray, S., Huguet, P., Grynszpan, O., Tartour, E., . . . Fossati, P. (2014). A meta-analysis of the anterior cingulate contribution to social pain. *Social Cognitive and Affective Neuroscience, 10*(1), 19–27. doi:10.1093/scan/nsu110

12. Aïte, A., Barrault, S., Cassotti, M., Borst, G., Bonnaire, C., Houdé, O., . . . Moutier, S. (2014). The impact of alexithymia on pathological gamblers' decision making. *Cognitive and Behavioral Neurology, 27*(2), 59–67. doi:10.1097/wnn.0000000000000027

Index

Note: Italicized page locators refer to illustrations; tables are noted with *t*.